Castiglione

CASTIGLIONE

The Ideal and the Real
in Renaissance Culture

Edited by
ROBERT W. HANNING
and
DAVID ROSAND

Yale University Press
New Haven and London

Published with assistance from the Kingsley Trust Association Publication Fund established by the Scroll and Key Society of Yale College.

Designed by Nancy Ovedovitz and set in VIP Baskerville type.
Printed in the United States of America by The Alpine Press, Inc., Stoughton, Mass.

Library of Congress Cataloging in Publication Data
Main entry under title:
Castiglione : the ideal and the real in
    Renaissance culture.

    Includes index.
    Papers presented at a conference celebrating the five-hundredth anniversary of Baldesar Castiglione's birth, held at the Casa Italiana of Columbia University on Oct. 27–28, 1978, and sponsored by the Casa Italiana with the cooperation of the Columbia University Program of General Education.
    1. Castiglione, Baldesar, conte, 1478–1529. Libro del cortegiano—Congresses.
2. Courts and courtiers—Congresses. 3. Courtesy—Congresses. 4. Renaissance—Italy—Congresses. I. Hanning, Robert W. II. Rosand, David. III. Casa Italiana.
IV. Columbia University.
BJ1604.C33C37   170'.2'02   82-6944
ISBN 0-300-02649-8   AACR2

10   9   8   7   6   5   4   3   2   1

Contents

Preface

"Castiglione: The Ideal and the Real in Renaissance Culture," a conference to celebrate the five-hundredth anniversary of the birth of Baldesar Castiglione (1478–1529), was held at the Casa Italiana of Columbia University on 27–28 October 1978. Sponsored by the Casa Italiana with the cooperation of the Columbia University Program of General Education, the event proved to be a success well beyond the expectations of its organizers.* For the two days of the conference the auditorium of the Casa overflowed with a public whose enthusiasm matched that of the participants. Clearly, Castiglione and his *Libro del Cortegiano* continue to strike a resonant chord in the modern world.

As the title of the conference suggests, we were eager to elicit from our invited speakers a series of papers embodying large responses to Castiglione, his achievement, and his world; we sought papers that would prove exciting and enlightening to a broad audience comprising not only Castiglione specialists or Italianists but also students of Renaissance culture in general. Proposing Castiglione as a central figure in the interplay, or tension, in Renaissance civilization between the formulation of optimistic ideals and the recognition of complex, often harsh realities allowed the participants a wide range of possible approaches to the subject and maximum freedom in treating several aspects of his work, traditions, and cultural context. Above all, that proposition seemed to us an appropriate way to celebrate his genius.

*We would like to acknowledge the special debt we owe to those colleagues and students who helped make that conference the success it was. In particular, we wish to thank Professor Joan M. Ferrante, then director of the Casa Italiana, and Professor Daniel Javitch, who worked so closely with us in organizing the event. The Columbia University Program of General Education provided much needed financial assistance, and several of our colleagues on the Columbia Committee for the Castiglione Conference proved most gracious hosts to our invited guests.

To celebrate Castiglione means, of course, to celebrate his book. At the heart of our conference—and hence of the present volume—was the *Book of the Courtier*. We ourselves had come to appreciate this classic as so much more than a compendium of manners and ideals, than a courtly book on etiquette, when we made it a basic text in a seminar we teach in Columbia College on themes in the art and literature of the Renaissance. In reading and rereading Castiglione's dialogue with our students, we continued to discover how beautifully rich and complex it was, how highly nuanced and ominously perceptive, how profoundly moving a reflection of and response to life. Serving as a gauge for so many aspects of Renaissance culture—from language and literature to art and music, courtiership and politics to humor and feminism, Neoplatonic idealism to the most cynical realism—the *Courtier* in the full integrity of its whole, in the contradictions of its dialogic structure, offered the most satisfying image of experience, of the precariousness of life and of the tenuous balance necessary for survival. We found in the text levels of the highest linguistic self-consciousness opening into the most profound situations of drama; we and our students were totally engaged.

Castiglione stands as the truest, because most complex, reflection of the complicated cultural phenomenon and historical moment we call the High Renaissance. The peculiar nature of his achievement in the *Book of the Courtier* lies in its presentation of multiple viewpoints without advancing any one as definitive—without, that is, enshrining within the dialogue among the courtiers of Urbino a single hierarchy of meanings, reflecting the author's convictions, that would make some of the protagonists figures of absolute authority while reducing others to the status of straw men. Castiglione's use of dialogue to create a dialectic abounding in theses and antitheses, but lacking syntheses, makes of the *Courtier* a profoundly equivocal work, one that repeatedly forces us, in effect, to internalize the dialogue and to seek to reconcile and synthesize its unresolved, opposing perspectives. Synthesis comes in reading, in the reader's full engagement with the dialectic of the dialogue.

Almost every opinion about the ideal courtier (or court lady) espoused by one of the interlocutors in the *Courtier*'s dialogues is contested by partisans of other viewpoints. Underscoring and justifying this lack of canonic pronouncement or argument is the conviction (expressed by many of the speakers and by the Castiglionesque narrator *in propria voce*) that life itself allows for no absolute values. The circumstances in which each individual finds himself change constantly; each person and situation encountered has its own peculiar features and requires an equally idiosyncratic response. In matters of behavior as of language it is usage, ever changing usage, that determines appropriateness. Furthermore, as Castiglione tells Alfonso Ariosto in the prefatory remarks to book 2 of the *Courtier,* the values with which we endow the world cannot exist or be defined in isolated essence but only in relation to other, opposite values. All values are relative; all opinions are ad hoc and subject to constant revision.

Castiglione's constant relativism is clearly incompatible with Platonic (or Neoplatonic) idealism. (The Aristotelian ethics frequently enunciated by speakers in the dialogue are more congenial to the *Courtier*'s overall analysis of its world, since the consensual norms on which such an ethics is based can change without subverting the whole system.) Despite the fact that the after-dinner setting of the four evenings of discussion at Urbino, the unexpected, noisy entrance of the prefect at the end of book 1, and Bembo's famous love discourse in book 4 all clearly recall Plato's *Symposium*; although all the discussions in book 4 concerning the best form of government, the nature of the ideal ruler, and the role of the courtier in teaching the prince virtue, derive from the *Republic*; and even given Castiglione's debt to Cicero's Platonically conceived dialogue, the *De oratore* (wherein notable orators of the Roman republic meet at a villa and discuss the proper training for the man of perfect eloquence)—despite this strong element of Platonic thought and technique, the *Book of the Courtier* cannot accurately be called a document of Renaissance Neoplatonism. There is no Socratic figure shaping the dialectic toward the author's doctrinal and didactic end, no authorial surrogate, no "man of greet auctoritee" to guide us to a changeless level of truth above the elegant fray, the war of words, in the chamber of the duchess of Urbino.

In transforming the Platonic dialogue to meet the needs of his equivocal vision, Castiglione turned for inspiration to the greatest prior achievement of Italian literary prose, Giovanni Boccaccio's *Decameron*. (His disavowal with respect to Boccaccio in the preface of the *Courtier*—"I could not imitate him in subject matter, since he never wrote anything at all like these books of the Courtier"—should be taken no more seriously than the antecedent denial that the "portrait of the Court of Urbino" deserves comparison with painted portraits by Raphael or Michelangelo.) From the *Decameron* Castiglione borrowed the idea of a series of verbal interchanges among a group of accomplished young men and women united by a common social station and by an agreement about the rules of their holiday game and conduct. (By contrast, the participants in the *Symposium* represent a cross section of Athenian professional life, while those in Cicero's *De oratore* are professionally, rather than socially, homogeneous.) Like the conversation of the courtiers of Urbino, that of Boccaccio's *brigata* balances license and decorum; the freedom of many of the stories, both sexually and satirically, is carefully distinguished from the always proper behavior of the men and women who tell them. The play space of the suburban villa owes its luster not only to the attractiveness of its temporary inhabitants and the beauties of nature, but also to the contrast between it and the Florentine world of plague and social breakdown which the young people have fled and to which they must return, lest they give scandal and ruin their reputation by extended, unchaperoned absence. The suggestion in the *Decameron* that values are social and relative rather than moral and absolute—that they reflect circumstances and are defined in contrast to their opposites—supplied Castiglione with canonic literary validation for his own representation of relativism and pragmatism in a world of brilliant conversational virtuosity that shines all the more brightly because there exists, beyond its carefully circumscribed borders, a world of political absolutism and tyranny, of capitulation to foreign invaders, and above all of Fortune's cruel, constant assault on human merit and happiness, made manifest with particular force in the person of Guidobaldo da Montefeltro, the crippled duke of Urbino. Within the *Decameron*'s temporary and fragile holiday world the real world's deficiency of authority, so graphically illustrated in the description of lawlessness in plague-ridden Florence, is compensated for by the daily appointment of a new "monarch" whose task is as much to allow as to abridge freedom, albeit within certain ad hoc rules of the game. Similarly, as we shall see, Castiglione places his courtiers in a situation of authority both complex and equivocal to make up for deficiencies in real (that is, political) authority.

In fact, the nature of authority in the world of the courtier (and of the *Courtier*) provides a major opportunity for Castiglione's equivocation between a Platonic view of the world and other, competing perspectives. Instead of embodying authority in the moral and intellectual superiority of a Socrates, Castiglione fragments the concept into three levels.

The first level is the absolute power of the prince—in this case Duke Guidobaldo. However, Guidobaldo's ill health prevents him from exercising his responsibility as a leader, either on the battlefield or in the after-dinner conversations on which his courtiers thrive; yet his absence from these two spheres of authority has very divergent effects. Forced to function as an observer, instead of a performer, of warlike deeds and public affairs, Guidobaldo, as a result, has become a connoisseur of courtiership: "Even though he could not engage personally in chivalric activities as he had once done, he still took the greatest pleasure in seeing others so engaged; and by his words, now criticizing and now praising each man according to his deserts, he showed clearly how much judgment he had in such matters." The blows of Fortune have accentuated and refined Guidobaldo's perceptions and thereby intensified the competition among his dependents for his approbation: "Wherefore . . . in all exercises befitting noble cavaliers, everyone strove to show himself such as to deserve to be thought worthy of his noble company." The illness that forces the duke's absence from the daylight world of war and politics renders him paradoxically more present to its dramatis personae in his role of arbiter of professional courtiership.

On the other hand, Guidobaldo's withdrawal from the world of purely social, recreational courtiership is absolute and has the effect of creating a play space for the court. Such freedom, however, like all else in the *Book of the Courtier,* is relative. After dinner Guidobaldo's authority resides in his duchess but not, Castiglione tells us, because of a formal devolution of power. Rather, the duchess owes her ostensibly absolute command over the gathering of courtiers and court ladies to their admiration for her qualities; to the commitment all share to create and maintain an ideal, temporary, and pain-exempt world of banter and repartee under her direction each evening; and to the respect (indeed, reverence) she commands from masculine society because of her sex. However, the very game-like nature of the duchess's domain endows her "subjects" with license beyond what they could expect to enjoy vis-à-vis authority in the real world. Lacking power to enforce her rule, the duchess must rely on subtler methods of control: laughter, shame, and extremely indirect coercion. The resultant ludic polity is very tenuous; at any moment, insufficient authority could lead to chaos and loss of coherence in the group of court comrades (the conversational game could dissolve into mere chatter) while too much or too strict a rule could lead to hard feelings and a withdrawal from the company by the aggrieved member or members.

To further complicate the issue of authority, the duchess, in effect following her husband's example, transfers her authority for much of the evening to her courtly subordinate, Emilia Pia, although she remains ready to intervene when requested by the latter, or when decorum seems to warrant, to preserve the game from threatened encroachment by dark reality (e.g., when one of the courtiers refers to her life as the "widow" of the crippled duke).

We can understand these first two levels of authority in the *Book of Courtier* in terms of a series of contrasts: male vs. female, political vs. social, earnest vs. game. One authority derives from fealty and political obligation and holds out the possibility of tangible, considerable rewards or punishments. The other depends upon a stylized veneration for women (coexisting with a strong vein of antifeminism within the dialogue among the courtiers) and a desire to keep the game circle together, to maintain its delicately balanced social harmony, its mix of the ideal and the cynical, the serious and the playful. The duchess rules as much by knowing when not to exercise authority as when to do so, and by relying on a (usually) unspoken consensus as to what topics of conversation are to be avoided as indecorous for the occasion. This second, contingent, relative, decorum-motivated authority is equivocal in the extreme and reflects the ambiguous position of women in the courtier's world, as discussed in book 3: at once placed on a pedestal and deprived of freedom, at once the inspiration and the downfall of men. But even the overt, statutory authority of the prince, because it is actualized in the observations and judgments of a crippled connoisseur, is far less objective than might at first appear. Books 1 and 2 make clear (and anatomize) the perfect courtier's obligation to calculate carefully his actions at court and on the battlefield, always taking into account his audience and manipulating its responses to his own advantage.

We see, then, that authority lacks absoluteness and possesses elements of ambiguity and equivocation that conform to, rather than limiting or opposing, Castiglione's world of contingency and relativism. Authority figures simultaneously establish and blur boundaries; they create a system of competiton without defining absolute standards for competing, except for the standards of prudence and flexibility. It is important to realize that Castiglione derives these models of authority from his medieval political heritage of feudalism and chivalry and medieval social heritage of courtliness and courtly love—all of which represent ideals foreign to Platonism and to classical antiquity generally. Castiglione raises, but leaves open, many questions about the compatibility and inherent antagonism of his classical and medieval antecedents. Would Plato and Aristotle have qualified, or wanted to qualify, as courtiers? Is the perfect courtier to instruct or applaud his prince? Is he to be a philosopher, schoolteacher, or cavalier, admonisher or flatterer? Should he simply use his opportunities as an adviser to advance himself, or should he take the moral high road and accept the responsibility of forming his prince in accord with an ideal of the good ruler? There are eloquent statements on both sides of all these questions, but no resolutions after the four nights of reported dialogue or after the countless further nights that Castiglione's open-ended text invites us to imagine as having succeeded them.

The third level of authority in the *Book of the Courtier* is occupied by the courtier of Urbino himself, who draws upon his expertise and experience to delineate a model of courtiership or court-ladyship—though here again, as we have seen, there is no final synthesis, no absolute agreement among the opinions throughout the four books. The courtier-as-authority in effect mediates between the Platonic model of authority based on philosophical insight and the medieval model of political authority inherent in the prince's office or the mock-political authority of the great, revered, almost worshiped court lady. He does this by embodying a view of life and mode of action calculated to enhance personal stature while recognizing—and by manipulating—the centers of external power that affect one's life and well-being. The courtier's program of self-aggrandizement specifically grows out of and reflects Castiglionesque relativism; it depends on constant, careful analysis in a series of public performances designed to deceive, please, or astonish the audience—be it the masses, fellow courtiers, or the prince himself—at which the particular performance is directed.

To present his courtier—both real and ideal—as a master of flexible, pragmatic, strategic role playing, Castiglione turned to yet another segment of his cultural inheritance: the Ovidian tradition of *cultus* behavior, or what Richard Lanham calls the "rhetorical view of life." In Ovid's works of love expertise Castiglione found the ludic perspective, the ideal of art excelling because it hides its existence, the insistence that artfulness can and should extend to all human social activity, and the genial commitment to self-aggrandizement by manipulation of the environment and the self.

Ovid's conception of the protean self—most clearly enunciated at the end of the first book of the *Ars amatoria*—mirrors the poet's insistence in the *Metamorphoses* on the primacy of change throughout the universe and accommodates the notion of flux to urban society and urbane strategies of personal success. The relevance of such a view to Castiglione's convictions about a world without permanency or absoluteness should be obvious, as should the Ovidian inspiration (via the insistence that the best art hides itself) of the ideal courtier's celebrated *sprezzatura*, that counterfeiting of graceful ease which hides the hard work underlying his successful performance and leaves the audience believing that, with effort, he could do even better. The notion, in book 3, that a woman should aim at possessing an ostensibly natural beauty with discreet use of cosmetics also descends from the *Ars amatoria*. All such social deception finds its ultimate justification in the concept of cultus, the improvement of nature by human effort and ingenuity that pervades human life from agriculture to city planning, the arts, and face painting. The application of cultus to urban social relations involves manipulating every situation encountered every day so that it becomes part of a drama of which you are the producer, director, and star player. Accentuate your strengths and hide your weaknesses, Ovid the *magister amoris* tells his pupils; use the cityscape strategically; make yourself over in the image of the one you are seeking to please. Be flexible, not dogmatic. In sum, the germ of the Castiglionesque system of courtiership lies exposed in Ovid's love expertise; even the error of *affettazione* (affectation; strained or too obvious effort) has its antecedent in the dreaded Ovidian *rusticitas* ("rural," i.e., unrefined, behavior).

Of course, Ovid's playful cynicism and irony are themselves metamorphosed in the *serio ludere* of the *Book of the Courtier*. A

refined pathos and a mood of political near despair haunt
many a page of the later work, rendering the Ovidian model
equivocal in its effect, even as that model renders the Platonic
idealism of Bembo eternally suspect. Ultimately, the Platonic,
Ovidian, courtly-medieval, and pathetic-nostalgic perspectives
coexist, interact, and clash throughout the four nights, four
books, or four hundred and fifty years that define Castiglione's
monument to himself and his culture. The task of choosing
among them (or perhaps the wisdom of refusing to choose)
remains ours.

Bibliographical Note

The text of *Il Libro del Cortegiano* cited throughout is that of B. Maier (2d ed., Turin, 1964); this edition also contains a selection of Castiglione's other works and letters. The translation used is that of Charles S. Singleton (Garden City, 1959), unless otherwise stated. Although there is no complete bibliography on Castiglione or on the *Book of the Courtier*, several recent publications contain extensive lists of editions, translations, and studies. These include Daniel Javitch, *Poetry and Courtliness in Renaissance England* (Princeton, 1978); Wayne Rebhorn, *Courtly Performances: Masking and Festivity in Castiglione's* Book of the Courtier (Detroit, 1978); J. R. Woodhouse, *Baldesar Castiglione: A Reassessment of "The Courtier"* (Edinburgh, 1978); and the article on Castiglione by C. Mutini in the *Dizionario biografico degli Italiani*, 22: 53–68 (Rome, 1979). Other important recent works include Richard Lanham, "The Self as Middle Style: *Cortegiano*," chapter 7 of *The Motives of Eloquence* (New Haven, 1976); Joan Kelly Gadol, "Did Women Have a Renaissance?" in Renata Bridenthal and Claudia Koonz, eds., *Becoming Visible: Women in European History* (Boston, 1977), pp. 137–64; and the essays in *La corte e il Cortegiano: I. La scena del testo*, ed. Carlo Ossola; II. *Un modello europeo*, ed. Adriano Prosperi (Rome, 1980). A new edition of Castiglione's letters is being prepared by Guido La Rocca, of which the first volume has appeared: *Le lettere* (1497–Mar. 1521) (Verona: Arnoldo Mondadori, 1978).

Chronology

This listing is adapted from the fuller chronology prepared by Guido La Rocca for his edition of Castiglione's letters. See *Le lettere*, volume 1, pages xcv–cix.

1478 Dec. 6	Baldesar Castiglione is born in the family house at Casàtico (Mantua).
1491 Jan.	At Milan he is presented by his parents to Isabella d'Este, the young bride of Francesco II Gonzaga, both of whom were there for the wedding of Beatrice d'Este and Ludovico (il Moro) Sforza.
1494	Castiglione studies Latin under Giorgio Merula and Greek with Demetrio Calcondia. In the same year he may have entered the court of Ludovico il Moro.
1499 Sept. 2	The French drive Ludovico il Moro from Milan. Castiglione, through the good offices of his mother, enters the service of Francesco Gonzaga, marquis of Mantua.
Oct.	In the cortège of Francesco Gonzaga, Castiglione is present at Pavia and at Milan when the Italian princes render homage to Louis XII of France.
1501 Apr.	Castiglione goes on his first diplomatic mission for the marquis of Mantua, to the Pio da Carpi, the house of Emilia Pia.
1503–04 Dec.–Apr.	Returning from a campaign around Naples, and with the permission of Francesco Gonzaga, Castiglione stops over in Rome and there enters into relations with Guidobaldo da Montefeltro, duke of Urbino, who has recovered his state following the election of Pope Julius II. Through the mediation of Cesare Gonzaga, who is already in the service of Guidobaldo, Castiglione agrees to serve the duke.

1504 Sept. 6 Castiglione receives permission from the marquis of Mantua to enter the service of the duke of Urbino (brother-in-law of the marquis) and is warmly received at court by the duke, the duchess, and Emilia Pia.

1505 Jan. 5–July 30 In the service of Guidobaldo da Montefeltro, Castiglione is in Rome to confer with Pope Julius II regarding the dukedom of Urbino. At this time Castiglione learns that he will soon be sent to England, there to receive, as Guidobaldo's proxy, the honor of the Order of the Garter, bestowed upon the duke by King Henry VII.

1506 carnival For the festivities at court Castiglione, in collaboration with Cesare Gonzaga, composes a "favola pastorale," *Tirsi*—in the recitation of which he himself plays two roles.

Sept.–Nov. Castiglione departs for England. Leaving Milan, perhaps on September 4, he proceeds through France by way of Lyons. On November 6 he writes from London of his safe arrival. At Dover there had been a solemn ceremony at his disembarkation; other ceremonies continued at the royal court in London, where, as proxy to the duke of Urbino, Castiglione is invested with the Order of the Garter.

1507 Feb. 9 Having returned to Italy from England, Castiglione writes to his mother from Milan. He then continues to Bologna, where Duke Guidobaldo has joined the company of Pope Julius II, who has wrested the city from the Bentivoglio rulers.

Mar. 3 Julius II, on his return to Rome, is accompanied by duke Guidobaldo to Urbino, where he sojourns with his retinue until March 7, when he sets forth again. "The day following the pope's departure" is the fictional date of the first of the four evening gatherings in the duchess's quarters of the palace at Urbino; hence those days can be exactly dated as being March 8–11, 1507. Castiglione, having returned from his mission to

England, was actually present at the court of Urbino during that period and would thus have been present at the imagined gatherings—had they not been imaginary.

June 6   At Milan Castiglione serves as envoy of the duke of Urbino to King Louis XII of France, participating in the act of homage rendered by the Italian princes to the French monarch on his invasion of Italy.

Nov.   Castiglione receives a proposal that Clarice de' Medici, daughter of Piero di Lorenzo de' Medici and Alfonsina Orsini, become his wife; in May of the following year the proposal is renewed with greater insistence by Cardinal Giovanni and Giuliano de' Medici. Such negotiations persist up to December 1508, but nothing comes of it in the end.

1508 Apr. 11   Guidobaldo da Montefeltro, duke of Urbino, last of the Montefeltro dynasty, dies. He is succeeded by his nephew and "adoptive son," Francesco Maria della Rovere. Castiglione remains in Urbino, in the service of the widowed duchess and the new duke.

1509–12   During these three years Castiglione engages in several military campaigns.

1513 carnival   In the ducal palace at Urbino Castiglione stages Cardinal Bibbiena's *Calandria*, for which he is thought to have written the prologue.

1513 Feb.   Upon the death of Pope Julius II, Castiglione is sent by the duke of Urbino to serve as his ambassador to Rome.

Mar. 11   Castiglione follows closely the conclave that elects to the papal throne Cardinal Giovanni de' Medici, who takes the name of Leo X.

Sept. 2   For his distinguished services and for other meritorious activities, Castiglione is invested by the duke of Urbino with the *contea* (countship) of Novilara (near Pesaro) for himself and his descendants; the act is recognized by Leo X with a letter of congratulations dated November 3, 1514, signed by Pietro Bembo and, on November

22, by a confirmation from Jacopo Sadoleto, the pope's new secretaries.

1514   Castiglione resides continuously in Rome as *oratore* of the duke of Urbino, and there establishes close friendships with Bembo, Sadoleto, Bibbiena, Raphael, Michelangelo, and many others, including Federico Fregoso, archbishop of Salerno. He is known to be working on the first redaction of *Il Libro del Cortegiano*; work on the manuscript may have begun in the preceding year.

1515 autumn   Castiglione composes the prologue to the first redaction of his *Cortegiano*, dedicating it to Francis I, king of France, *Il Re Cristianissimo*. That dedication, however, will be changed in subsequent versions.

1516 June   Francesco Maria della Rovere, duke of Urbino, is excommunicated and divested of all his power and his property by Pope Leo X, who proceeds to install as the new ruler of the dukedom his own nephew, Lorenzo di Piero de' Medici, grandson of Lorenzo il Magnifico. The deposed duke and duchess go into exile in Mantua, whither Castiglione follows them.

Oct. 19   Castiglione marries Ippolita Torelli, daughter of Count Guido and Francesca Bentivoglio. Francesco Gonzaga, marquis of Mantua, holds a public festival in celebration of the marriage, with jousts, tournaments, and feasts.

1518 autumn   Castiglione completes the second redaction of the *Cortegiano* and sends it, in the care of Ludovico da Canossa, to Sadoleto and Bembo. It seems never to have reached Bembo, however, for there is a letter to him inquiring about this possibility.

1519   The letter to Leo X on the archaeological ruins of Rome is drafted by Castiglione in collaboration with Raphael. For his wife Castiglione composes the *Elegia qua fingit Hippolyten suam ad se ipsem scribentem*.

Apr. 5   Death of Lorenzo di Piero de' Medici, usurper

of the dukedom of Urbino. Castiglione is dispatched to Rome for an extended residence, to frequent the papal court and do all he can to help restore Francesco Maria della Rovere to the rulership of Urbino.

May   Following the deaths of the Emperor Maximilian, Francesco Gonzaga, and Lorenzo di Piero de' Medici, Castiglione's main concerns in Rome are the interests of the young Federico Gonzaga, new marquis of Mantua, and the return of Urbino to Francesco Maria della Rovere.

June 28   Castiglione writes to the marquis of Mantua to rejoice over the election of Charles V as Holy Roman Emperor.

1520 Jan. 15   Having received no response from Pietro Bembo to the revised redaction of the *Cortegiano*, Castiglione writes again, begging for a copy of the letter in which Bembo presumably had expressed a judgment.

Apr. 7   The death of Raphael. In July Castiglione completes the elegy *De morte Raphaelis pictoris*.

Aug. 25   Castiglione's wife dies in childbirth, but the child, a daughter, lives. The widower is thus left with three children, one son and two daughters.

1520–21   Completion of the "definitive" version of the second redaction of the *Cortegiano*.

1521 June 9   In the Belvedere palace near St. Peter's, Castiglione is inducted into the Order of the *Tonsura* and by such act is given ecclesiastical status.

Dec. 1   Castiglione writes to inform the marquis of Mantua of the sudden death of Pope Leo X and of the possibility that he was poisoned. He remains in Rome for the funeral services and to follow the conclave by which Pope Adrian VI is elected.

1522 Jan.–Feb.   Castiglione participates in the secret negotiations seeking to bring about the return of Urbino to Francesco Maria della Rovere.

1523 Aug. 4   An alliance is formed between the pope, the emperor, the king of England, and the Vene-

	tians against Francis I of France. Castiglione prepares to follow the marquis of Mantua to military encampment.
Nov. 15	Cardinal Giulio de' Medici is elected Pope Clement VII. Castiglione is sent back to Rome by the marquis of Mantua as his ambassador in residence.
1524 May	Castiglione completes the first version of the third redaction of the *Cortegiano*. Rome, he writes, is terribly stricken by the plague.
July 19	Pope Clement VII informs Castiglione of his intention to send him to Spain as apostolic nuncio at the court of Charles V; the pope charges him to deal "not only with the Sede Apostolica, but with all matters concerning Italy and the whole of Christianity." Castiglione asks and receives permission of the marquis of Mantua to accept this appointment.
1525 Mar. 11	Castiglione is received at the imperial court in Madrid.
1526 Jan. 28	The widowed Duchess Elisabetta Montefeltro Gonzaga dies at Urbino.
1527 Mar. 6	The Sack of Rome. Clement VII is imprisoned in Castel Sant'Angelo.
Apr. 9	Castiglione writes to Cristoforo Tirabosco to tell him that he has sent to Venice the completed manuscript of the *Cortegiano*, addressed to Battista Ramusio, secretary of the Venetian Republic, who will arrange for the printing of the book by the heirs of Aldus Manutius. He directs Tirabosco to see to an edition of 1,030 copies of the book, 30 of which are to be printed on the finest paper available in Venice. From a recently discovered letter, written by the mother of Tirabosco, we know that Castiglione chose as the last reviser of the *Cortegiano* for final printer's copy, not Pietro Bembo as has generally been assumed, but Giovan Francesco Valerio (Valier).
Nov. 26	The actual printing of *Il Libro del Cortegiano* begins.

1528 Apr.   Castiglione instructs Girolamo Tiraboschi concerning the distribution of the newly printed copies of the *Cortegiano*.

May 20   Emilia Pia dies at Urbino, having received, but a few days before, a printed copy of the *Cortegiano* and having had the opportunity to discuss it with Ludovico di Canossa.

1529 Feb. 8   Baldesar Castiglione, stricken by violent fever, dies in Toledo at the age of fifty. He is buried in the cathedral of the city, with a great procession that includes the Emperor Charles V and his court along with many dignitaries of the Church. The emperor pronounces the famous words: "I tell you that one of the best *caballeros* of the world is dead."

1

Il Cortegiano and the Choice of a Game

Thomas M. Greene

The narrative of the *Libro del Cortegiano* involves at once subdued drama and slightly risky play. It begins with a game whose
purpose is to propose a second game that will occupy the company at Urbino for the rest of the evening. This elaborately
two-tiered pastime suggests immediately the centrality and formality of play for this group and throws the dramatic focus on
the question of a given proposal's suitability. The reader does
not know what criteria will determine the excellence of the
winning invention but he is allowed to participate in the consideration of each. Thus in this preliminary contest Gasparo
Pallavicino makes a proposal, and then Cesare Gonzaga another;
then the buffoon Fra Serafino and the poet, the Unico Aretino,
each makes a kind of nonproposal in bad faith, which has to be
dealt with by the arbitress, Emilia Pia. Then the contest re-
sumes with another proposal by Ottaviano Fregoso, and then
another by Pietro Bembo. Each of the four legitimate proposals
is ingenious and imaginative; each might be in fact amusing to
play; most of them kindle some enthusiasm among the assembled company. Each game might, in another book, conceivably have furnished matter for a witty and revealing scene.
But in this book the arbitress chooses none of them and simply
turns in silence to the next speaker whose turn it is, Federico
Fregoso, a gentleman who begins by saying that he would gladly
approve any of the games already described, but if obliged to

A version of this essay appeared in *Renaissance Quarterly*, 32 (1979).

suggest another, he would propose forming in words a perfect courtier. Before he has finished defending this somewhat irregular idea, decidedly unlike all the others, Emilia interrupts to decree that this will indeed be the evening's recreation. "This, should it please the Duchess, shall be our game for the present" (1.12).

It might be said that this contrivance of a preliminary game before the principal one constitutes a leisurely and somewhat circuitous entry into the main business of the book. We have no way of knowing with assurance why Castiglione chose it, any more than we can know what motives led his creature Emilia to pass over those other amusing suggestions and to make the unconventional choice, loaded with hidden implications, that in fact she made. But as readers we can reflect on the character of the five proposals, four of them stillborn, barren of the ghostly gaiety they might have provoked, and the fifth so seminal, so contagious, so resistant to conclusion, that its enjoyment continues for at least five evenings and perhaps for many more. It is worthwhile reflecting on the loaded consequences of Emilia's impulsive decision because Castiglione did choose to begin with all five alternatives as well as those two nonproposals which he also thought fit to introduce.

There are of course obvious narrative advantages in this particular kind of opening. It permits the writer to acquaint us with several of the most articulate members of his gathering; it permits him to establish from the start the complex and fascinating division of roles between the sexes in this community; it permits him to establish the special tone of its talk, the mingled banter and formality, the byplay that is almost ceremonial, the rituals of command and obedience which are both pretense and reality. But the rejected games are of interest in themselves. The first, invented by Pallavicino, is about self-deception: Since all lovers deceive themselves, he says, let each one say what special virtue he would wish to find in his beloved, and which fault; in this way the judgment of the lover is likely to be less beguiled. Gonzaga's game is about folly: Since each of us perceives his neighbor's folly but not his own, let each examine himself and reveal what his own true folly is, thus gaining self-knowledge. Ottaviano's game is about anger and scorn: since some suffer and some find sweetness in their lady's displeasure, let each one say "in case she whom he loves must be angry with him, what he would wish the cause of that anger to be" (1.10), thus presumably coming better to understand her hostility and his own response to it. Bembo's game finally is also about the lady's anger, justly or unjustly based: "Each should tell, if she whom he loves must be angry with him, where he would wish the cause of her anger to lie, in her or in himself" (1.11). Thus one might learn whether giving or receiving displeasure causes more suffering.

These are all distinctly different inventions but they bear a certain family resemblance; they all deal with the socially aberrant, with private passions and imbalances and blindnesses which could threaten the harmony of the group, that magic chain which, we have been told, binds all members together in bonds of love (1.4). The games suggest the presence of the potentially dangerous (of self-deception, cruelty, folly, and hostility) just as the pseudogame proposed by Serafino hints at indecencies and the pseudogame proposed by Aretino reveals in him a self-advertising and manipulative affectation. All of this emerges from the proposals, but what emerges with equal clarity is the therapeutic capacity of the group to cope with this potential venom. All four original games are calculated to function as measures of healing, to induce self-knowledge and understanding, to contain the antisocial deviations that in the recurrent phrase "go beyond bounds." Emilia's disposition of Aretino, here and elsewhere, is itself a brilliant model of tactful containment in the subtlety of its ironies and the indirection of its reproof. Thus at this early stage of the book the drama of social cohesion appears already as a testing of the company's *power of containment,* and this drama will be sustained when the final game is approved and played to its inconclusive ending.

All four original games stem from a recognizable genealogy that is old and astonishingly stable, a tradition that straddles literary and social history. The tradition has its source, as far as we know, in the medieval *cours d'amour* and the Provençal *jocs partitz,* which latter institution confronted two poets arguing opposed solutions to a subtle question drawn from the codified doctrine of *fin amors.* The questions were chosen clearly to admit of no final judgment beyond appeal. Which are the greater, the joys or the sorrows of love? Must a lady do for her lover as much as he for her? Which is the most in love, the one who speaks of his lady everywhere or the one who remembers her in silence? Which lover shall a lady take, one who confesses his love or one who does not dare to?[1] Scores of similar teasers are extant from the refined casuistry of the Provençal intelligence, and many more from its Italian disciples. Trecento literary reflections of the tradition appear in Boccaccio's *Filocolo* and the *Paradiso degli Alberti* by Giovanni di Prato. It is no surprise to read that the courtiers at Urbino amuse themselves with *belle questioni.* Of the four original games proposed, the latter two are quite simply *questioni* in the medieval tradition and the first two merely variants.

This of course is not the case of the game that is chosen for play, and if we had any doubts about *its* provenience, the author's prefatory letter would remind us that its models are in Plato, Xenophon, and Cicero. The medieval *questione* is exchanged for the ancient dialogue, the Socratic or in this case the far more influential Ciceronian conversation about a hypothetical ideal. This gesture toward Cicero as the main authenticating model is sustained by the number of allusions and echoes that appear throughout the body of the *Cortegiano,* chiefly from the *De oratore.* Emilia Pia, in making the choice she does, rejects the familiar game of erotic litigation, a game that in Urbino seems to be contrived as personal and social therapy; she chooses in its place an unfamiliar game, rich in classical associations, a game whose limits and whose drift no one as yet can fully foresee. It commits the players to try to define the ideal that underlies their own approved conduct, the authorized version of behavior that has regulated their day-to-day activity but has heretofore regulated it tacitly. The choice to form a courtier commits them to examining their own values and norms, with the opportunity to criticize those norms and so to acquire a self-consciousness as a community. This Ciceronian game assumes a capacity for mature self-criticism as well as a firm, stable society capable of questioning its own foundations. If there is anything radically insecure or hypocritical, any area where norm and reality diverge too widely, it could be a destructive experience; it could confront the company with truths it might not be able to face. So the questions that hang over the drawing room as these elegant people begin to play are first, whether the game will actually lead to more self-understanding, but also whether it will lead to so much that it will destroy the delicate fabric of their social equilibrium.

Two structural oppositions underlie the distinction between "medieval" and "classical" game. First, the medieval *questione* is fundamentally deductive. One begins with certain norms, certain rules, which are taken for granted, and one then analyzes specific cases, specific problems or aberrations, in the light of these sacrosanct assumptions. In the classical game, one begins with a certain praxis, with what is done, and out of that praxis one elicits the norms, inductively; this constitutes the game. The second structural opposition stems from the first. The medieval game, because it rests on the sacrosanct, can never legitimately overflow its boundaries. Although in a juridical sense, closure is difficult because there is always more to say, because the question is contrived to invent endless debate, nonetheless in a structural sense closure is tight because the debate proceeds within limits which by definition can never be called into question. This however is not the case in the classical game, which is to say the game that more or less makes up Castiglione's book. There the boundary is vague between the area that is "serious," untouchable, outside the play, on the one hand, and on the other that area where the play can range freely. Because there is no code, traditionally defined, to focus and delimit the talk, this is a parlor game which can expand indefinitely, which can become coextensive with all that is normally nonplay. Indeed if it were permitted by its arbiters, this game could conceivably swallow up everything outside itself.

We think normally of a game as a detached figure against a background of the serious, the nonludic, but in this case the ground becomes the content of the figure. In Plato and Cicero this situation does not arise because the conversation in each case is not regarded as ludic, as enjoying that special isolation from context we attribute to games. But the *Libro del Cortegiano* insists on its ludic purpose, thus possibly risking the comment which the Grand Turk's brother makes on jousting: "Too much if done in play and too little if done in earnest" (2.66). It risks also that ambiguity which is said to arise when a prince masquerades as a prince: "If he were to perform in play what he must really do when the need arises, he would deprive what is real of its due authority, and it might appear that the reality were mere play" (2.11). Because *bounds* matter so much at Urbino, one test of the players will be their ability to sustain the game as a game, to protect it from this ambiguity which might subvert play and reality alike.

It has been asserted of course that this ambiguity is fundamental to play. If, as was argued by Schiller and Huizinga and later by others, the play impulse lies at the root of human culture, then clearly the ludic is inseparable from all that we think of as most meaningful in civilization. Huizinga was in fact criticized with some justice by Jacques Ehrmann because Huizinga seemed always to maintain a category of nonludic seriousness while demonstrating simultaneously how deeply that serious activity was pervaded by the play element. Ehrmann's alternative is more radical.

> In an anthropology of play, play cannot be defined by isolating it on the basis of its relationship to an *a priori* reality and culture. To define play is *at the same time* and *in the same movement* to define reality and to define culture. As each term is a way to apprehend the two others, they are each elaborated, constructed through and on the basis of the two others.[2]

If Ehrmann was right, if play, culture, and reality are ultimately inextricable, then the particular game at Urbino will tax even more severely the power of its players to segregate it as a *diversion*.

To be sure, this segregation of the ludic is made easier by its physical disposition: everything that occurs is contained within four walls. We first meet the players in the flesh after they have taken their places in a certain drawing room, an actual room that still exists today, and we remain with them in that room, *only* in that room, until the conclusion. The last voices we hear on the last page belong to individuals who are just about to leave the room but have not yet done so. The sense of enclosure is very strong, and this sense is only heightened by that magical and unexpected moment at the end when a window is opened. This sense of enclosure powerfully affects the reader's impression of the society and the game. Whether or not there is structural closure, there is strong physical containment. This concrete delimitation of a play space is of course one of those essential elements stipulated by most theoreticians of play, a space that must be fixed and separate in order for the game to define itself. This separation exists at Urbino to a degree that might in another work almost become claustrophobic. All we know of the court, of the society, of the world at large beyond it, reaches us through this rigid and compressed mediation. And the very sharpness of this ludic circumscription reflects of course something significant about the group enclosed. The artistic sealing of this drawing room comes unavoidably to represent a community itself turned inward, flawless in the perfection of its withdrawal, protected momentarily by its mountains, its palace, its style, its harmony, from the violence and vulgarity beyond it. A chrysalis of a culture seems to exist in its own static, circumscribed self-sufficiency and proposes to mirror its contentment by a game of autocontemplation.

We can measure that degree of enclosure by comparing the *Cortegiano* to a work far less substantial and complex written a century earlier: the *Ad Petrum Paulum Histrum Dialogus* by Leonardo Bruni.[3] At the opening the narrator, Bruni, meets Niccolò Niccoli at an Easter service in Florence, and the two humanists decide spontaneously to pay a call on their revered chancellor Colluccio Salutati. On their way they meet a friend, Roberto Rossi, who joins them. During the talk that ensues, Salutati recalls the spontaneous visits *he* had paid as a younger

man to the theologian Luigi Marsili. The four Florentines
discuss the state of modern learning and agree to meet the
next day at Rossi's villa beyond the Arno, where they will be
joined by a fifth friend. Before recommencing the discussion at
Rossi's, they take a turn in the villa's garden and pause to
admire the dignity of their city in the distance. These indications of spontaneous movement by independent citizens
through the streets and squares and faubourgs of Florence
receive no special prominence in Bruni's little work, but they
reflect all the more tellingly the open converse, the mobile
liberty of the commune. They bespeak a different organization
of space without circumscriptions or enclosures, a space actually closer than Urbino's to that of the *De oratore*, where recreation is not firmly segregated from the rest of experience. To
draw this contrast is not to diminish the peculiar grace of the
Urbinese court but rather to underscore its will or its compul-
sion to turn so insistently inward. Its play space is not a public
space.

The drama of the game, as it is played out in this space, will
be again a drama of containment but no longer the containment of passion or folly but rather the containment of insight.
It is healthy doubtless for a community to confront itself, but
when the community rests upon unsteady political and ethical
props, too much illumination can be destructive as well as enlightening. This holds true even for so brilliant, so articulate,
and so poised a set as these talkers of the *Cortegiano*. We can
follow the progress of the game in terms of the potentially
threatening or divisive issues it raises, in terms of the doubts it
flirts with, the embarrassments it skirts, the social and political
and moral abysses it almost stumbles into, the dark underside
of the authorized truth it sometimes seems about to reveal.
This threat is really double. There is an intellectual threat to
the minds of the players, but there is also a social threat that
the conversational surface might be ruffled irreparably; there
is a threat that the talk might reach a point that would destroy
its quality as game, as amusing conversation between ladies and
gentlemen. So we can measure the resiliency of the group to

these implied threats by the way it heads off the threatening while protecting its governing mythologies and its social tone. The game really becomes a contest between the community's will to understand itself, to examine and know itself, and conversely its will to protect itself from excessive knowledge in order to function politically and socially. One way to gauge the threat to the social surface at any given moment is to note the presence or absence of laughter. It is extraordinary how many speeches are introduced with the participle *ridendo*. The presence of this participle is an indication that the playful dimension of the conversation is intact. Laughter proves that the discussion of norms and ideals can coexist with banter, that "serious" talk represents no danger to the social occasion. Laughter is a guarantee of the polish of the conversational surface, and when it is silenced for an immoderate time one can detect a tension; one should be alert to the potentially intrusive.

Count Ludovico da Canossa hits upon a potentially explosive issue at the outset by raising the question of the courtier's aristocratic birth. The courtier requires it because, says the count, birth acts as a spur to achievement, deters one from dishonor, and implants a hidden seed which lends distinction to an aristocrat's conduct. He speaks of aristocratic *grazia* almost as though it came through the genes. Whereupon Gasparo Pallavicino, who tends to play the role of the demystifier throughout, asserts that many aristocrats are vicious while many people of humble birth have become illustrious; he also suggests that Fortune has as much to do with eminence as does Nature. Curiously and significantly, Ludovico in rebuttal fails to defend his earlier assertions but falls back on the pragmatic argument that the courtier will encounter less hostility and will make a stronger first impression if he is well born. This little difference of opinion, followed by a partial retreat, signals a soft spot in authorized opinion, a genuine rooted ambivalence which the dialogue structure reveals. The ambivalence is dangerous because it threatens one of the principles of selection on which this company has been assembled. It also clearly threatens the company's ostensible function. If in fact the alleged superiority of birth is only a myth, what is the rationale of a community serving a nobleman whose power is inherited? We are not surprised when the subject is dropped for other, less controversial gifts by which to adorn the court's hypothetical archetype. The subversion has been headed off and the group's resiliency, the game's resiliency, have been quietly vindicated.

But during the second evening another test arises, and this time the challenge is blunter and uglier. The younger Fregoso remarks that the courtier should devote "all his thought and strength of spirit to loving and almost adoring the prince he serves above all else, devoting his every desire and habit and manner to pleasing him" (2.18). But Fregoso is told that he has described nothing but a flatterer. A few minutes later he is told that his vision of a modest and retiring courtier falsifies reality; only presumptuous courtiers win advancement. Fregoso's reply concludes with the statement that the courtier must hold to what is good, only to meet further skepticism about the nature of princes, who look not for goodness but for willing instruments of their despotic wills. Should one obey a dishonorable command? No, says Fregoso, but some commands only appear dishonorable. Here the players almost expose themselves to a perception of the corruption endemic to the system they live by, the perception of a courtier essentially passive, dependent on the whim of a master who may be evil and is likely to be a despot. A vision almost takes shape of the very condition of courtiership as potentially or inherently corrupting. The vision flickers briefly and obliquely but unmistakably, and for a while there is no laughter. Mercifully the subject is changed to dress, but that too leads to a painful admission: Italians have given up their own styles, as though to symbolize their helplessness before foreign invasion. The talk remains dogged by the morally equivocal but finally will be saved by Bibbiena's discourse on jokes, by the return of that saving laughter which proves a game is still being played.

On the third evening a different kind of threat emerges, a threat to that balance between the sexes which has governed the decorum of Urbinese social ritual. To denigrate the status of women in any group that contains them will clearly place a strain on its cohesion. But in this company the insult is more scandalous because the court takes its fundamental character from the dominant presence of women, and in particular one woman. The creative male figure, Federigo da Montefeltro, the founding father, is dead. In his place there exists a vacuum. Duke Guidobaldo, the putative male leader, is indisposed and absent. He never enters the stage, the game space of the drawing room, and he fails to play the centrifugal, out-thrusting role that his father had played and that would open up the rigid enclosure of the court's withdrawal. The distinction of this society, its felicity, its *dolcezza,* that which justifies its memorialization in a book, all stem from the radiating presence of the Duchess Elisabetta. The author has told us this quite explicitly from the beginning, where he pays her a tribute of remarkable resonance: "It seemed that she tempered us all to her own quality and fashion, wherefore each one strove to imitate her style, deriving as it were a rule of fine manners from the presence of so great and virtuous a lady" (1.4). To deny the worth of women is to attack from another direction the foundations of this company's particular grace. Yet in fact this attack on the feminine enclosing power never succeeds in suspending the laughter of the play spirit as had the attack on the masculine corrupting power. This is true despite the social injustices suffered by women which the discussion reveals, despite the double standard applied to sexual conduct, and despite the sexual hostility which surfaces repeatedly. Once this almost leads to blows: "At a sign from the Duchess, many of the ladies rose to their feet and all rushed laughing upon signor Gasparo as if to assail him with blows and treat him as the bacchantes treated Orpheus" (2.96). There is plenty of hostility here, but again the key word is *ridendo.* Nobody among those present, including the women, wants that laughter to fade; nobody wants to pass that limit beyond which hostility would banish play, just as nobody expects a woman to take over the defense of her sex from the male champions who assume it so articulately. The women of Urbino do not want an interchangeability of social roles; what they want is respect for the distinct roles society has assigned them. And because ultimately their position in this faintly effete community is so strong, the challenge to their dignity is contained like the earlier challenges to the authorized version. But again, the insecurities and inconsistencies of that version have been exposed; the court and the game have been tested; the tension of containment has betrayed its strain.

The fourth book and fourth evening call into question much more visibly and explicitly not only the authorized version but the game that has reflected it. The elder Fregoso is in no playful mood, and he brands most of the ideal courtier's accomplishments, so carefully compiled, as nothing but "frivolities and vanities" (4.4). Here is yet another subversion, the most systematic, the most articulate presented thus far, and it is hard to see how this dismissal of frivolity could fail to include the game, the diversion which is still going on and which frames the repudiation. Ottaviano's discourse represents an effort to salvage courtiership at a higher level of moral responsibility, but it is not in its turn free from flaws of argument that might, once exposed, give away more than it gains. Ottaviano argues that the courtier's several accomplishments are justified only if they serve a higher end, namely, the moral and political education of the prince. He attempts to beat off the doubts raised concerning the prince's educability, and he evokes a quasi-divine portrait of the model prince to balance the more familiar portrait of the demonically cruel and rapacious tyrant. But he cannot deny that the tyrant is by far the more common figure, and later in his discourse he confesses that some princes are not in fact redeemable. There is one especially telling Freudian slip when the duchess puts a hypothetical case to him. "Let us assume," says the duchess, "that you have won [your prince's] favor completely, so that you are free to tell him whatever comes to mind" (4.25). Whereupon Ottaviano laughs and replies: "If I had the favor of some of the princes I know, and I were to tell them freely what I think, I fear I should soon lose that favor" (4.26). That laughing remark in its context cancels out a good deal of Ottaviano's argument, and it leaves the courtier suspended between the frivolity of his style and the futility of his political vision. This long discourse repudiates the elegant dilettante of the drawing room without convincingly establishing the adviser of the council chamber. Thus it constitutes the most formidable threat we have seen to the court and its play. Yet it too is contained, doubtless because no one present is disposed to press the negative implications all the way, to go beyond bounds. The court chooses to accept what is palliative in the discourse, chooses to settle for the partial self-consciousness that will permit it to continue.

At one point Ottaviano retells the myth of Epimetheus he found in Plato's *Protagoras*. At the end of that myth Zeus takes pity on primitive men who are the victims of wild beasts because, lacking civic virtue, they do not congregate in cities. So he orders Hermes to bring justice and shame to all men in order that civic life will become possible. Fregoso's repetition of this myth betrays a nostalgia for that kind of community where the civic virtue of all citizens does determine its destiny—communities such as the Athenian *polis,* which inspired the myth, or the Roman republic Cicero defended, or the commune of Bruni's Florence. The Platonic myth is pathetically or tragically anachronistic at Guidobaldo's Urbino; it points precisely to what the little Urbinese state lacks, the creative interplay of free and equal men in shaping the policy of the city. Here in this brilliant and worthy company the one thing not attainable is the civic virtue of the polis and the commune. For that to be present, the play space of the drawing room would have to yield to what Hannah Arendt called a "public space," that place where equal and distinct individuals create a shared tradition of integrity. "The *polis,*" writes Arendt, ". . . is the organization of the people as it arises out of acting and speaking together, and its true space lies between people living together for this purpose."[4] The courtiers of Urbino play but do not act together, in Arendt's sense, which is why the Platonic myth is cruelly inappropriate. But the will to self-consciousness which produced their game is not so strong as to confront that anachronism.

According to the psychiatrist D. W. Winnicott, there is an area of experience that mediates between the inner psychic world and the outer objective world. Winnicott calls this the area of play, which begins in infancy and "expands into creative living and into the whole cultural life of man."[5] He locates this area in the potential space between the individual and the environment; it is made possible, he argues, by the child's trust in its mother, which permits a distinction between the self and the nonself. The pain of the separation is averted by filling the potential space with creative play and that which will later become cultural life. For our purposes, the significant word in Winnicott's theory of development is the verb *expand*. As the experience of trust is confirmed, the area of creativity widens. This widening leaves the maternal space behind for a broader, agonistic public space. But in the *Cortegiano* the trust in a broader scope of activity is weak; the role of the soldier has become vestigial; each of the four prefaces bespeaks a helpless consciousness of mutability, loss, and death. Here the play space has failed to expand; the area for creation has remained constricted, dominated by a benevolent but authoritative woman.

It is precisely that sense of mutability, that unavailability of political interplay, that beleaguering force of enclosure which defines the quality of the laughter in this book. The laughter is so perfect that it is poignant; it almost brings one close to tears. It has its own purity and its own courage even if that courage falls short of the full lucidity which would render this purity impossible. It remains to the last sentence. The final test of the court's resiliency is the rhapsodic hymn to love by Bembo, which brings to the book and the company a spiritual element they had conspicuously lacked. But in the privacy and intensity of its mysticism, it constitutes the supreme denial of the company, the game, and the society behind them. It is the extreme assault. When Bembo's eloquence finally pours out of him, he falls silent as though he were rapt. There is a moment of sublime silence that is a terrible silence, a moment when the collective heartbeat has stopped, when the game is no longer being played. No one has anything to say. The social surface that has withstood all other threats has finally been torn. It is only a moment, and then Emilia Pia leans forward and gently tugs Bembo's sleeve, saying, "Take care, messer Pietro" (4.71). He replies to her, and then the others begin to speak and the crisis has passed. A moment later we hear Emilia laughing, and we hear plans for the discussion the following evening. The play and the society have absorbed this last accession of blinding light; the choice of the game has been vindicated; one can be confident that nothing will be said on the fifth evening which the resiliency of this circle will not contain.

NOTES

1. These examples are taken from Thomas Frederick Crane, *Italian Social Customs of the Sixteenth Century* (New Haven, 1920), p. 10.
2. "Homo Ludens Revisited," *Yale French Studies*, No. 41 (1968), pp. 31–57.
3. Contained in *Prosatori Latini del Quattrocento*, ed. Eugenio Garin (Milan and Naples, n.d.), pp. 44–98.
4. *The Human Condition* (Chicago, 1970), p. 198.
5. *Playing and Reality* (London, 1971), p. 102.

2

Il Cortegiano and the Constraints of Despotism

Daniel Javitch

When I was young, I used to scoff at knowing how to play, dance, and sing, and other such frivolities. I even made light of good penmanship, knowing how to ride, to dress well, and all those things that seem more decorative than substantial in a man. But later, I wished I had not done so. For although it is not wise to spend too much time cultivating the young toward the perfection of these arts, I have nevertheless seen from experience that these ornaments and accomplishments lend dignity and reputation even to men of good rank. It may even be said that whoever lacks them lacks something important. Moreover, skill in this sort of entertainment opens the way to the favor of princes, and sometimes becomes the beginning or the reason for great profit and high honors. For the world and princes are no longer made as they should be, but as they are.

— Francesco Guicciardini, *Ricordi* (1530)

One of the chief novelties of the *Cortegiano*, and a basic reason for its tremendous fortune in the sixteenth century, is that it set forth an art of conduct tailored to the social and political exigencies of Renaissance despotism. This pragmatic and forward-looking aspect of Castiglione's code has been obscured by modern commentators who have tended to dwell on the book's idealistic, escapist, and nostalgic features.[1] To be sure, the game of fashioning a perfect courtier that constitutes the book allows Castiglione's speakers to fabricate a composite ideal that, at best, can only be partly approximated in actual society. But even though this game permits its participants to ignore many

claims of daily existence, Castiglione's speakers rarely disregard
the real constraints of the autocratic political order to which the
courtier belongs. As I want to show in the following observations, the proper conduct they recommend reveals their full
awareness that the model individual they fashion has to depend
on his ruler's favor for his existence and that his prime objective, therefore, is to secure or preserve such favor.

The pragmatism of the *Cortegiano* can be more fully appreciated once it is recognized that Castiglione's speakers *cloak* the
fact that the pressures of autocratic rule shape the norms of
conduct they advocate. Until Federico Fregoso mentions it on
the second evening of discussion, it is left to be assumed that
the courtier has to "devote all his thought and strength of spirit
to loving and almost adoring the prince he serves above all else,
devoting his every desire and habit and manner to pleasing
him" (2.18). And except for Federico's brief treatment of the
matter (2.18–20), the speakers give no explicit consideration
to the courtier's subservient duties as prince pleaser—despite
their paramount importance. Ludovico da Canossa points out
near the beginning of his talk that *grazia* must be "an adornment informing and attending all his actions" in order for the
courtier to show himself "worthy of the company and the favor
of every great lord" (1.14). But it is virtually the only time he
indicates that the courtier's graceful self-display is primarily
intended to win the prince's approbation. In general, when
Castiglione's speakers recommend various stylistic attributes
that the courtier must possess, they rarely, if ever, point out
that these attributes are especially desirable because they are
pleasing to the prince. One might think that they, not their
sovereign, are the principal arbiters of graceful conduct at court.
This deceptive impression is further reinforced, of course,
by the absence of Urbino's ruler, Duke Guidobaldo, from the
parlor game taking place in his palace. Appearances to the
contrary, however, the ruler is not excluded from the conversations at Urbino: Castiglione's speakers obfuscate but never
ignore the prince's decisive influence while they fashion their
model individual. For if we consider some of the courtier's

principal stylistic attributes and try to establish why they are
valued, it gradually becomes apparent that these attributes are
not simply advocated because they appeal to the social and
esthetic tastes of a courtly elite but, more importantly, because
they are necessary and effective means of maintaining a favorable relationship with the prince.

Consider an attribute such as *mediocrità*, the difficult moderation deemed so graceful an aspect of the courtier's style and
personality. Basically, mediocrità consists of balancing with their
opposites predominant traits determined by habit, inclination,
office, age, or state of mind. For instance, older men display it
when they temper their gravity with lighthearted wit, younger
ones when they balance their boisterousness with sober calm.
So, mediocrità can be achieved by moderating seriousness with
jest, pride or presumption with modesty, fervor with detachment, or exhibitionism with reticence. Because this requires the
individual to behave in ways contrary to his natural inclinations, or to disguise innate tendencies with their opposites,
mediocrità calls for enormous flexibility. Castiglione's speakers
stipulate that the courtier display this flexibility in his opinions
and attitudes as well as in his external behavior. Exemplified by
Ludovico da Canossa in the course of the debates he provokes
in book 1, the tempered style demands that the courtier be
ready not only to concede the validity of views contrary to his
own but also to moderate his beliefs so that they will accommodate contrary views.

As Castiglione portrays them, the courtiers at Urbino show
little tolerance for earnest partisanship or single-mindedness
of any kind, but prize, instead, flexibility and even paradox
in demeanor and points of view. It is consistent, therefore,
that they should advocate and value mediocrità. Moreover, the
claims of politeness and deference that are shown to prevail in
courtly company—and made all the more pronounced by the
presence and participation of women—demand the balanced
restraint and flexible accommodation that define mediocrità.
But the main reason for possessing such moderation and flexibility—namely, that the courtier has to master mediocrità to

win or retain the favor of his ruler—remains virtually unstated by the discussants. Unyielding tenacity on the part of a courtier may provoke criticism and mockery from his equals, but what inhibits such obstinate behavior even more is that the prince will simply not tolerate it in his subordinates. Conversely, the courtier's elasticity may win admiration among his peers but he has to possess it primarily because, as companion and servant of his ruler, he must always be ready to accommodate himself to the latter's changing and unpredictable whims. I maintained earlier that the company at Urbino devotes little specific discussion to the courtier's ingratiating conduct in the company and service of his sovereign. However, when Federico Fregoso does offer some brief advice on the subject (2.18–20), pliability is the first quality he recommends for maintaining a good relationship with the ruler. Federico proposes that the courtier must always be ready to accommodate his ruler's wishes for playful diversions. "Ed a questo voglio," he explains,

> che il cortegiano *si accomodi, se ben da natura sua vi fosse alieno,* di modo che, sempre che 'l signore lo vegga, pensi che a parlar gli abbia di cosa che gli sia grata; il che interverrà, se in costui sarà il bon giudicio per conoscere ciò che piace al principe, e lo ingegno e la prudenzia *per sapersegli accommodare, e la deliberata voluntà per farsi piacer quello che forse da natura gli despiacesse.* [2.18, italics mine]
>
> [And I would have our Courtier *bend himself to this, even if by nature he is alien to it,* so that his prince cannot see him without feeling that he must have something pleasant to say to him; which will come about if he has the good judgment to perceive what his prince likes, and the wit and prudence *to bend himself to this, and the considered resolve to like what by nature he may possibly dislike.* . . . .]

Mediocrità, as I said, calls upon the individual to perform in ways contrary to his natural inclinations. But until Federico offers the above advice, one might forget how indispensable this quality becomes in the company of the rulers and, hence, a main reason for valuing it as a courtly attribute. So, when Federico goes on to warn against presumption and obstinacy in conversations with the prince, one more fully realizes that unyielding single-mindedness is deemed undesirable not only because it violates the mediocrità required in polite company but because it is bound to alienate the prince.

Federico's discussion of the courtier's proper relationship with the ruler does not last very long. Still, it suffices to help the modern reader recognize that political motives underlie most of the courtier's beautiful stratagems. For instance, Federico goes on to stipulate that

> se 'l cortegiano, consueto di trattar cose importanti, si ritrova poi secretamente in camera, dee vestirsi un'altra persona, e differir le cose severe ad altro loco e tempo ed attendere a ragionamenti piacevoli e grati al signor suo, per non impedirgli quel riposo d'animo. [2.19]

> [if a Courtier who is accustomed to handling affairs of importance should happen to be in private with his lord, he must become another person, and lay aside grave matters for another time and place, and engage in conversation that will be amusing and pleasant to his lord, so as not to prevent him from gaining such relaxation.]

One is led to suppose, before this brief directive, that the ability to shift from gravity to facetiousness, or to embody them simultaneously, is an aspect of mediocrità desired by the courtiers as a group rather than by the ruler dominating the group. Certainly Urbino's courtiers display a marked intolerance of unrelieved seriousness. Given their admiration of the individual's capacity to embody opposites, they consider it much more graceful to blend seriousness with levity. From their point of view this blend does not jeopardize serious intention but rather makes it more attractive. In fact, the very activity engaging them as a group—fashioning an ideal of civilized man while playing a parlor game—serves to exemplify the *serio ludere* they consider so attractive an aspect of the courtier's tempered style. Yet, again, as Federico's above directive indicates, it is primarily in order to relieve and delight his prince that the courtier must know how to offset gravity with play. Norms of elegance at court may well call for an ability to treat serious matters playfully, but more essential for the courtier's social and political survival is the fact that this ability can serve to enhance his relationship with this ruler. Similarly, because the courtier wins admiration among his equals by balancing seriousness with jest, one can understand why so much discussion is devoted to the means and range of joking at the end of book 2. But if one keeps in mind the courtier's duty to engage in "ragionamenti piacevoli e grati al signor suo," it becomes even clearer why the capacity to raise laughter has to be one of his necessary talents. In general, it is because the ruler's favor or assent can be won more easily by appealing to his pleasurable instincts that the courtier must possess and develop artistic and recreative skills.

Federico devotes most of his brief account of the courtier's relationship with his prince to proper ways of suing for favors. The courtier, he warns, must particularly avoid aggressive or importunate solicitation. He must wait

> che i favori gli siano offerti, più presto che uccellargli così scoper-tamente come fan molti, che tanto avidi ne sono, che pare che, non conseguendogli, abbiano da perder la vita. (2.19)

> [until favors are offered to him rather than fish for them openly as many do, who are so avid of them that it seems they would die if they did not get them.]

Modest but studied reticence, on the other hand, will prove much more effective in obtaining princely rewards:

> Dee ben l'omo star sempre un poco più rimesso che non comporta il grado suo; e non accettar così facilmente i favori ed onori che gli sono offerti, e rifutargli modestamente, mostrando estimargli assai, con tal modo però, che dia occasione a chi gli offerisce d'offerirgli con molto maggior instanzia; perché quanto più resistenzia con tal modo s'usa nello accettargli, tanto più pare a quel principe che gli concede d'esser estimato. . . . (2.19)

> [A man ought always to be a little more humble than his rank would require; not accepting too readily the favors and honors that are offered him, but modestly refusing them while showing that he esteems them highly, yet in such a way as to give the donor cause to press them upon him the more urgently. For the greater the resis-tance shown in accepting them in this way, the more will the prince who is granting them think himself to be esteemed.]

Prescriptive comments made earlier in the book already establish the comeliness of ironic reticence and studied indirection.
But it takes Federico's directives to remind us when and how
the courtier's *sprezzatura* and *disinvoltura* can be put to most
effective use. His recommendations serve to remind us, moreover, that fierce competition for favors is a pressing and an
ever present condition of courtly existence. Again, this constant
rivalry for preferment is left to be inferred in previous conversations. For example, when Ludovico da Canossa initially recommends that the courtier "put every effort and diligence into
outstripping others in everything a little, so that he may be always recognized as better than the rest" (1.21), he neglects to
mention that such competitiveness is prompted by the need to
impress the ruler and thereby win his preferment. To be sure,
the ruler's desire to keep his subordinates in check, as well as
the court's standards of polite refinement, compel its members
to subdue or at least mask their aggressive and competitive
drives. That is why such qualities as reticence, detachment, and
understatement are so valued at court. Castiglione's speakers
repeatedly suggest that the more sprezzatura and disinvoltura
the courtier displays when disguising his efforts at outperforming others, the more admiration he will win from his peers. For
instance, on an earlier occasion, when Federico speaks of the
courtier's musical skills, he says,

> Venga adunque il cortegiano a far musica come a cosa per passar
> tempo e quasi sforzato; . . . e benché sappia ed intenda ciò che fa, in
> questo ancor voglio che dissimuli il studio e la fatica che è necessaria
> in tutte le cose che si hanno a far bene, e mostri estimar poco in se
> stesso questa condizione, ma, col farla eccellentemente, la faccia es-
> timar assai dagli altri. (2.12)

> [Let the Courtier turn to music as to a pastime, and as though
> forced. . . . And although he may know and understand what he
> does, in this also I would have him dissimulate the care and effort
> that is required in doing anything well; and let him appear to es-
> teem but little this accomplishment of his, yet by performing it
> excellently well, makes others esteem it highly.]

Such displays of sprezzatura, however, are not simply recommended to the courtier because they will delight his peers. It

must be kept in mind that the courtier exhibits his various skills
in order to impress his sovereign and win his good graces.
His displays of virtuosity are, in effect, bids for preferment
and, just like his actual requests for favor, they are likelier
to be effective when disguised by apparent reticence and nonchalance. As Federico subsequently makes clear, the prince's
intolerance of presumptuous self-promotion on the part of his
suitors makes it particularly important to master sprezzatura
and disinvoltura. The deference, moreover, that the courtier
must show in the presence of his ruler demands that he veil
and underplay his various talents in order not to outshine his
superior. Too open a display of his skills or virtues might expose by contrast his sovereign's lack of such qualities, thereby
calling into question a supremacy that the courtier cannot af-
ford to challenge. Furthermore, when one keeps in mind how
unpredictable and whimsical the sovereign's bestowal of grace
can be, the need for sprezzatura and disinvoltura becomes all
the more apparent. Despite his real merits, however appealing
his prince-pleasing strategems, the courtier can never be sure
to obtain his patron's grace and favor. He always faces the risk
that, for reasons beyond his control, the efforts he exerts to
gain such favor will be ignored or discounted. His ability therefore to disguise and minimize such efforts when outperforming
others becomes indispensable if he is to avoid losing face and
status whenever these efforts fail or are simply unacknowl-
edged by his ruler.

Indirection is so prized in the courtier's world, and obvious-
ness so unseemly, that dissimulation has to characterize most
aspects of his conduct. Sprezzatura, considered one of the chief
sources of grazia, always requires deliberate subterfuge because
it entails making artifice seem natural, studied effort seem easy
and casual. Even mediocrità is deceptive because it often demands that the courtier consciously disguise a particular disposition by cultivating an appearance of its contrary. In general,
the courtier's conduct is deemed most graceful when it is most
ironic, when his actions or stances subtly imply their opposites.
Why do the courtiers at Urbino prize such discrepancy between

being and seeming? Or conversely, why do they show such distaste for plain and perspicuous conduct? Sheer esthetic preference aside, it seems very consistent that an aristocratic elite, seeking to exclude all but a privileged few, should cherish and promote all ornamental behavior or discourse that refines, obscures, and even defies common usage. Castiglione's speakers repeatedly indicate that the pleasure derived from the covert and ironic guises they recommend will escape individuals of plainer and therefore baser taste. To some extent, then, the courtier's tactics of indirection and deception are ploys by which he asserts his social superiority and refinement. But to an equal, if not greater extent, these ploys are conditioned by the prudential relation he must maintain with his sovereign and even his peers. Transactions with a despotic ruler require ingratiating deceit. Again, lest we might forget, Federico's directives on currying favors from the prince remind us how ineffective and risky undisguised truth can be at court. Federico tells the courtier:

> Rarissime volte o quasi mai non domanderà al signore cosa alcuna per se stesso, acciò che quel signor, avendo rispetto di negarla così a lui stesso, talor non la conceda con fastidio, che è molto peggio. Domandando ancor per altri, osserverà discretamente i tempi; . . . ed assetterà talmente la petizion sua, levandone quelle parti che esso conoscerà poter dispiacere e facilitando con destrezza le difficultà, che 'l signor la concederà sempre, o se pur la negarà, non crederà aver offeso colui a chi non ha voluto compiacere. (2.18)
>
> [Rarely or almost never will he ask of his lord anything for himself, lest his lord, not wishing to deny it to him directly, should perchance grant it to him with ill grace, which is much worse. And when asking something for others, he will be discreet in choosing the occasion; . . . and he will so frame his request, omitting those parts that he knows can cause displeasure, and will skillfully make easy the difficult points, so that his lord will always grant it, or do this in such wise that, should he deny it, he will not think the person whom he has thus not wished to favor goes off offended.]

Obviously, a relation that calls for this kind of obfuscation would only be jeopardized if the courtier chose to be plain and

direct with his master. As Ottaviano remarks on a later occasion, "If I had the favor of some of the princes I know, and if
I were to tell them freely what I think, I fear I should soon lose
that favor" (4.26). The courtier, such observations make apparent, inhabits a world where graceful deceit is not only valued
for its intrinsic delight but because the despot who governs that
world makes it imperative.

The ties between the courtier's ingratiating deceits and the
exigencies of despotic rule are finally made explicit on the last
evening of discussion, when Ottaviano Fregoso takes his turn as
main speaker. Ottaviano attempts, it will be recalled, to transform the model courtier from the beautiful parasite he thinks
his colleagues have fashioned into a moral counselor of the
prince. However, he is sagacious enough to recognize that modern princes, accustomed to the fawning ways of their servants,
would react most adversely if they had to countenance the
"orrida faccia della vera virtù." So even though he considers
insufficient the graceful style and accomplishments the other
speakers have prescribed, he realizes that without them the
courtier would be quite unable to exert any moral influence on
his prince. As he laments,

> Poiche oggidì i principi son tanto corrotti dalle male consuetudini e
> dalla ignoranzia e falsa persuasione di se stessi, e che tanto è difficile
> il dar loro notizia della verità ed indurgli alla virtù, e che gli omini
> con le bugie ed adulazioni e con così viciosi modi cercano d'entrar
> loro in grazia, il cortegiano, per mezzo di quelle gentil qualità che
> date gli hanno il conte Ludovico e messer Federico, po facilmente e
> deve procurar d'acquistarsi la benivolenzia ed adescar tanto l'animo
> del suo principe. (4.9)
>
> [Since the princes of today are so corrupted by evil customs and by
> ignorance and a false esteem of themselves, and since it is so dif-
> ficult to show them the truth and lead them to virtue, and since men
> seek to gain their favor by means of lies and flatteries and such
> vicious ways—the Courtier, through those fair qualities that Count
> Ludovico and messer Federico have given him, can easily, and must,
> seek to gain the good will and captivate the mind of his prince.]

And he goes on to stipulate that the courtier use his beautiful
and ingratiating talents as a "salutary deception" by means of

which he can edify his sovereign (4.10). However idealistic the courtier may be, Ottaviano recognizes that dissimulation must remain his most characteristic habit of style. Eventually Ottaviano's attempt to transform the courtier into a didactic agent becomes too unrealistic, but even when he is carried away by his own moral fervor he remains aware that, given the fallibility of princes, didactic persuasion demands even more guileful subterfuge than the courtier's other rhetorical intents.

Ottaviano displays exemplary mediocrità when he tempers his idealism and acknowledges that the courtier's likelihood of edifying his sovereign depends on the cunning and deceit he is previously asked to cultivate. Although he is more idealistic than the previous speakers, he reveals the pragmatism that he shares with them by acknowledging more openly than they do that the political pressures of an autocratic order make necessary the artful behavior advocated in the book. On the other hand, his more open recognition of such political exigencies entails, as we can see, a criticism of modern princes that such despots would find intolerable to hear. This undisguised criticism makes us aware, in retrospect, of why speakers such as Ludovico and Federico are relatively silent about the political constraints that shape their stylistic prescriptions—for the very same reasons that they stipulate indirection and subterfuge. To point out the unpleasant realities of despotic rule that determine their norms of conduct would contradict the prudential cunning they recommend. In other words, by so often leaving us to construe that their primary objective is to fashion a cunning prince pleaser, they exemplify the covertness that must perforce be practiced under princely rule. This deliberate resemblance between the speakers' conduct and the graceful manners they advocate was, of course, Castiglione's own subtle way of commemorating the civilized refinement that he had seen achieved at Urbino. For it showed that the behavior of its courtiers in reality could approximate an ideal of courtiership imagined in a game.

As I have tried to show, however implicit they remain for most of the book, the constraints of an autocratic order shape the art of conduct set forth in Castiglione's book. The *Cortegiano* is,

in effect, an art of prince pleasing since virtually every beautiful attribute the courtier is asked to cultivate can be success-
fully used to win the good will of a sovereign or to preserve it.
This pragmatic aspect of the book needs to be emphasized, if
only to explain the tremendous success of the *Cortegiano* in
Renaissance Europe. We, as modern readers, may feel dis-
mayed by the growing sense that most of the beautiful manners
advocated in the book are made necessary by the loss of sincer-
ity and free expression, by the sycophancy and servitude that
individuals are made to bear in a despotic political system. Yet
in the sixteenth century, when autocratic rule gained such as-
cendance in Europe, when despotic courts became the centers
of power and fashion, was it not precisely because Castiglione
provided an ideal of artful behavior tailored to suit the dictates
of such institutions that readers found his book so pertinent
and instructive?

NOTES

1. For an exaggerated and polemical account of Castiglione's escapist idealism, see Giuseppe Prezzolini's introduction to his edition of B. Castiglione—G.
Della Casa, *Opere* (Milan and Rome, 1937). Similar, if less extreme, claims that
Castiglione's ideal is divorced from reality recur in modern discussions of
the *Cortegiano*, especially whenever it is compared with Machiavelli's *Principe*.
Among interpretations that emphasize the work's elegiac or nostalgic character,
see Giuseppe Toffanin, *Il "Cortegiano" nella trattastistica del Rinascimento* (Naples,
1960?), pp. 37–39, and, more recently, Wayne Rebhorn, *Courtly Performances:
Masking and Festivity in Castiglione's Book of the Courtier* (Detroit, 1978), especially pp. 91–115.

In my *Poetry and Courtliness in Renaissance England* (Princeton, 1978) I have
already proposed that the pressures of Renaissance despotism shaped the behavior of Castiglione's ideal courtier, but after reconsidering my discussion of
the *Cortegiano* in that earlier study (see pp. 18–49) I felt that it needed this
supplementary essay to demonstrate more precisely and more emphatically the
extent to which Castiglione's norms of conduct are determined by these political pressures.

3

Politics and the Praise of Women: Political Doctrine in the *Courtier*'s Third Book

Dain A. Trafton

The sixteenth century in Europe was one of reduced political options.[1] Monarchy was in the ascendant almost everywhere. Here and there, older traditions of feudal aristocracy, civic autonomy, and republicanism retained some vigor, but the pressures tending to focus power in the figure of a strong central monarch and his court dominated the age. As a result, a young man of political virtue and ambition, taking his bearings around 1500 in Milan, Naples, Vienna, Paris, or London (and a bit later in Madrid), saw two main paths open before him: to become a prince or a courtier. Only a rare young man, obviously, found in circumstances or in himself what it took to become a prince. For him the century produced, by its second decade, a book of instruction that stands out above all other such books written before or after: Machiavelli's *Prince*. For the others—the young men of ambition whose virtue had not been transformed into *virtù* or whose spirit was simply of a different order—there appeared, about the same time as the *Prince*, another preeminent guide to conduct: Castiglione's *Book of the Courtier*. It is said that the Emperor Charles V, who seems to have grasped as well as anyone the peculiar character of the age, kept both these books along with the Bible by his bedside. Perhaps he thought of the *Prince* and the *Courtier* as repositories of an essential political wisdom analogous to the spiritual

29

wisdom of Holy Scripture. Indeed, the *Courtier* and the *Prince* might be considered the fundamental political testaments of the sixteenth century.

That the *Courtier* is in some sense a political book will be readily granted; it instructs in the arts of getting along at court and thus reflects the political realities of the age. But can the book be described as political in the strict sense of the word? Does Castiglione offer more than a superficial examination of the essential fact of sixteenth-century politics: princely rule itself? Does he provide any truly practical suggestions about how courtiers ought to participate in that rule? The *Courtier* invites these questions. At the beginning of the fourth book we are told that the courtier's highest duty consists in teaching his prince to be a better ruler (4.5). We are told further that the courtier must couch his teaching in a cautious, oblique style (4.9–10). What the content of that teaching should be, however, remains disappointingly vague. Beyond a few pious generalities—a prince must be temperate and virtuous (4.16), must participate in the contemplative as well as the active life (4.26), must obey the laws and set a good example (4.33), and must reward the good while punishing the bad (4.34)—book 4 has nothing to say about the actual business of ruling. Such truisms hardly constitute an adequate guide to the slippery and dangerous world of Cesare Borgia and Julius II. Must we conclude, then, that the preeminent book about courtiers is radically deficient, that it fails precisely when it comes to the most important matter, to the courtier's function as political counselor? I think not. In this essay I shall try to demonstrate that the *Courtier* does in fact supply practical political instruction aimed at preparing courtiers who must guide princes. I intend to assert Castiglione's claim as a serious writer of political doctrine.

My approach will be to focus on what might at first seem an unlikely element in the *Courtier*'s structure: the discussion of women in the third book. One might expect the attempt to describe the court lady, which induces the company to turn away from the courtier himself at the end of the second book, to lead to something quite different from politics—to the social graces, perhaps, or chastity, or courtly love. While touching on all these matters, however, the third book also contains an extended commentary on rule. Indeed, it is the most truly political of the *Courtier's* four books. It goes directly to the heart of sixteenth-century politics and raises the most searching question about the courtier's function. Beneath the camouflage of the court lady and assorted tales of good women, the third book reveals the fundamental orientation of Castiglione's political thought. As we shall see, that thought is not so different from Machiavelli's as most commentators have concluded or assumed.[2] The *Courtier's* political doctrine cannot be reduced to dully edifying platitudes; it is informed by a spirit of boldness, flexibility, and pragmatism. At the same time, book 3 enables us to establish some important distinctions between Castiglione's boldness and pragmatism and those of his less moderate Florentine contemporary. Castiglione's readiness to fight evil on its own terms, "to make good use of the beast as well as the man,"[3] is restrained by a firmly traditional sense of limits. Because his affinity with Machiavelli has not been understood, the originality and vigor of Castiglione's allegiance to tradition have also been missed.

The third book opens with an analogy that hints at the political seriousness of what follows. Castiglione first describes the ingenuity by which Pythagoras was able to determine the probable size of the body of Hercules. Since the Olympic stadium at Elis was known to be 625 times as long as Hercules' foot, while other stadiums were 625 times as long as the foot of an ordinary man, Pythagoras concluded that Hercules' body must have been larger than an ordinary man's body in the same proportion as the stadium at Elis was larger than other stadiums. "Thus you," Castiglione goes on, addressing Alfonso Ariosto, "by the same reasoning may clearly know, from this small part of the whole, how superior the Court of Urbino was to all others in Italy, considering how much these games, which were devised for the relaxation of minds wearied by more arduous endeavors, were superior to those practiced in the other courts of Italy. And if these were such, imagine what the other worthy pursuits were to which our minds were bent and wholly given over" (3.1). Through this analogy the *Courtier* reminds its readers that the games it records, refined and fascinating though they are, do not represent the real business of courtiers. Those games may, as some critics have suggested, provide an image of the workings of a high civilization, with its love of style, its sublimated eroticism and aggression, its cult of individual perfection.[4] As a social and political organization, however, no court is self-sufficient; ultimately, no court justifies itself in itself but rather in its role as head and heart of a larger social and political structure where courtly gentility does not predominate, where sublimation and a sense of style cannot be depended upon to create order. In this greater and harsher world, men have to be ruled; the heroic energy and force of a Hercules (the whole man, not just his foot) are needed. To the portrait of the courtier's foot, furnished by books 1 and 2, the third book's discussion of women adds the rest of the body, especially the head, heart, and strong right arm.

After some preliminary uncertainty, discussion on the third night settles into the Magnifico Giuliano de' Medici's attempt to describe a court lady who can be considered the equal of the courtier as he has emerged from the first two books. Initially the description proceeds along familiar lines established during the previous nights. The Magnifico makes passing reference to practically every virtue known to moral and political philosophy but locates the court lady's specific excellence in "a certain pleasing affability . . . whereby she will be able to entertain graciously every kind of man with agreeable and comely conversation suited to the time and place and to the station of the person with whom she speaks" (3.5). Challenges from Gaspar Pallavicino, however, soon force abandonment of this neatly limited approach. Some of these challenges simply reflect Gaspar's role, which he obviously relishes, as the group's sacrificial misogynist but others cannot be so easily dismissed. At one point, drawing attention to the disparity between the Magnifico's casual references to the highest virtues and his stress on "affability," Gaspar remarks, "Since you have granted letters and continence and magnanimity and temperance to women, I am quite surprised that you do not wish them to govern cities, make laws, lead armies, and let the men stay home to cook and spin" (3.10). The Magnifico promptly replies, "Perhaps that would not be so bad either," and finds himself drawn rapidly into a discussion that cuts through mere affability to serious intellectual, moral, and political issues.

At first the discussion takes the form of an abstract and almost scholastic debate over the nature of women. Gaspar unlimbers some of the big guns in the arsenal of traditional misogyny: woman is a "defect" or "accident" of nature; man can be compared to "form" and woman to "matter," and since "form" is superior to "matter" man must be considered superior to woman; men are by temperament warm, women cold, and "warmth is far more noble and more perfect than cold." To each of these and other similar points, the Magnifico offers a careful and thoroughly convincing rebuttal (3.11–19). There can be no doubt that here and elsewhere the *Courtier* asserts the dignity of women and their essential equality with men. In itself, of course, this assertion amounts to a political teaching of great consequence, and among the *Courtier*'s many influences on later European civilization, its contribution to an increasing recognition of, and respect for, women might be traced. Within the dramatic economy of the dialogue, moreover, the Magnifico's skillful rebuttal of misogyny serves to raise him above the general run of Urbino's courtiers. We see for the first time the qualities of mind that establish him in the course of book 3 as one of Castiglione's chief spokesmen—a figure comparable in authority to Ottaviano Fregoso or Pietro Bembo. In addition, the Magnifico's demonstration that both sexes must be considered equally capable of virtue serves as a necessary preparation for what follows: his elaboration of a series of tales about good women into a vehicle for political ideas intended to have a general applicability to both sexes.

Between the demonstration and the tales, however, the Magnifico introduces a digression that is of great importance for

understanding the design of book 3. Lamenting the plight of
women whose goodness remains unknown "because the poor
creatures are kept shut in," the Magnifico suddenly launches
into a tirade against a certain group of "accursed hypocrites
among men," who by their wiles win a false reputation for piety
and virtue. These hypocrites make a show of holiness, going
about with bowed heads and ragged habits, while in fact they
are bent upon seductions, forgeries, murders, treacheries, and
"every sort of villainy." The Magnifico refrains from naming
the group he means but his unstated point is not lost upon
Emilia Pia. She promptly identifies the object of his attack as
the friars and reproaches him for speaking ill of them. "Then,"
Castiglione tells us, "the Magnifico laughed and said: 'How,
Madam, have you guessed so well that I was speaking of friars
when I did not name them?'" (3.20). Through this digression
Castiglione alerts us to a dimension of the Magnifico's rhetoric
that is essential to an interpretation of his stories about women.
He knows how to speak through hints and implications; he
does not always make his main point explicit. To catch his full
intention we must, like Emilia Pia, be prepared to perceive
what is implied clearly enough even when it is not named.

Of the Magnifico's stories of good women, some amount to
little more than the citation of a famous name; others are presented in enough detail to be understood even by a reader
unfamiliar with their sources. The latter are the more revealing. Although all support the contention that women are capable of the highest virtue, the more fully developed stories illustrate the particular qualities that not only women, but men
too, need in order to rule and function as advisers to rulers. In
the very first of these stories the Magnifico confronts the young
courtier abruptly with the political world that awaits him beyond
the sheltering walls of the palace. In compiling a list of women
who "have been as worthy of praise as the great men whose
wives or sisters or daughters they were," the Magnifico first
names several well-known Roman ladies and then extols at
length the "prudence" of Alexandra, wife of Alexander, King of
the Jews (3.22). After the death of the tyrannical Alexander,

the people rose in arms, eager to revenge themselves by killing his children. Grasping the danger, Alexandra acted promptly, boldly, and effectively. She had her husband's body thrown into the public square and addressed the mob, commiserating with them, inviting them to tear her husband to pieces and feed him to the dogs but begging them "to have mercy on her innocent children." Her words "were so effective that the fierce wrath prevailing in the minds of all the people was at once mitigated and converted to such a feeling of pity that with one accord they not only chose those children as their rulers, but they even gave a most honorable burial to the body of the dead man." Alexandra's story carries with it the bracing odor of the real world of power and violence—an odor that pervades the *Prince* but that has been for the most part absent from the *Courtier* up to this point. Alexandra is faced not with the obstreperousness of a Gaspar but with an enraged mob, out for her children's and perhaps her own, blood. And she triumphs not through learned wit and charming raillery but by confronting ruthlessness with ruthlessness, by boldly and impiously encouraging a mob to desecrate her husband's body in the hope that this will satisfy their passions and win them to her side. Her bold impiety, which the Magnifico characterizes as "prudence," succeeds. Here is a tale to be pondered by courtiers who would instruct princes. The Magnifico does not call attention to the fact that his very first extended example of a virtuous woman introduces a new and more realistic tone into the discussion. As in his description of the friars, he lets the style and substance of his account speak for themselves. At least one of his reasons for such indirectness can be readily understood. Speaking ill of friars may arouse Emilia; to describe as "prudence" Alexandra's throwing her husband's body to the mob (even granting that he was a tyrant) might be considered much more subversive. It implies that ordinary decency may be irrelevant and even a hindrance to the real business of ruling.

Many of the stories that follow prompt similar reflections. A thread of political realism and pragmatism runs throughout the Magnifico's examples, distinguishing book 3 from the rest of the *Courtier* as well as from conventional handbooks of politics and courtesy. When the Magnifico recounts how the Trojan women with Aeneas "helped in the founding of Rome," his tale stresses not only their benefaction but also the trickery by which it was achieved (3.29). The fugitives from Troy had landed near the mouth of the Tiber. While the men were away in search of provisions, the women, who were weary of traveling and had remained behind, burned the ships so that their husbands would not be able to reembark. Thus the men were forced to accede to the wishes of the women and to found the city that became Rome. In fact, the Magnifico asserts, following Plutarch, the very name of the city honors a certain Roma, the leader of this female meeting.[5] From an act of conjugal deception, an act that would be blameworthy on moral grounds, it appears that salutary political consequences as well as fame may result. A student of the ways in which courtiers should deal with princes might also remark in this story about women the implication that such deception can be especially helpful when the weak seek to influence the strong.

From the story of Rome's founding, the Magnifico proceeds immediately to the story of its preservation through the Sabine women. Of the various rapes by which Romulus supplied the city with women, the Magnifico comments simply—and rather surprisingly in view of his role as a defender of women—that Romulus succeeded in most of them "since he was a man of ability" (3.30). As is well known, however, the Sabines were less easily exploited than some of their neighbors. The Sabines attacked Rome in an effort to free the captured women, and the battle was still undecided when the women themselves rushed between the armies and persuaded them to lay down their weapons. The Magnifico lauds the Sabine women's "piety and wisdom" in thus accepting their rape and in reconciling the men of their native city to the fait accompli. Furthermore, he goes on to describe how Romulus repaid those "wise and courageous women": "When he divided the people into thirty wards, he gave to these the names of Sabine women." Here again, as in his accounts of Alexandra and the Trojan women, the Magnifico delicately, but nonetheless clearly, indicates that political success requires a degree of freedom from morality. From a political perspective, "piety," "wisdom," and the acquisition of fame may depend upon ignoring the strict demands of honor and justice, not to speak of chastity.

Christianity too, the Magnifico indicates, may be politically enfeebling. The story about "a gentleman in Pisa whose name was messer Tommaso," his wife madonna Argentina, and his son Paolo (3.27) can be read as a warning to the courtier against the tendency to rely upon Providence rather than one's own strength and skill. On a trip to Sicily messer Tommaso had fallen into the hands of Barbary pirates. In defending himself before his capture, he had killed the brother of a pirate captain, and in revenge the victors had determined to hold him without ransom. Freed prisoners returning from North Africa had informed madonna Argentina of her husband's sufferings, and all had concluded that his situation was hopeless "unless God should miraculously help him." Messer Tommaso himself had come to accept his enslavement. At that point, however, "it came to pass that a sedulous piety so spurred the wit and daring of one of his sons, whose name was Paolo, that the youth took no thought of any kind of danger and resolved that he would either die or free his father; and in this he succeeded and brought him out so secretly that he was in Leghorn before it was known in Barbary that he had escaped." Unfortunately, the unexpected joy of this event proved too intense for madonna Argentina; upon learning the news, she "raised her eyes to heaven and, calling her husband's name, fell dead." Ostensibly this story illustrates women's capacity for faithful love. In fact, the Magnifico's telling focuses not on madonna Argentina's passive faith but on the vigor and self-reliance of Paolo. When everyone else had decided that only a miracle could save his father, Paolo took matters into his own hands. His "sedulous piety" was not of the kind that resigns everything into God's hands—the kind that Machiavelli thought had so debilitated the ancient virtue in Italian hearts.[6] Paolo's was a "piety" that exercised itself in "wit and daring." Only that kind, the Magnifico leads his readers to infer, is of practical political value in a world infested by pirates.

Consistent with the implications of the story of messer Tommaso is the emphasis on arms that emerges from a proportionally large number of the Magnifico's examples.[7] He introduces the theme with two stories about the women of Chios (3.32). The first tells how they were so angered by an insulting enemy that they took arms and overcame him themselves when their husbands proved unable to do so. The second extols their fierce independence in adversity. Having been defeated by the Erythraeans, the men of Chios agreed to depart into exile "dressed only in their cloaks and tunics." When the women learned of the agreement, however, they reproached the men for abandoning their weapons and persuaded them "to leave their clothes behind and to carry their shields and spears; and to tell the enemy that these were their attire. And so," the Magnifico concludes, "following their women's advice, they undid in great part the shame from which they could not entirely escape." Later stories underline the political lesson. The Magnifico assembles an impressive collection of women who benefited their countries because they understood (often better than their men) the need for martial virtue: Persian women who shamed a routed Persian army into returning to battle (3.32); Spartan women "who rejoiced in the glorious death of their sons . . . who disowned or even slew their sons when they saw them act like cowards" (3.33); women of Saguntum who fought against Hannibal (3.33); Pisan women "who in the defense of their city against the Florentines showed that generous courage, without any fear whatever of death, which the most unconquerable spirits that ever lived on earth might have shown" (3.36); Queen Isabella of Spain, to whom "alone is the honor of the glorious conquest of the kingdom of Granada to be attributed" (3.35).

Behind these and the Magnifico's other stories in book 3 lies, it is true, no systematic political program—no blueprint for uniting Italy against the barbarians, no scheme for revitalizing Italian arms,[8] not even a comprehensive list of the virtues necessary for rule. Rather, the Magnifico's political teaching seems to aim at the inculcation of certain fundamental insights and attitudes essential to political success. Above all, it seems, the courtier, and the prince whom he instructs, must not allow the elegant, civilized sublimations of the court to obscure the fact that cruder passions and ugly dangers inform the outside world of politics; those passions and those dangers cannot be laughed away with raillery but must be subdued by bold cunning and force. Both the courtier and the prince must know how to confront brutality on its own terms; they must be prepared to fight ruthlessness with ruthlessness, to counter strength with strength, or with deception, to make the best of indecent necessities, and to depend upon themselves instead of Providence. They must cultivate freedom from too fastidious a morality and from the potential enervation of piety.

In view of the bold and potentially shocking character of this political teaching, Castiglione's decision to camouflage it in the rhetoric of a character adept at speaking obliquely is understandable. To express such ideas openly would have been imprudent for a man who was himself a courtier moving in the highest circles and who was serving, at the time of the book's publication, as papal nuncio to the court of Charles V. Self-protection, however, does not provide a complete explanation of the third book's subtle art. Castiglione's indirection also reflects the essential conservatism that informs the *Courtier* as a whole—the love of style, the respect for the decorous and decent, and the idealism that are such striking features of the work's surface texture. Unlike Machiavelli, Castiglione does not revel in the harsh, ugly, and shocking facts of life. He is fully aware of those facts and realizes that they must be understood by courtiers who advise rulers, but he refuses to engage in an assault upon traditional values and pieties in the name of realism. By concealing rather than trumpeting his view that those traditional vaues and pieties are sometimes politically inadequate, Castiglione upholds them, albeit in a qualified manner. Praise of constancy, love, continence, chastity, and the values of the classical–Christian synthesis carries a dominant weight throughout book 3 and the rest of the *Courtier*, in spite of the

Magnifico's indications that a darker knowledge too is needful. Machiavelli takes his political bearings by the extreme cases of brutality—Romulus's murder of Remus, Hannibal's "inhuman cruelty," and Cesare Borgia's *virtù* at Sinigaglia;[9] Castiglione wants courtiers to meditate upon such cases and grasp their implications for the problem of ruling but not to make them an excuse for the abandonment of established values. For Castiglione virtù appears to complement, but does not replace, virtue.

Indeed, one of the Magnifico's longest and most impressive stories (the story of Camma [3.26]) is designed to stress this point and to suggest the limits that a courtier must try to impose upon a ruler's freedom to deviate from conventional norms. Camma was a very beautiful married woman who had the ill luck to arouse the lust of a certain Sinoris, a man "who was almost tyrant of the city where they lived." Having tried in vain every means of seduction, Sinoris finally had Camma's husband murdered and offered to marry her. She refused, but her parents, impressed by the advantages of such a match as well as the dangers of refusing it, kept urging her to reconsider. At last she pretended to accept and on the wedding day took her revenge with a poisoned drink she had prepared: "Before Diana's image and in the presence of Sinoris, she drank half of it; then with her own hand (for such was the custom at marriages) she gave the rest to the groom, who drank it all." Before dying herself, she had the satisfaction of learning that the tyrant had already expired. In light of the worldly pragmatism that informs so many of his stories, the Magnifico's moralizing tone, with no hint of ulterior meanings, surprises here. The predicament of Camma might remind us of the Sabine women whose adaptation to an advantageous rape the Magnifico approves, and Sinoris might seem not so different from the enterprising and apparently unscrupulous Romulus. However, a crucial dissimilarity separates the two stories. Both Romulus and the Sabine women acted as they did for truly political ends—the preservation of the city—whereas Sinoris had nothing in view beyond his private pleasure, and nothing except personal advantage could have resulted from Camma's acquies-

cence. By censuring Sinoris while approving Camma's firm re-
jection of moral compromise, the Magnifico establishes the standard that must control the doctrine of pragmatism that he
teaches elsewhere. That doctrine is strictly political in scope; it
is not meant to provide an excuse for private greed and lust.
For the Magnifico, only the public good—true political necessity—can justify deviations from strict morality.

One detail in the story of Camma indicates, furthermore,
that the Magnifico's teaching about the limits of pragmatism
has a special pertinence for courtiers. Sinoris is described as
"almost the tyrant of the city." We learn that he is able to
arrange for the murder of Camma's husband and to use his
rank to intimidate her parents. In resisting him, Camma resists
not simply private lust but the lust of a public man who is
willing to exploit his public position for private ends. Among
other lessons, the Magnifico's praise of Camma conveys a subtle
encouragement to resist tyranny. The importance of this lesson
within the Magnifico's political teaching as a whole is revealed
by the fact that resistance to tyranny appears as the theme of
two of his other stories: the stories of Epicharis and of Leona
(3.23). According to the Magnifico, Epicharis was "a Roman
freedwomen, who, being privy to a great conspiracy against
Nero, was of such constancy that, although racked by the worst
tortures imaginable, she never betrayed any of her accomplices;
whereas many noble knights and senators, in the same peril,
timorously accused brothers, friends, and the dearest and near-
est they had in the world." To Leona, the Athenians "dedicated
a tongueless lioness (*leona*) in bronze before the gate of the
citadel" because she too endured torture without betraying
a plot against tyranny. Near the beginning of the *Courtier*'s
fourth book, Ottaviano Fregoso pronounces a stern judgment
on "the princes of today," describing them as full of "extreme
self-conceit," interested only in power, and antagonistic toward
"reason" and "justice" (4.6–9). He might be describing Sinoris;
such princes are plainly tyrants. Nevertheless, Ottaviano remains apparently optimistic that many of them can be changed
for the better by the gentle and artful persuasion that he rec-

ommends to courtiers (4.9–10, 47).[10] The stories of Camma,
Epicharis, and Leona suggest that the Magnifico does not share
this optimism. There are times, these stories warn, when a
courtier will have to resist tyranny by force, will have to put the
arts of courtiership per se—the jousting, the dancing, the loving,
even the giving of good counsel—behind him and call upon
sterner political virtues. At such times, concern for the common good must weigh more heavily than any merely pragmatic
consideration of personal advancement. Like the good women
whom the Magnifico praises, the courtier must be prepared
to be killed and to kill; he must exhibit the heroic spirit of
Hercules, who, according to Ottaviano, "waged perpetual and
deadly war" against tyranny (4.37).[11]

Now we are in a position to grasp even more clearly the
prudential considerations that underlie Castiglione's conceal-
ment of his teaching about rule. Exhorting courtiers to tyran-
nicide not only contradicts the *Courtier's* prevailing emphasis
on the normal rather than the extreme cases but also subverts
the fundamental understandings on which a book of advice to
courtiers rests. When courtiers turn rebels they cease to be
courtiers. The Magnifico's praise of Camma, Epicharis, and
Leona leads ultimately to an understanding of the limits of
courtiership, to an awareness of the point beyond which one
cannot be both a good courtier and a good man. The Magnifico's instruction in the bold pragmatism necessary to rule is
not, it seems, intended only as advice to be passed on to princes.
Such instruction also provides courtiers with the understanding
that they will need to combat tyrants. Indeed, it might not be
too much to say that the Magnifico intends to provide courtiers
with the understanding necessary in the extreme case to make
themselves princes. These are dangerous ideas, especially in
light of Ottaviano's description of the tyrannical proclivities of
"the princes of today." One wonders what Charles V thought as
he reflected upon the Magnifico's tales of good women. If that
prince penetrated the third book's veiled political doctrine,
perhaps he recognized the benign as well as the self-protective
motive behind the veiling. Perhaps his own experience and po-

sition made him sympathetic to the political temper of a man who looked unflinchingly at the base facts that absorbed Machiavelli, who acknowledged the necessity implicit in those facts, but who still preserved an allegiance to the humane ideals of tradition. Of course there is no way to know exactly what Charles made of the *Courtier*, but if we bear in mind the dimension of the book that has been described here, we may discover a special poignancy in the eulogy that we are told the emperor pronounced upon learning of Castiglione's death: "Yo vos digo que es muerto uno de los mejores caballeros del mundo" ["I tell you that he who is dead was one of the greatest gentlemen in the world"].

NOTES

1. For fuller accounts of the political situation described in the opening paragraph of this essay, see H. G. Koenigsberger and George L. Mosse, *Europe in the Sixteenth Century* (New York, 1968), pp. 212–44 (there is a useful bibliography on pp. 212–13); Denys Hay, *The Renaissance: 1493–1520*, New Cambridge Modern History, I, ed. Denys Hay (Cambridge, 1957), pp. 5–10; and G. R. Elton, "Constitutional Development and Political Thought in Western Europe," in *The Reformation: 1520–1559*, New Cambridge Modern History, II, ed. G. R. Elton (Cambridge, 1958), 438–63. Cf. Lauro Martines, "The Gentleman in Renaissance Italy: Strains of Isolation in the Body Politic," in *The Darker Vision of the Renaissance: Beyond the Fields of Reason*, UCLA Center for Medieval and Renaissance Studies, Contributions, VI, ed. Robert S. Kinsman (Berkeley, 1974), 77–81.

2. See Ralph Roeder, *The Man of the Renaissance* (New York, 1933), pp. 213–312; Erich Loos, *Baldessare Castigliones "Libro del Cortigiano": Studien zur Tugendauffassungen des Cinquecento* (*Analecta Romanica*, II; Frankfurt am Main, 1955), 26, 72–156, 183–210; Alfredo Bonadeo, "The Function and Purpose of the Courtier in *The Book of the Courtier* by Castiglione," *Philological Quarterly*, 50 (1971), 36–46; and Martines, "Gentleman in Renaissance Italy," pp. 87–93.

3. See the *Prince*, trans. and ed. Mark Musa (New York, 1964), chap. 18, p. 145: "You should know, then, that there are two ways of fighting: one with the law, the other with force: the first way is peculiar to man, the other to beasts; but since the first in many instances is not enough, it becomes necessary to resort to the second. Therefore, a prince must know how to make good use of the beast and the man."

4. See especially the excellent work of Wayne A. Rebhorn: "Ottaviano's Interruption: Book IV and the Problem of Unity in *Il Libro del Cortegiano*,"

Modern Language Notes, 87 (1972), 37–59, and *Courtly Performances: Masking and Festivity in Castiglione's* Book of the Courtier (Detroit, 1978).

5. Plutarch, "Mulierum Virtutes," in *Moralia* (243F), ed. F. Dübner (Paris, 1861), 1, 301.

6. See especially Machiavelli's discussion of the connection between religion and political liberty in *Discourses* 3.2.

7. Cf. the *Prince*'s stress on possessing arms of one's own (especially chaps. 6, 7, 12–14, 24).

8. Cf. J. R. Hale's remarks on Castiglione's lack of military experience (pp. 146–59, below).

9. See the *Prince*, chaps. 7 (Sinigaglia), 17 (Hannibal's "inhuman cruelty"), and *Discourses* 1.9 (Romulus's murder of Remus).

10. That Ottaviano's optimism is not unqualified is indicated by his remark that "if I had the favor of some of the princes I know, and if I were to tell them freely what I think, I fear I should soon lose that favor" (4.26). See Thomas M. Greene's comment on this passage (pp. 12–13, above).

11. Ottaviano's reference to Hercules' fame as a destroyer of tyrants aims explicitly at inspiring princes. Coming to the passage after an attentive reading of book 3, however, one cannot help reflect that courtiers too may emulate Hercules.

4

Grazia, Sprezzatura, Affettazione in the *Courtier*

Eduardo Saccone

Grazia, sprezzatura, affettazione—these three words have long claimed the particular attention of students of Baldesar Castiglione's *Book of the Courtier*. Although the first of them has generally been the object of most frequent and intensive investigation, careful readers have generally recognized that there exists among all three an interrelation and interdependence. The scrutiny to which they have consequently been subjected has been, in a sense, excessive, and not without unfortunate results. For many illustrious scholars have concentrated, not on the function of these key terms in their proper context—the total verbal universe of the *Book of the Courtier*—but on their role as indicators of or partakers in some larger theoretical frame.

As examples of this problematic tendency, I will mention three well-known attempts to place Castiglione's "theory of grace" in the respective contexts of the history of Renaissance philosophy, the overall history of ideas, and the development of "classical art theory." Eugenio Garin dedicates a section of the chapter on "Platonism and the philosophy of love" in his study *L'umanesimo italiano* to the problem of grace; in it he speaks of "two great theorists of grace, Castiglione and Della Casa," and, using dubious supporting texts and arguments, attempts to show how the "concept" of grace presented by Castiglione, as the very cornerstone and premise of the *Book of the Courtier,* depends on Ficino or more broadly on Neoplatonic thought.[1]

Much more recently, in the article on "grace" in the *Diction-*

ary of the History of Ideas, Rudolf Wittkower begins by survey-
ing the concept of *venustas* in classical authors from Cicero to
Quintilian and the Elder Pliny as the antecedents of the more
modern grazia, "the irrational element in works of art" that
defies "rational analysis." He continues: "From the XVI century
onward classical art theory was permeated with this concept.
'Grace' for the Italians from Baldesar Castiglione to Vasari and
beyond was *un non so che,* which in the French theory of the
XVII century became the *je ne sais quoi* and in England, in
Pope's immortal phrase, 'a grace beyond the reach of art.'"[2]
Wittkower in turn makes explicit reference to the most significant study of grace from the history of ideas perspective, that
of Samuel Holt Monk.[3] Here again there is much that we might
wish to question, although this is not the place to do so.

Finally, in Anthony Blunt's *Artistic Theory in Italy 1450–1600,*
we learn that Vasari, "the first writer to elaborate the theory of
grace in connection with painting, . . . only applied to the arts
the conception of grace as a necessary part of behaviour which
had been evolved by the writers of manners, particularly those
of the Neoplatonic school, such as Castiglione." But Blunt later
states, "'Grace' is that extra quality which is added to the more
solid 'properties' and 'conditions' which can be acquired by precept. Grace, on the other hand, cannot be learnt; it is a gift
from heaven; and it comes from having a good judgement."
Blunt attempts to clarify this point as follows: "It will vanish if a
man takes too much pains to attain it, or if he shows any effort
in his actions. Nothing but complete ease can produce it. And
the only effort which should be expended in attaining it is an
effort to conceal the skill on which it is based; and it is from
sprezzatura . . . that grace springs."[4] So grace is an "extra quality," not to be acquired by precept because it is a gift from
heaven. On the other hand (and here the logic of the argument
escapes me) it derives from good judgment, from that effort to
conceal skill that is sprezzatura.

I have not lingered over details of these instances, since it has
been my sole intention to illustrate arguments about Castiglione's terminology quite different from my own in the extra-

textual focus of their definitions. In the present essay I will try not to limit discussion of *grazia, sprezzatura,* and *affettazione* to a relatively narrow semantic field, that of aesthetics, or to flee from the complex reality of the text in search of definitions but rather to adhere to it as far as possible. I will, in short, start not from disembodied ideas (which often can be made to seem deceptively clear and distinct) but from the materials of which literary texts are made, that is, the words themselves. Beginning first of all, as we must, with *grazia,* let us, before considering its use in the *Courtier,* note the characteristic ambivalence of the Italian word, and antecedently of the Latin *gratia,* from which it derives.

The broadest, most fruitful, and most complex definition, but also the most precise that I know—applicable as well to the Italian as the Latin—is to be found in the *Thesaurus Linguae Latinae*:

> *gratia* proprie favorem significat, i. inclinationem animi ad bene faciendum alicui, colendum aliquid tam ultro quam ob beneficium ante acceptum. hinc transfertur ad statum eius personae, cui hic favor accidit. similiter de qualitate rerum, quae placent, adhibetur.[5]

> [Strictly, *gratia* signifies favor, i. the inclination of the soul toward doing well to someone, or toward cherishing something, as much gratuitously as because of any benefit previously accepted. Whence it is transferred to the condition of the person to whom this favor pertains. Similarly it is applied to the quality of the thing that pleases.]

In insisting on the meaning of *gratia* as "favor," this definition puts the stress (as to some extent do all other dictionaries, both Latin and Italian) on the semantic alternation, equally present in the Latin *gratus* and the Italian *grato,* made evident by the active and passive uses of the word. Thus, for example, an expression such as "Io ti son grato" can mean either "I am welcome, or appreciated, I am acceptable to you," or "I feel gratitude towards you." The definition also points out the twofold value, abstract and concrete, of the term. *Grazia* is an attribute, or rather a gift, that presupposes two parties: one who attributes, gives, or offers and another who takes, receives, or accepts; he who favors and he who is favored. It is a process, an operation, therefore, that necessarily implies a beginning and an end or, rather, an intention and an object. It is interesting to note that this structure is substantially retained even in the specifically Christian usage of the word. The only real distinction is relatively unimportant in this context, though essential in its own: that is, that the two parties in Christian usage are specified as God and man, with the concomitant gratuitousness of the gift. What counts, however, is the retention of the structure. We may also remark that in either case (Christian or non-Christian) there is a tendency to reify the term in a substance or a quality, in some more convenient and simplified identity that obscures its progressive character, sacrificing as well its dynamism and adaptability and rendering it static and determinate.

The semantic alternation implicit in *grazia* is explicitly recalled in the *Courtier* when Cesare Gonzaga declares "the very meaning of the word," by which "it can be said that he who has grace finds grace" ("si po dir che chi ha grazia quello è grato") (1.24). On the other hand, in confirmation of the definition given in the *Thesaurus,* which insists, as we have seen, on the fundamental sense of "favor," here is the first occurrence of the word in Castiglione's text, where it appears in significant relation to the final end immanent in the formation of the perfect courtier: "Now, you have asked me to write my opinion as to what form of Courtiership most befits a gentleman living at the courts of princes, by which he can have both the knowledge and the ability to serve them in every reasonable thing, thereby winning favor from them and praise from others [acquistandone da essi grazia e dagli altri laude]: in short, what manner of man he must be who deserves the name of perfect Courtier, without defect of any kind" (1.1).

The grace at issue here is that of the prince and is to be distinguished from "praise," which ought to come from "others." In chapter 7 of book 2 this distinction appears to be reaffirmed: "noble birth," "talent," "bodily disposition, and comely aspect" ("grazia dell'aspetto") are all very well, says Federico

Fregoso, but more is required "to win praise deservedly, and a good opinion on the part of all, and favor from the princes whom he serves" ("e grazia da quei signori ai quali serve"). It appears, in other words, that we should here reserve for grace a specifically vertical relationship, one, that is, that moves exclusively from the prince "down" to his courtier. This insistence should not be viewed as a casual component in the strategy of the book; certainly it anticipates the end of the courtier's profession as it is delineated in the fourth book, where the theory is set out of the courtier's function as counselor and almost preceptor to the prince, a situation that is obviously owing to the "favor acquired by his good accomplishments" ("la grazia acquistata con le sue bone qualità"), as we read there (4.5). Thus grace becomes, from an end in itself, the means in turn to another and higher end, to that "good end" ("bon fine") that is the education and direction of the perfect prince.

This vertical application of grace is not, however, universally valid throughout the *Book of the Courtier*. In another passage (2.17) we read: "But in the end all these qualities in our Courtier will still not suffice to win him universal favor with lords and cavaliers and ladies" ("per acquistar quella grazia de' signori, cavalieri e donne").[6] Here the vertically directed lord–courtier relationship no longer pertains but is replaced by a horizontal dimension. The favor or grace desired by the courtier must come as well from "cavalieri e donne," that is, from the other members of the class to which the courtier belongs.

Up to this point, it will be noted, the examples I have listed have this in common: They all refer to the object of, or rather the end to, the final moment of a process, the moment when grace is achieved (*acquistata*—the verb recurs in all these passages). We ought now to consider the other pole of the process, from the end to the beginning, as it were, or from the other to the self. But first we must establish a further necessary element of the definition of *grazia,* the neglect of which lies at the heart of various noteworthy misunderstandings about its meaning and is certainly responsible for some of the ambiguities particularly evident in the critical passages cited above, especially

those of Wittkower and Blunt. It will be recalled that the former spoke of grace in works of art as an "irrational element," a
non so che, while the latter went so far as to call it a "gift from
heaven." Neither formulation sees the word as an element of
Castiglione's larger plan (one that is essential to the pedagogical
scheme of the *Courtier*): to delimit an area of human activity
that can serve as an Aristotelian middle ground between two
exceptional conditions, the "mean" between absolute perfection
and imperfection, between "eccellente grazia" and "insensata
sciocchezza" ("I say that there is a mean to be found between
such supreme grace on the one hand and such stupid ineptitude on the other, and that those who are not so perfectly
endowed by nature can, with care and effort, polish and in
great part correct their natural defects" [1.14]). One could perhaps even say that for Castiglione such an area occupied the
territory between the divine and the brutish, and hence the
territory that a humanist might deem specifically human. To
establish one border of the territory (the only one in which we
may speak of truly human social behavior),[7] Castiglione (through
Count Ludovico da Canossa) invoked Don Ippolito d'Este, cardinal of Ferrara, exemplifying the divine or, rather, representing those who "seem not to have been born, but to have been
fashioned by the hands of some god, and adorned with every
excellence of mind and body" (1.14). At the opposite extreme
stand the "many others so inept and uncouth that we cannot
but think that nature brought them into the world out of spite
and mockery." Just as for the representatives of the first category the "summit of the highest excellence" is an attribute, an
original grace, the others, on the contrary, "yield little fruit
even with constant diligence and good care" ("assidua dili-
genzia e buona crianza poco frutto per lo più delle volte possono fare").

As I have already suggested, however, the discussion in the
Courtier applies not to the especially gifted or the absolutely
ungifted but indeed to those who, without being "so perfectly
endowed by nature," can nevertheless, "with care and effort,
polish and in great part correct their natural defects." What is

required, in other words, is a minimal but necessary basis from which to build, that will comprise, according to the desideratum of Ludovico da Canossa, "besides his noble birth, . . . [his being] endowed by nature not only with talent [ingegno] and with beauty [bella forma] of countenance and person, but with that certain grace which we call an 'air' [una certa grazia e, come si dice, un sangue], which shall make him at first sight pleasing and lovable [grato ed amabile] to all who see him; and let this be an adornment informing and attending all his actions, giving the promise outwardly that such a one is worthy of the company and the favor [del commerzio e grazia] of every great lord" (1.14).

This comment by Ludovico is especially interesting for the differing uses that are made of the word *grace* in the two places where it occurs. The second instance, in which the *grazia,* or favor, is the end or object of a behavioral process, coincides in meaning with the preceding examples given from the *Book of the Courtier.* At the beginning of the speech, however, the "certa grazia e, come si dice, un sangue" seems ambiguous, consisting on the one hand of an initial quality that determines the desired result ("un sangue, che lo faccia al primo aspetto a chiunque lo vede grato ed amabile"), while, on the other, coinciding with the *non so che* described by Wittkower. I would, however, argue that a more precise definition is possible. This grace, coming as it does at the end of a list of virtues ("nobilità, . . . ingegno e bella forma di persona e di volto") and preceded by a "but" that, rather than opposing, seems to comprehend and color all the preceding qualities, signifies not so much a particular quality as a modality, an ability: the graceful using of qualities so as to provoke grace ("and let this be an adornment in forming and attending all his actions, giving the promise outwardly that such a one is worthy of the company and the favor [grazia] of every great lord"). A modality, thus, instead of a fixed, identifiable quality: here is an important, even fundamental distinction that will recur in the treatment of that other grace which a courtier can and must learn, and more generally in the treatment of his learning and exercise of the profession of courtiership, which, in Richard Lanham's words, consists not in learning "a pattern of concepts, of whatever sort, but a skill."[8] From yet another, Aristotelian perspective, we may describe the courtier's grace as a virtue, resulting from habit, become in itself a habit: a habitual state. We can therefore scarcely be surprised that this first level of grace, which we may identify as natural, is explicitly distinguished from beauty. In 1.19 Bibbiena makes a distinction between the "beauty of [his] person," which he doubts, and "the grace of countenance" ("la grazia del volto"), which, as Canossa declares, "you can truly be said to have." "Although the features of it are not very delicate, . . . we do see beyond any doubt that your aspect is very agreeable [gratissimo] and pleasant to all"; and he adds that Bibbiena's face "has something manly about it, and yet is full of grace [grazioso]."

But let us come at last to the other grace. Canossa has already recommended several qualities to be required of an excellent courtier: the use of arms, honor, faith, discretion in praising himself, agility in every physical exercise, wrestling, fencing, horsemanship, and so on. While setting out his requirements he has two or three times included the caveat that the courtier must temper "his every action with a certain good judgment and grace [un certo bon giudicio e grazia] if he would deserve that universal favor which is so greatly prized" (1.21).[9] At this point Cesare Gonzaga intervenes to request an explanation, or, more precisely, Canossa having "aroused" in his audience an ardent desire ("un'ardente sete") to attain this grace, which he has added "as that seasoning without which all the other properties and good qualities would be of little worth" (1.24), Gonzaga now invites him to satisfy it ("estinguerlo") with his teaching. It is well to note that Gonzaga, in formulating his request, has reaffirmed the distinction we have observed between those few who possess grace by "a gift of nature and the heavens," and so have no need for teachers, being already "not only pleasing [grati], but admirable to everyone," and the many "who are less endowed by nature and are capable of acquiring grace only if they put forth labor, industry, and care." This being the case, "by what art, by what discipline, by what method" can the latter "gain this grace, both in bodily exercises, . . . and in every other thing they do or say [come in ogni altra cosa che si faccia e dica]"?

Canossa, being called upon thus peremptorily to extinguish Gonzaga's "ardent thirst," does not excuse himself from the "obligation" put upon him, but, in a manner characteristic of Castiglione's strategy in the text, anticipates stating the *form* of his doctrine by offering an *example* of it to demonstrate grace in action. Hence he effects a *correctio* with a gesture that is perhaps analogous to the author's choice for the book of a dialogue or portrait form in preference to the catechistical form of a treatise. "'I am not bound,' said the Count, 'to teach you how to acquire grace or anything else, but only to show you what a perfect Courtier ought to be. . . . So I, perhaps, shall be able to tell you what a perfect Courtier should be, but not to teach you what you must do to become one'" (1.25). Canossa's restatement of his charge, including as it does a refusal to take on the ungracious task of teaching grace, has already all the earmarks of sprezzatura, of which he is about to speak. In effect the model to be imitated (himself, clearly, in this case) has already been displayed, but covertly, that is to say, without affectation. Now he suggests the mode of imitation to be used, one akin to assimilation, which will call to mind as its exemplar not the ape but the bee.

> Chi adunque vorrà esser bon discipulo, oltre al far le cose bene, sempre ha da metter ogni diligenzia per assimigliarsi al maestro e, se possibil fosse, transformarsi in lui. E quando già si sente aver fatto profitto, giova molto veder diversi omini di tal professione e, governandosi con quel bon giudicio che sempre gli ha da esser guida, andar sceglendo or da un or da un altro varie cose. E come la pecchia ne' verdi prati tra l'erbe va carpendo i fiori, così il nostro cortegiano averà da rubare questa grazia da que' che a lui parerà che la tenghino e da ciascun quella parte che più sarà laudevole; e non far come un amico nostro, che voi tutti conoscete. (1.26)
>
> [Therefore, whoever would be a good pupil must not only do things well, but must always make every effort to resemble and, if that be

possible, to transform himself into his master. And when he feels that he has made some progress, it is very profitable to observe different men of that profession; and, conducting himself with that good judgment [bon giudicio] which must always be his guide, go about choosing now this thing from one and that from another. And even as in green meadows the bee flits about among the grasses robbing the flowers, so our Courtier must steal his grace from those who seem to him to have it, taking from each the part that seems most worthy of praise; not doing as a friénd of ours whom you all know."]

We cannot doubt that we are dealing here with the exercise of an art, or rather of *areté* in the Aristotelian sense. And insofar as it is an art, exactly like those of painting or speaking referred to elsewhere in the *Courtier,* Castiglione holds the observation and imitation of existing models, the best possible models, to be essential to it. In his dedicatory letter to Don Michel de Silva, bishop of Viseo, Castiglione, pronouncing himself in favor of *lingua cortigiana,* proposes to take account of "la consuetudine del parlare," "the idiom of the other noble cities of Italy where men gather who are wise, talented, and eloquent, and who discourse on great matters pertaining to the governing of states, as well as on letters, war, and business." We may take this declaration as a noteworthy, if not definitive, indication of what the "bona consuetudine," the "good usage in speech" of chapter 35 in book 1 can mean.[10] In the light of the letter to Don Michel de Silva we can say that this language pertains manifestly to a class. It has "grace," that is, *grata.* Here, as elsewhere, the question of grace cannot be propounded absolutely but only relative to Castiglione's specific time, place, and intended audience. Even if the *Book of the Courtier* reaches out, in the course of its discussions, beyond the court of Urbino, the Italy of Castiglione's day in which he worked and wrote, and beyond the class (his own) whose portrait and apology he makes, still these coordinates must continually be borne in mind if we wish to understand his text. For this reason we may find it more misleading than helpful to elucidate Castiglione's *grazia* (or *sprezzatura* or *affettazione*) by means of words and concepts either anterior or posterior to the context he establishes for them: the *cháris* of Demetrius Phalareus or Dionysus of Halicarnassus, for example, or the *venustas* of the Elder Pliny or Quintilian, the *decor* of Cicero, the *grazia* of Firenzuola, Della Casa, or Vasari, and so forth. Not that the meaning of the word *grazia* in Castiglione is divorced from, or independent of the Greco-Latin tradition: not at all. But it is certainly significant that he was constrained to invent a new word, *sprezzatura*, to express an idea that was not unknown either to the Greeks or to the Latins. Why a new word, then, and why that particular word?

The famous passage in book 1, chapter 26, has been quoted a thousand times but I cannot avoid recalling here, in my turn, its most salient features. Ludovico says, "But, having thought many times already about how this grace is acquired (leaving aside those who have it from the stars), I have found quite a universal rule which in this matter seems to me valid above all others, and in all human affairs whether in word or deed." At this point the discussion appears to be maintained on a very general level: "una regola generalissima," dealing with "tutte le cose umane che si facciano e dicano." Yet it is precisely at this moment that the word *grace* comes to be delimited and assumes its special meaning for the work. The "universal rule" begins with a negative prescription: "and that is to avoid affectation in every way possible as though it were some very rough and dangerous reef." Whenever did grace come to consist in the avoiding of affectation? If we wish to make the *venustas* of Pliny and Cicero or the *gratia* of Quintilian the ancestor of Castiglione's *grazia* and *sprezzatura*, we should also not forget that in Pliny the *nimia diligentia* ("too much care") that cancels *cháris*, *venustas*, refers only to art and more precisely to the painting of Apelles as opposed to that of Protogenes;[11] by the same token in Cicero (*Orator* 23.78) it is a question of the oratory of Lysias, in which "quaedam etiam neglegentia est diligens" ("there is such a thing even as careful negligence"), and, just as with women who go "unadorned," yet "are said to be more beautiful," so also in the Greek orator "there is something . . . which lends greater charm, but without showing itself;" again in Quintilian the reference is once more to Apelles in *Institutio Oratoria* (12.10.6) and to Lysias (9.4.17), and then to Horace and Terence.[12] We are still very far from "all human affairs whether in word or deed" ("tutte le cose umane che si facciano o dicano").

All the same, if this enormous extension of *grazia*, or rather of the possible areas to which this word is applicable, is real, it is not yet indiscriminate or undetermined. Just who are they that do or say "tutte le cose umane"? On reconsideration it appears that they are almost exclusively the members, actual or potential, of the courtly "club" memorialized in the *Book of the Courtier*.[13] Castiglione did not make of his book the treatise on human nature that Burckhardt, citing those of its parts that might belong in such a treatise, could claim it to be; instead, he restricted his investigation to a single class whose ambition is to lead. And yet, in describing how the making of the courtier involves the search for a certain perfection within the context of a predetermined social sphere and a distinctive ideology, Castiglione often consciously refers to, and finds himself in accord with, the most classical ethical formulations. This is, as I have indicated, most particularly true with respect to Aristotle. In many ways, indeed, the very aim of the *Book of the Courtier* is to portray *areté*, and to demonstrate its basis in *mesótēs*, the "giusto mezzo," the *mediocritas* referred to several times in the text:[14] the proper mean that in respect to worth is also, as Aristotle describes it, an apex and an extreme.[15] And for Castiglione as for Aristotle, *areté* depends on three factors: nature (*physis*), habit (*ethos*), and science (*logos*).[16] We may even perhaps add that the more aristocratic character of the *Courtier* has led the writer to go back and reappropriate elements antecedent to the Aristotelian synthesis itself, as for example the insistence on nobility and the dependence of *areté* on the approbation of the group, and its definition (as in Pindar and Theognis) as a successful activity (*eupragia*).

But, we asked, what need is there for a new word, and why that word? Turning back now to book 1, chapter 26, we find that Canossa, having described what is to be avoided "in every way possible as though it were some very rough and dangerous reef"—that is, affectation—continues: "and (to pronounce a new word perhaps) to practice in all things a certain *sprezzatura,* so as to conceal all art and make whatever is done or said appear to be without effort and almost without any thought about it." What is the novelty of this word that it should have given such endless trouble to translators? In order to understand it properly, I think we must consider the nature of this disdain, misprision, or depreciation that the etymology suggests. At the most immediate and evident semantic level, these terms apply to (and qualify) *diligentia,* the very art that is put into operation by the practitioner. Hence comes the oxymoron: an art without art, a negligent diligence, an inattentive attention. The contrary and enemy of sprezzatura, Castiglione tells us plainly, is affectation, which consists in overstepping the "certain limits of moderation" ("certi termini di mediocrità"), wherein resides the "excellence" of sprezzatura.

Here we may observe the exact repetition of the Aristotelian scheme mentioned above. It will be worthwhile for our purposes, however, to refer more precisely than we have yet done to book 2 of the *Nicomachean Ethics,* where the philosopher, turning his attention to those virtues and vices relative to interpersonal relations, identifies the virtue that he calls *alḗtheia,* or truthfulness, as proper measure, its two extremes being on the one hand boastfulness, *alazoneía,* and on the other *eirōneía,* or irony. Both the latter imply *prospoíesis,* dissimulation, pretense. The difference between them is that whereas the former goes too far in the direction of excess, *epì tò meizon,* whereby a man makes claim to merits he does not possess and inflates those he does, the latter lags too far behind, tending toward paucity, *epì tò élatton,* so that it intentionally diminishes those merits and takes the form of understatement.[17] Aristotle's attitude toward eirōneía is, however, singular, and, I should say, ambiguous. Although he does not hesitate to condemn alazoneía, he is extremely cautious with respect to irony. When speaking of magnanimity in book 4 of the *Ethics,* Aristotle repeats his praise of the *alḗtheutikós* and *authekastós,* of the truthful and straightforward character, which the magnanimous man will evince in all his words and actions. His language will be truthful and straight-forward, "unless when he has recourse to irony, which will be his tone in addressing the generality of men."[18] Again in 4.7.9, after repeating that both *eíron* and *alazón* are insincere and hence blameworthy, he goes on to say that if a frank and truth-ful man is obliged to deviate from the truth, he should have recourse to understatement in preference to exaggeration. The reason, interestingly enough, that Aristotle gives for this pref-erence is that irony seems to have more grace, it has a more elegant effect, as opposed to the crudity, the distastefulness that must accompany any excess. Once again in 4.7.14, we read that ironic persons give an impression of superior refinement "because we feel that their way of speaking is not dictated by greed or gain but by the desire to avoid showing off."[19] Thus, if men employ irony in moderation and when the subject is not too banal and obvious, they appear to posess distinction, cháris, and so make a pleasant impression. Here it will be well also to recall the passage in the *Rhetoric* on wit, of which some varieties are deemed appropriate for use by a gentleman but others not. In this context Aristotle affirms that irony is more fitting for a gentleman than buffoonery. In using irony, indeed, he seeks his own amusement; in playing the buffoon that of others.[20]

Why then did Castiglione, who almost certainly was familiar with these passages, choose to ignore the proper mean of Aris-totle, which in this case was *alétheia,* and, while continuing to speak of "certain limits of moderation" and *mediocritas,* to priv-ilege instead the word corresponding to *eirōneía, sprezzatura?* It may be useful here, if perhaps not entirely necessary after so much has already been said, to repeat with G. C. Sedgewick, the author of a good study *Of Irony, especially in Drama,* that, even though the notion of irony "as understatement—a mere rhetorical figure—derives from Aristotle, it was not the centre of his idea of *eironeia.* In the *Ethics eironeia* is a pervasive mode of behaviour, a constant pretence of self-depression, of which understatement is only one manifestation."[21] But again, why did

Castiglione abandon the orthodox (I refer to the etymology) *alḗtheia* for the paradox of *sprezzatura*?

The answer, I believe, will be found in a certain sense implicit in some of the observations of Aristotle, especially in those, shall we say, embroiled pronouncements on *eirōneía* that I have cited above. When the philosopher speaks of distinction, of elegance, of finesse, he seems to reveal in the use of this word an attitude to class values that we must call aristocratic. We have already particularly noticed how the magnanimous man will have recourse to irony in his dealings with the generality of men, the masses. It might further be interesting to note that traditionally writers treating the subject of irony have dwelt almost exclusively on its polemic as opposed to its playful aim.[22] But in our case, or rather that of Castiglione, against whom is the polemic directed, against whom the misprision, and who is the butt of the joke?

We know that the essential thing for the practice of irony, as also of sprezzatura, is dissimulation: a trick, or at any rate always a detachment, a discrepancy between being and seeming. A dissimulation obviously is intended to the disadvantage of someone. Whose, and of what sort, is this deception? What are its characteristics and its limits, if limits they are? Let us try to articulate the structure of the communicative process with which we are dealing. The success of irony, as of sprezzatura, or as of a witticism, obviously depends on its reception. The public is the arbitrator of grace, that is, of the success or failure of sprezzatura. This we know, but what public? Will it be the generality, the mass, or a more restricted, qualified public, the "happy few"? This is the crucial point but also the least attended to. Indeed, to tell the truth, it has been completely ignored in the treatment of the *Book of the Courtier*.

In order to understand this communicative process (which is the same, to a certain extent, for wit as it is for irony), it is necessary, in my opinion, to postulate a structure that is not simply dyadic (emitter–receiver) but at least triadic. We must admit, in the case in question, a bifurcation of the receiver, the public, into two parts, one of which is not necessarily present on the scene. One of these parts will recognize an instance of sprezzatura or irony for what it really communicates, and thus sanction its success; the other will take the action or affirmation at its face value, admire, without recognizing, the sprezzatura or irony. In other words it will serve as its victim. The price it pays will be its exclusion from the club of the happy few. To put it differently, sprezzatura is the test the courtier must pass in order to be admitted to this club, to obtain the recognition of his peers. This division of the public into general and restricted exists above all to remind us that what is at play is a contest for distinction, with the ever-present and actual risk of failure. The enemy, the seeming adversary, would be affectation or exaggeration of any kind. But to combat such an adversary, as Aristotle foresaw, alétheia would be sufficient. The real enemy of sprezzatura is something else again: the lack of sprezzatura, the quality of being explicit instead of implicit, direct instead of indirect. Sprezzatura functions like a set of inverted commas that it would be unpardonable to omit. The inverted commas are there although they remain invisible for those who have not the skill to see. The appeal of sprezzatura is to those who have that skill.

The interpretative scheme I have attempted to set out is no more than that, a scheme, which can only simplify a textual reality that is much richer and more complex, and at times indeed even contradictory. Yet such as it is, the scheme still seems to me to be able to render some account of specific textual difficulties that would otherwise remain inexplicable, and at the same time to distinguish and set in a historical context the grace that is the preoccupation of Castiglione's courtier.

The grace of the courtier, Canossa is made to say, depends on sprezzatura, that is, on a certain excellence, in itself rare and difficult, that gives the impression of facility. This impression, given the difficulty understood to reside in the attainment of such excellence ("because everyone knows the difficulty of things that are rare and well done" [1.26]) provokes wonder and admiration. In whom? At this point it would be fair to say in the public in general without distinction of kind. But why must the art be concealed? And what does it signify that it must? "Because if it is discovered, this robs a man of all credit and causes him to be held in slight esteem" is Canossa's answer. Here the text follows with an example in order to demonstrate the validity of this observation. The example itself, however, is problematical and can be applied to our case only if we refer it to just one part of the public:

> E ricordomi io già aver letto esser stati alcuni antichi oratori eccellentissimi, i quali tra le altre loro industrie sforzavansi di far credere ad ognuno sé non aver notizia alcuna di lettere; e dissimulando il sapere mostravan le loro orazioni esser fatte simplicissimamente, e più tosto secondo che loro porgea la natura e la verità, che' l studio e l'arte; la qual se fosse stata conosciuta, arìa dato dubbio negli animi del populo di non dover esser da quella ingannati. (1.26)

> [And I remember having read of certain most excellent orators in ancient times who, among the other things they did, tried to make everyone believe that they had no knowledge whatever of letters; and, dissembling their knowledge, they made their orations appear to be composed in the simplest manner and according to the dictates of nature and truth rather than of effort and art; which fact, had it been known, would have inspired in the minds of the people the fear that they could be duped by it.]

It is evident that we must distinguish here between two publics, as also between fiction and reality. Obviously the orations to which Canossa refers must have been very differently received by the members of the public who were to be persuaded and those in the know—fellow advocates, for instance. The former are deceived in earnest (it is not the question here whether this deception be to a good end); the latter will admire the art of the orator and in him recognize an excellent compeer. But what if this artifice were evident or were exposed? The result would be doubly catastrophic. The first public would recognize the trick and refuse to let themselves be persuaded; the other would moreover find deplorable (affected, inelegant, strained, perhaps even unprofessional) the performance of their colleague. For this restricted public of the competent, sprezzatura consists, beyond doubt, of a performance, like a conjuring act, which they attend, knowing full well that there is some trick: there must be, even if they canot find it out. The other public do not even guess that there is a trick. Their wonder may seem alike but it is not; it belongs, in effect, to a completely different order. The ideal, then, is "that pure and charming simplicity which is so appealing [grata] to all" (1.27), but the group in the know are well aware that they must not take the words literally, because their "simplicity" and "nature" are artificial constructions.

If we go a little further in the *Courtier* (1.28), we find that Canossa adds a significant codicil:

> Questa virtù adunque contraria alla affettazione, la qual noi per ora chiamiamo sprezzatura, oltra che ella sia il vero fonte donde deriva la grazia, porta ancor seco un altro ornamento, il quale accompagnando qualsivoglia azione umana, per minima che ella sia, non solamente sùbito scopre il saper di chi la fa, ma spesso lo fa estimar molto maggior di quello che è in effetto; perché negli animi delli circunstanti imprime opinione, che chi così facilmente fa bene sappia molto più di quello che fa, e se in quello che fa ponesse studio e fatica, potesse farlo molto meglio.

> [Thus, this excellence (which is opposed to affectation, and which, at the moment, we are calling *sprezzatura*), besides being the real source from which grace springs, brings with it another adornment which, when it accompanies any human action however small, not only reveals at once how much the person knows who does it, but often causes it to be judged much greater than it actually is, since it impresses upon the minds of the onlookers the opinion that he who performs well with so much facility must possess even greater skill than this, and that, if he were to devote care and effort to what he does, he could do it far better.]

Who are these "onlookers"? To which public does this refer? Without doubt to the general rather than the restricted. The latter know perfectly well that the result they witness implies "care and effort." Sprezzatura, which results in grace—as indeed in every other worthy activity of man—derives from the

so-called giudicio naturale or bon giudicio (1.44), which is by
no means natural, or solely natural, but is also the fruit of
education, experience, and reason. Above all, it is the index of
the courtier's preoccupation with his social image, or, to be
more precise, his "grado," and the dignity and distinction inherent there.

Take the problem raised in chapters 9 and 10 of book 2,
whether it is suitable for a gentleman to participate in "a country festival . . . where the spectators and the company were
persons of low birth." Federico Fregoso is of the negative opinion, and if at the end he concedes such activities to the courtier,
it is only with the greatest caution and, in particular, as regards
dancing or partaking in "public spectacles, either armed or
unarmed," only if he adopt a disguise:

> ma in publico non così, fuor che travestito, e benché fosse di modo
> che ciascun lo conoscesse, non dà noia; anzi per mostrarsi in tai cose
> nei spettaculi publici, con arme e senza arme, non è miglior via di
> quella; perché lo esser travestito porta seco una certa libertà e lic-
> ienza, la quale tra l'altre cose fa che l'omo po pigliare forma di
> quello in che si sente valere, ed usar diligenzia ed attillatura circa la
> principal intenzione della cosa in che mostrar si vole, ed una certa
> sprezzatura circa quello che non importa, il che accresce molto la
> grazia: come saria vestirsi un giovane da vecchio, ben però con abito
> disciolto, per potersi mostrare nella gagliarda; un cavaliero in forma
> di pastor selvatico o altro tale abito, ma con perfetto cavallo, e leg-
> giadramente acconcio secondo quella intenzione; perché sùbito l'an-
> imo de' circonstanti corre ad imaginar quello che agli occhi al primo
> aspetto s'appresenta; e vedendo poi riuscir molto maggior cosa che
> non prometteva quell'abito, si diletta e piglia piacere. (2.11)

> [but not in public, unless he is masquerading [fuor che travestito],
> for then it is not unseemly even if he should be recognized by all.
> . . . Because masquerading [lo esser travestito] carries with it a cer-
> tain freedom and license, which among other things enables one to
> choose the role in which he feels most able, and to bring diligence
> and a care for elegance into that principal aim, and to show a cer-
> tain *sprezzatura* in what does not matter: all of which adds much
> charm [accresce molto la grazia]; . . . as for a cavalier to dress as a
> rustic shepherd, or in some other such costume, but astride a per-

fect horse and gracefully attired in character: because the bystanders immediately take in what meets the eye at first glance; whereupon, realizing that here there is much more than was promised by the costume, they are delighted and amused [si diletta e piglia piacere].]

Even in this instance it is ostensibly a question of sprezzatura and grazia. But here the detachment between being and seeming introduced by the use of disguise functions in a manner different from our previous examples. Now clearly the public is homogeneous, not divided; it is the general public or, to be precise, a public socially inferior to the actor. The disguise functions not literally but very much as a sign that gradually becomes visible to all. The structure of this process is no longer that of irony or sprezzatura, as we have outlined it in the preceding discussion, but might better be classed with that of allegory just because it unfolds in time and requires a period of unraveling. True sprezzatura, it seems to me, like irony or wit, requires no passage of time for its effect, which is instantaneous.

The dissimulation of sprezzatura, like that of irony, is ambiguous and equivocal, and it cannot be otherwise,[23] and any attempt to circumscribe its dangerous possibilities would be in vain. As Friedrich Schlegel wrote of irony, one does not play, "one absolutely must not play" with irony.[24] It is a weapon, doubtless, and double-edged, and its use, though rhetorical, does not therefore pertain any less to reality. What the courtier is playing at is no game, or if it is, it is like that of the trapeze artist, who plays without the net. There are no inverted commas to catch him, to keep him safe from disastrous slips. Besides, as in any other communicative process, there are no rules or recipes to guarantee success. The actor must possess "prudenza," "discrezione," and "bon giudicio" (2.6). But for the performance to be a success, prudence, discretion, and good judgment must also be found in the public for whom the spectacle is destined.

NOTES

1. Eugenio Garin, *L'umanesimo italiano* (Bari, 1964), p. 137.
2. "Genius: Individualism in Art and Artists," in Philip P. Wiener, ed., *Dictionary of the History of Ideas* (New York, 1973), II, 304.

3. "A Grace beyond the Reach of Art," *Journal of the History of Ideas*, V (1944), 131–50.

4. Anthony Blunt, *Artistic Theory in Italy 1450–1600* (Oxford, 1940), pp. 97–98.

5. *Thesaurus Linguae Latinae* (Leipzig, 1934), VI, 2205. An exhaustive study on *gratia* and its family is that of Claude Moussy, *Gratia et sa famille* (Paris, 1966). It is interesting from our perspective to read there that "le sens de la majorité des dérivés de [la] racine [*g^{w}er-(ə^2)] se rattache à celui de 'louange'," 35; also that "un des caractères essentiels de cette louange est qu'elle n'est pas désintéressée et, comme l'exprime bien la formule proposée par G. Dumézil: *laudo ut des* [cf. *Servius et la fortune*, p. 89], qu'elle contraint en quelque sorte celui à qui elle s'adresse à répondre par des bienfaits" (p. 37). We may further learn that the variety of semantic fields in which words from this family, and *grātia* in particular, can be found (from religion to justice, gratitude, friendship, politics, and aesthetics) is not as dispersive as it appears to be. "Les différents significations prises par *grātia* ont toutes un lien entre elles: toutes se rattachent d'une façon ou d'une autre à la pratique de la bienfaisance, toutes s'expliquent à partir des sens fondamentaux de 'reconnaissance' et de 'paiement en retour'. L'extension des valeurs de la famille de *grātia* depuis la sphère religieuse jusqu'aux domaines moral, social, politique peut se schématiser ainsi: cette famille de mots a servi d'abord à exprimer les relations entre les hommes et les dieux, puis les relations des hommes entre eux, relations dont on peut affirmer dans les deux cas, sans vouloir restreindre la religion des Romains à la pratique du *do ut des*, qu'elles sont fondées essentiellement sur le couple que constituent le bienfait et la reconnaissance" (p. 475). As for the seeming contradiction between an expression like *grātiam referre*, for instance, and words like *grātiīs, grātuītus, grātuītō*, one must consider, as Moussy rightly points out, that for Roman law the two notions of gratuitousness and remuneration are not "antonymes, mais solidaires; toutes deux se fondent sur la réprocité: le don gratuit, comme toute autre prestation, appelle une compensation, un contre-don." (On the obligatory character of this exchange, which in archaic societies was certainly more evident than in Roman society, see É. Benveniste, "Don et échange dans le vocabulaire indo-européen," *Année sociologique*, 3d ser. [1948–49], pp. 7–20, and M. Mauss, "Essai sur le don, forme archaïque de l'échange," *Année sociologique*, new ser., I [1923–24]).

Finally, even if it is certainly true that the Greek *cháris* is behind the two meanings late to develop of the word *gratia*, that is, the aesthetic and the Christian, there is nothing surprising in this development: "les mots de la famille de *grātia* sont souvent joints à des termes qui expriment la joie, et servent parfois eux-mêmes à l'expression de la joie," and "l'association de la joie et de la reconnaissance est on ne peut plus naturelle dans les paroles, comme dans l'âme, de qui a vu exaucer ses voeux" (p. 480). More specifically, for Christian *grātia*: "Outre son équivalence avec *cháris* et ses valeurs anciennes de 'faveur', de 'bienfait', ce qui prédestinait en quelque sorte le mot à devenir le nom latin du 'don gratuit' qu'est la grâce de Dieu, c'est avant tout que l'expression de la gratuité était étroitement liée à la famille de *grātia*" (Moussy).

6. Many other places in the text treat as well of the "grazia . . . dei principi" (4.10) or "grazia e favore" of the prince (4.6).

7. This is obviously restricted to the aristocratic class, of which the prince himself is a part. Hence the book's insistence—required by the logic of the argument—on the prerequisite for the courtier of a noble birth, for him to be born in a "nobile e generosa famiglia" (1.14).

8. Cf. Richard A. Lanham, *The Motives of Eloquence: Literary Rhetoric in the Renaissance* (New Haven, 1976), p. 149: "Reading *The Courtier* is like learning to ride a bicycle, not like learning about Renaissance Platonism." What follows, however, is less convincing: "So, here, Castiglione tries to teach us a skill, an intuitive not a conscious, considered response."

9. And in 1.22: "If such agility is accompanied by grace, in my opinion it makes a finer show than any other;" and also "let him do all that others do, yet never depart from comely conduct [dai laudevoli atti], but behave himself with that good judgment [bon giudicio] which will not allow him to engage in any folly; let him laugh, jest, banter, frolic, and dance, yet in such a manner as to show always that he is genial and discreet [ingenioso e discreto]; and let him be full of grace [aggraziato] in all that he does or says."

10. In 1.35, class qualification may seem to be absent whereas it is actually only less explicit. Canossa states there in a more general way that "good usage in speech . . . springs from men who have talent, and who through learning and experience [dottrina ed esperienza] have attained good judgment [il bon giudicio]." But note that the latter, deriving from "dottrina ed esperienzia," is immediately and equivocally, it seems, redefined as follows: "and who thereby [con quello, i.e., il bon giudicio] agree among themselves and consent to adopt those words which to them seem good; which words are recognized by virtue of a certain natural judgment and not by any art or rule." "Natural," however, must be understood as "diventato naturale," "that has become natural," if it is a product of doctrine and experience. The same should be said of Canossa's polemic against "grammatical rules," to which "figures of speech" ("le figure del parlare") are opposed, consisting precisely of "abusioni," "abuses of grammatical rules." These are said to "give so much grace and luster to discourse [grazia e splendor alla orazione]" but only if "accepted and confirmed by usage," this being qualified obviously as above. The polemic here is clearly directed against absolute and metaphysical values in the name and favor of history and usage: of uses and conventions that are historical.

11. C. Plinii Secundi, *Nat. Hist.* 35.79–80, in K. Jex-Blake and E. Sellers, eds., *The Elder Pliny's Chapters on the History of Art* (Chicago, 1976), p. 120.

12. M. Tulli Ciceronis, *Ad M. Brutum Orator*, John E. Sandys, ed. (Cambridge, 1885), pp. 89–90; M. Fabio Quintiliano, *L'Istituzione Oratoria*, Latin text and Italian translation edited by R. Faranda (Turin, 1968), II, 678, 336.

13. Illustrious people from antiquity and artists, ancient and modern, are

clearly to be included among the potential members of this club. Their excellence is obviously responsible for their inclusion in both cases. A further distinction ought perhaps to be made, within the second group, between literary men and other artists. It seems certain, at any rate, that in the case of Giovan Cristoforo Romano, for instance, his opinion is asked for only in matters concerning his profession. On the other hand, if Bembo is given such a prominent part to play in the book, one cannot forget that the literary man was also a Venetian nobleman.

14. A "certain decorous mean" ("certa onesta mediocrità") is mentioned for instance in 1.41 while talking of the courtier; a "certain mean, difficult to achieve and, as it were, composed of contraries" ("certa mediocrità difficile e quasi composta di cose contrarie") in 3.5 while speaking of the court lady.

15. *Eth. Nic.* 2.6.17–18: "Thus, looked at from the point of view of its essence, . . . virtue no doubt is a mean; judged by the standard of what is right and best, it is an extreme" (J. A. K. Thompson's translation, in Aristotle, *Ethics* [Penguin Classics, 1955], pp. 66–67).

16. *Pol.* 7.12.39–40; *Eth. Nic.* 10.10.20–21.

17. *Eth. Nic.* 2.7.12: "Well then, as regards veracity, the character who aims at the mean may be called 'truthful' and what he aims at 'truthfulness.' Pretending when it goes too far is 'boastfulness' and the man who shows it is a 'boaster' or 'braggart'. If it takes the form of understatement, the pretence is called 'irony' and the man who shows it 'ironical'" (in Thompson's translation, p. 70).

18. *Eth. Nic.* 6.3.28.

19. Thompson, p. 132.

20. *Rhet.* 3.18.1419^b.6–9.

21. G. C. Sedgewick, *Of Irony, especially in Drama* (Toronto, 1935), p. 10. With this in mind, we may feel less surprised at Daniel Javitch's recent reminder, in his excellent *Poetry and Courtliness in Renaissance England* (Princeton, 1978), that authors such as George Puttenham and Fulke Greville recognized in Castiglione's courtier's behavior an affinity, if not an identity, with the procedures of classical rhetoric, in particular with that of irony.

22. Cf. Antonino Pagliaro, *Ironia e verità* (Milan, 1970), pp. 14–15.

23. On this in particular, see the discussion between Gaspare Pallavicino and Federico Fregoso in 2.40.

24. "Über die Univerständlichkeit," *Kritische Ausgabe* (Zurich, 1967), II, 369: "Mit der Ironie ist durchaus nicht zu scherzen."

5

The Enduring Word: Language, Time, and History in *Il Libro del Cortegiano*

Wayne A. Rebhorn

The debate on language in the first book of *Il Cortegiano* begins with Count Ludovico da Canossa's argument that the ideal courtier would appear affected if he spoke archaic Tuscan words. In reply, asserting the position that Bembo presents in his *Prose della volgar lingua,* Federico Fregoso declares that in writing as in speaking—for he and all the other courtiers assume no radical disparity between the two—one should not only use Tuscan words but "those only which have been used by the ancient Tuscans" (1.30).[1] Federico defends his preference by arguing for the authority that antiquity gives such words and for the majesty and gravity that they thus acquire. He wants a language that, possessing a certain difficulty by virtue of its archaic vocabulary, removes itself from easy comprehension by commoners and peasants and in this way achieves social as well as aesthetic status. Federico, however, comes off rather badly in the debate as he defends his preference for an ideally fixed and codified Tuscan language as the idiom for all Italians. Not only does his main opponent, Count Ludovico, defeat his arguments at every turn, but Castiglione rigs the debate against poor Federico by having the only two actual Tuscans in the group speak against him. First he makes the Magnifico Giuliano de' Medici declare haughtily that for his part, although he thinks the Tuscan dialect more beautiful than any other in Italy, he would never speak or write Tuscan words

69

use. When Federico then replies that the Mag-
~~er~~ Tuscans err in letting their old language per-
so that it is better known outside the city than in
it, the other Tuscan in the group, Bernardo Bibbiena, delivers
the coup de grace: "Those words which are no longer used in
Florence have remained with the peasants, and are rejected by
the gentry as words that have been corrupted and spoiled by
age" (1.31). How can Federico, a native of Genoa, maintain the
aristocratic superiority of ancient Tuscan when doing so only
gets him implicitly classed among the peasants by these two
famous Florentine nobles?

If Castiglione has given one side in the language debate a
seemingly unfair advantage—something he avoids doing in all
the other debates in his work—it is largely because he himself
has clearly taken sides in the contemporary "questione della
lingua" against those who argued that ancient, or modern,
Tuscan should be the national Italian language.[2] Like a number
of contemporary writers, including Pierio Valeriano, Mario
Equicola, and Giangiorgio Trissino, Castiglione favors the more
universal language he says is spoken throughout the noblest
cities and courts of Italy.[3] Vittorio Cian has argued, Mme Labande-Jeanroy to the contrary, that there really was such a
courtly language, citing a letter of 15 October 1513 written by
Gian Francesco Valerio, a friend of Castiglione, requesting an
unguent of some sort: "uno bossletto o bussolino non so come
chiamarlo cortegianamente di quella sua excellente mixtura"
("a *bossletto* or *bussolino* [little box], I don't know the courtly
term for it, of your excellent mixture").[4] And Giancarlo Mazzacurati, in a fairly recent article, has claimed that there really
was a large, widespread class of courtiers who opposed Tuscan
as the language of just one region and who, because they felt
themselves part of a universal, courtly culture rather than ad-
herents of local feudal courts, wanted a language that would be
equally universal and comprehensible throughout the peninsula.[5] These courtiers resisted the use of archaic Tuscan and
rejected the notion of language as a fixed system, a static entity
divorced from the flow of history. According to Mazzacurati,

for this class of Renaissance men and their views, Cast.
his *Cortegiano* became the most eloquent spokesman.

Castiglione characterizes language as a living and cha
system whose first principle is "uso" or "consuetudine" (1.2%
concept best translated as "current use" or "customary use."
Strikingly, Castiglione's prescriptions for language replicate
those for the general social behavior of his ideal courtier. Thus,
in order to avoid the vice of affectation, the courtier is instructed to adopt and adapt himself to the uses and customs of
contemporary social reality; he is neither to deny it nor to
imitate it slavishly but rather to master its grammar, lexicon,
and syntax, and then to use them as he creates an ideal *persona*
for himself. Castiglione's book aims, after all, at fashioning a
courtier to live in the real world of contemporary courts and
not, despite Castiglione's own comparisons of his book to works
by Plato and Xenophon, to inhabit an imaginary utopia. Consistently, and with a solid though perhaps intuitive grasp of
modern sociolinguistic conceptions, Castiglione treats the courtier's language as an aspect of behavior, as just another part of
the social-cultural system in which he lives. Or, to put the matter another way, Castiglione sees the linguistic system as a synecdoche for the larger social-cultural system of which it is a
part. Thus, he introduces consideration of it into book 1, when
discussion of the courtier's relation to that larger social system
has scarcely begun because the definition of the courtier's use
of language allows Castiglione to construct a fairly precise, de-
tailed, powerful model for all aspects of courtly behavior. The
principles of social behavior, Castiglione seems to imply, can be
more readily grasped and more easily universalized by readers
when presented in terms of a linguistic model than when presented in terms of the specific social-cultural system of Renaissance Italy. After all, even those who live in societies quite
different from Urbino's nevertheless speak and write languages.
A linguistic model is transferable; a social one may not be.

When Castiglione accepts language as a system that changes
constantly, which, like any organic entity, is capable of growth
and decay and even contamination (from other languages), he

implicitly conceives of it as an aspect of human and cultural
history seen as flux or process. This acceptance has led Mazzacurati to see in Castiglione's book not a yearning for the ideal
of some past golden age but, in a moment of expansion and
optimism, an exultant and exalted celebration of the present.[6]
Such a view, in which Castiglione's acceptance of history metamorphoses into a warm embrace, is, however, too simple. In
the first place it really misses the tone characterizing Castiglione's response to history; it misses his dissatisfaction with history as mere process, his dismay over its limitation, its finitude,
and his disenchantment that time, which he calls the father of
truth, is also "tempus edax rerum," time the devourer. Second,
the view that sees Castiglione embracing historical process also
oversimplifies his linguistic theory, ignoring those elements in
it which run counter to that doctrine. Specifically, it ignores
Castiglione's preference for the retention and cultivation of
Latinisms, a seemingly conscious archaizing tendency which
contradicts the notion that language must change constantly.
Finally, such a view forgets a major theme of Castiglione's work,
his celebration of art precisely because of its ability to transcend
history and preserve language in some measure from decay
and death. It forgets that the *Book of the Courtier* itself represents an attempt to transcend time and history even as it necessarily remains bound to its epoch and to the Renaissance Italian
language in which it was written.

As Count Ludovico develops his notions of use and mutability as the first principles of language, Castiglione has him present a minihistory in which he sees the Italian language devel-
oping out of the chaos and barbarism of the Middle Ages,
which corrupted and destroyed Latin, and emerging as the
tender, new vernacular in Tuscany. Ludovico continues:

> Nascendo poi di tempo in tempo, non solamente in Toscana ma in
> tutta la Italia, tra gli omini nobili e versati nelle corti e nell'arme e
> nelle lettere, qualche studio di parlare e scrivere più elegantemente,
> che non si faceva in quella prima età rozza ed inculta, quando lo

incendio delle calamità nate da' barbari non era ancor sedato, sonsi lassate molte parole, così nella città propria di Fiorenza ed in tutta la Toscana, come nel resto della Italia, ed in loco di quelle riprese dell'altre, et fattosi in questo quella mutazion che si fa in tutte le cose umane; il che è intervenuto sempre ancor delle altre lingue. (1.32)

[Then, from time to time, not only in Tuscany but in the rest of Italy, among wellborn men versed in the usages of courts, in arms, and in letters, a concern arose to speak and write more elegantly than in that first rude and uncultivated age when the fires of calamity set by the barbarians were not yet extinguished. Thus, both in the city of Florence itself and in all Tuscany, as well as in the rest of Italy, many words were abandoned, and others were taken up in their stead, thereby bringing about the change which takes place in all things human and has always taken place in other languages as well.]

Finally, the count concludes his brief history with the observation that Latin, like Italian, was not a static entity but went through a long and complicated development from rude beginnings down through the golden age of Virgil and beyond. Organizing Ludovico's conceptualization of these historical developments and determining the metaphors he uses to describe them is an unmistakable organic model: Language, like plants and men, is born, grows, reaches maturity, and finally is corrupted or decays and dies. Strikingly, although elsewhere Castiglione seems to treat language as part of the general behavioral or cultural system, his organic metaphors here suggest a basically different conception. Language is seen as belonging to the realm of nature, going through an inevitable, unavoidable life cycle. It is also seen, however, as potentially part of the domain of culture because it is something men can *cultivate*, using their art to bring it within the domain of civilization. Language is thus like the ideal courtier's physical appearance, talents, and mental capacity. It is the raw material of nature awaiting the dispositions of human artifice to make it into culture. Castiglione is at the opposite pole from the modern anthropologist, for whom language is always a primary datum of culture. For Castiglione, as for the Renaissance, culture is a

normative term, the achievement of man's art, and language
betokens culture only when culture has been achieved.

In the passage cited above Ludovico seems to speak in an
almost neutral tone. He presents his vision of languages—and,
by implication, of men and cultures—going through the cycle
of existence from birth to death certainly without melancholy
or regret; there may even be a hint of optimism since the
passage emphasizes the *birth* of Italian and its growth to maturity rather than the decay and death of Latin. Acceptance, similar to the kind that often attends pastoral contemplation of the
life cycle, may well be the word to describe Castiglione's response here.[7] Acceptance, however, is not generally an adequate
term, because elsewhere Castiglione cannot avoid the implications of his model, namely, that if his language and culture
flourish, they will also inevitably decay and die. Moreover, he
has the monumental history of Latin antiquity as a constant
reminder of the total pattern. Thus, in a later passage Count
Ludovico introduces a note of strong feeling into his organic
model as he contemplates the extinction of Oscan and Provençal as living tongues.

> Ma delle parole son alcune che durano bone un tempo, poi s'invec-
> chiano ed in tutto perdono la grazia; altre piglian forza e vengono in
> prezzo perché, come le stagioni dell'anno spogliano de' fiori e de'
> frutti la terra e poi di novo d'altri la rivesteno, così il tempo quelle
> prime parole fa cadere e l'uso altre di novo fa rinascere e dà lor
> grazia e dignità, fin che, dall'invidioso morso del tempo a poco a
> poco consumate, giungono poi esse ancora alla lor morte; perciò
> che, al fine, e noi ed ogni nostra cosa è mortale. (1.36)

> [But among words there are some that remain good for a time, then
> grow old and lose their grace completely, whereas others gain in
> strength and come into favor; because, just as the seasons of the
> year divest the earth of her flowers and fruits, and then clothe her
> again with others, so time causes those first words to fall, and usage
> brings others to life, giving them grace and dignity, until they are
> gradually consumed by the envious jaws of time, when they too go
> to their death; because, in the end, we and all our things are
> mortal.]

In this passage, although there is first a seemingly reassuring balance between death and life, before long the focus comes to rest on the envious jaws of time and the inevitable death of all things mortal. Clearly, the count's vision of the organic cycle of life is not so comfortable—and comforting—in this passage as it was in the earlier one.

Just how much emotional emphasis to place on the negative implications of Castiglione's metaphors may not be fully apparent in the passages cited. But when those passages are placed within the context of the entire work, an argument can indeed be made that the fate of languages, like all other aspects of human life and culture, is the occasion for nostalgia and melancholy lament, not acceptance, let alone optimism. First, it should be remarked that Castiglione views his own age—and hence, his language—less as a beginning than as the climax of a historical development, the beginning, in other words, of the end. To be sure, scattered throughout his work he has passages praising contemporary or recent rulers and their courts, and the second book even opens with an elaborate argument that contemporary courts are superior to those they superseded. However, also scattered throughout *Il Cortegiano* are numerous passages that point to a shared sense of contemporary decadence. For instance, all Castiglione's courtiers take the lack of a national form of dress as a symbol of Italy's lack of political independence (2.26). Moreover, all agree with Ottaviano's assertion that most contemporary princes are corrupt, unjust, and misled by flatterers (4.9). Most strikingly, as Ottaviano rejects the conception of the ideal courtier developed during the first three nights of discussion, he condemns as "frivolities and vanities" the ideal's dancing, singing, joking, and other courtly activities, for these activities, he declares,

> spesso non fanno altro che effeminar gli animi, corrumper la gioventù e ridurla a vita lascivissima; onde nascono poi questi effetti che 'l nome italiano è ridutto in obbrobrio, nè si ritrovano se non pochi che osino non dirò morire, ma pur entrare in uno pericolo. (4.4)

> [often serve merely to make spirits effeminate, to corrupt youth, and to lead it to a dissolute life; whence it comes about that the

Italian name is reduced to opprobrium, and there are but few who
dare, I will not say to die, but even to risk any danger.]

Notably, although the other courtiers attack Ottaviano's vision
of the courtly ideal, none of them says a word against his view
of their own age as hopelessly corrupt and decadent. Moreover, although none makes the connection, surely the reader
cannot help see that the contemporary domination of Italy by
"barbarians" invading from the north and the contemporary
decline of Italian courage and morality may properly be considered a replay of similar developments in the Middle Ages
for which Castiglione has used identical terms.

Even more than such scattered references to contemporary
decadence, the general mood of *Il Cortegiano*, a mood of nostalgia and lament, supports the idea that Castiglione views his
age as having reached its high point and begun its inevitable
decline. He establishes this mood in the opening letter to Don
Michel de Silva and in the opening chapters of his four books.
To be sure, those prologues focus on the excellence of Urbino
and sing the praises of its dukes Guidobaldo and Francesco
Maria. The last prologue in particular rejoices in the length of
time Urbino's glory has already endured and hopes for an even
more splendid future. Note, however, how Castiglione's optimism here is qualified as he stresses how much Urbino's future
depends on chance or fortune:

Però parmi che quella causa, o sia per ventura o per favore delle
stelle, che ha così lungamente concesso ottimi signori ad Urbino,
pur ancora duri e produca i medesimi effetti; e però sperar si po
che ancor la bona fortuna debba secondar tanto queste opere vir-
tuose, che la felicità della casa e dello stato non solamente non sia
per mancare, ma più presto di giorno in giorno per accrescersi. (4.2)

[It seems to me, however, that the cause, whether through chance
or favor of the stars, that has for so long given excellent lords to
Urbino, continues still to produce the same effects; and hence we
may hope that good fortune will so continue to favor these virtuous
achievements that the blessings of the court and the state shall not
only not decline but rather increase at a more rapid pace from day
to day.]

This qualified optimism is dispelled completely by the letter to de Silva as well as by what Castiglione generally says about the workings of fortune. In the cover letter he does not sing the continuing triumphs of Urbino but laments the deaths of Duchess Elisabetta and many of Urbino's most celebrated courtiers, all of whom were still alive when the prologue to book 4 was composed. Moreover, Castiglione says that the duchess's death has cast him into a "desert full of woes,"[8] an emotional state which suggests some vague but definitive separation from his beloved Urbino. In historical fact, by the time the opening letter was penned in 1527, Castiglione had long since left Urbino to return to the service of the dukes of Mantua, and the little court had been wrested from Francesco Maria by Pope Leo X and given to his nephew Lorenzo de' Medici. In 1527 Castiglione was actually in a kind of "solitudine," in spiritual exile at the Spanish court serving as papal nuncio and learning, much after the fact, that the Sack of Rome had occurred that spring. It is hardly surprising, then, that *Il Cortegiano* has a nostalgic tone, that Castiglione constructs it as a kind of memorial for Urbino, whose life and customs he always refers to in the past tense as *having flourished*. As he says at the start of book 3, there are many worthy men who "personally saw and knew the life and the customs that once flourished in that court" (3.1). Finally, it should be remembered that although Castiglione must have conceived his book in some measure as a didactic work, a behavioral guidebook for his contemporaries, he never claims explicitly to be writing for them. When he does define his purpose in writing *Il Cortegiano*, he identifies it as a desire to memorialize Urbino's court or to satisfy the personal requests of friends, and he locates his expected audience always in some fairly unspecific future. As he says at the start of book 3, he wishes his book to live "in the mind of posterity. . . . Wherefore, perhaps, in the future, someone will not be wanting who will envy our century for this as well" (3.1).

If Castiglione's supposed acceptance of life as flux must be qualified by his nostalgia for Urbino and his sense that he has already lived through the high point of a historical epoch, it

must also be qualified by his general vision of human life as the
plaything of the whimsical goddess Fortuna. Again and again
in his book, as he celebrates the accomplishments of his masters, friends, and fellow courtiers, he praises them for their
"virtù," by which he means their fortitude and courage and
endurance. Through their virtù they triumph over an exceedingly hostile "fortuna" and survive its worst predations. At one
point Castiglione blames fortune that even a perfect courtier
might fail to please his lord (2.32); at another, he denounces it
for keeping him from finishing his book (*Let.* 1.68). Most of all,
Castiglione condemns fortune for causing that chief source of
human misery and defeated hope—death. Thus, at the start of
book 4, as he laments the deaths of three fellow courtiers,
"even while they flourished in robust health and in hope of
honor," he broods: "How often Fortune in midcourse, and
sometimes near the end, dashes our fragile and futile designs
and sometimes wrecks them before the port can even be seen
from afar" (4.1; cf. 2.1). In the context created by such laments,
which frame the entire work and determine its general tone,
any passage that describes the life and death of languages in
however neutral a fashion cannot help being infused with melancholy and regret.

Castiglione's vision of human life cut short by a hostile fortune is made all the more uncomfortable by its rigorous exclusion of any Christian consolation. All the biographical evidence supports the contention that Castiglione in his life was
quite devout and fully merited the bishop's hat he was awarded
toward the end of it.[9] Nevertheless, his *Cortegiano* expresses no
hope that a Christian afterlife could compensate for the injustice of death and fortune in this world. Strikingly, in the passage
cited above, the "port" to which our fragile earthly vessels sail is
not identified with heaven; in fact insofar as it is the object of
our deceived hopes and vain designs, it seems reasonably identified as some form of worldly success or glory since heaven
would hardly involve deception or vanity. Indeed, throughout
Il Cortegiano Castiglione's courtiers insist that public recognition, fame, and glory are the true, the only, prizes for human

accomplishments. For instance, with scarcely a thought that virtue might be its own reward, let alone receive a heavenly prize, Gasparo Pallavicino and the others defend self-praise if the ideal courtier is to gain honor, for such public celebrity is the only reward conceivable to them for good deeds (1.18, 2.8). Certainly, Castiglione's characters nowhere display hostility to religion or to Christian institutions—the duchess even silences an exceptional, although mild attempt to criticize friars—but the absence of any otherworldly perspective from Castiglione's book, except fleetingly in Bembo's admittedly digressive speech in book 4, renders his vision of life a fully secular one.[10] And in this vision, although history is seen as moving through a succession of organic cycles that offer some sort of order, however uncomfortable, on the level of entire societies, for the individual the prospect is far grimmer because the whimsical operations of fortune so seldom allow him to live out the full, organic pattern of growth, maturity, and death.

Castiglione's complex, emotional response to history and life as flux helps to explain what might otherwise seem a strange contradiction in his linguistic theory. Although he establishes current usage as the first principle of language, he shows a decided preference in both theory and practice for Italian words that are close in form to their Latin roots. In his prefatory letter Castiglione himself attacks Tuscan because its words are often so far corrupted from their Latin originals—a charge hardly true in fact—and he says he prefers his native Lombard dialect because it sustains Latin words in forms that are "pure, whole, proper, and unchanged in any part." He sums up his preference by declaring, in a sentence notable for its Latinisms, that he has chosen to use "from my own country what is intact and genuine, rather than from another's what is corrupted and mutilated." In practice this preference means that Castiglione writes *contenzione* for *litigio, documento* for *insegnamento, eleggere* for *scegliere, exito* for *uscita, similitudine* for *somiglianza.* He spells Italian words according to the Latin roots: *diligentia, exemplo, satisfatione, amplo, ingenioso,* and *suave.* And he uses Lombardisms that have the form of Latinisms, particu-

larly: *bono, loco, novo, omo,* and *vale.*[11] In short, Castiglione's Latinisms seem to run directly counter to his principle of use; they
seem to imply a desire to give the language a fixed form, thus
denying history and change, which the drift away from Latin
epitomized. How can Castiglione mock Federico's call to the
Tuscans to preserve their language in its archaic form if he is
engaged in a much larger project of the same sort himself?

This problem, however, is only an apparent one, as a closer
examination of Castiglione's text reveals. First, he does not
argue for using Latinate forms on the grounds that they are
archaic and hence more dignified; apparently they were not
felt to be archaic within Castiglione's linguistic culture but were
simply considered possible alternatives to other forms.[12] Thus,
rejecting the notion of an elitist language incomprehensible to
the people because of its archaisms, Castiglione implicitly advocates the use of Latin forms preserved in the various Italian
dialects because they would actually be more comprehensible to
Italians from all regions than would idiomatic Tuscan forms
and usages. He observes that in Tuscany the people use many
words corrupted from Latin, words that "nella Lombardia e
nelle altre parti d'Italia son rimasti integri e senza mutazione
alcuna, e tanto universalmente s'usano per ognuno, che dalli
nobili sono ammessi per boni e dal vulgo intesi senza difficultà"
(*Let.* 2.74) ("in Lombardy and in other parts of Italy have remained intact and without change whatever, and are so universally used by everyone that they are admitted by the nobility to
be good, and are understood by the people without difficulty").
On the basis of the desirability of a universally understood and
usable Italian language, Castiglione concludes: The closer its
words to Latin, the better.

Castiglione's second and more extensively developed justification for his preference, however, has nothing to do with
linguistic ideals; it grows directly out of his emotional discom-
fort with history and life as flux. He argues that just as it is
presumptuous to retain old words for new ones in spite of
current use, it is equally presumptuous, although for a different reason, to "distruggere e quasi sepelir vivi quelli che dur-

ano già molti seculi, e col scudo della usanza si son diffesi dalla
invidia del tempo ed han conservato la dignità e 'l splendor
loro" (*Let.* 2.75) ("destroy and, as it were, bury alive those which
have already survived many centuries and have defended themselves with the shield of usage against the envy of time, and
have kept their dignity and splendor"). When the wars and
ruins of Italy have caused so many changes in language, build-
ings, clothes, and customs, to discard those relics from a sacred
Latin past appears nothing less than an "impietà." Castiglione
may join his courtiers in mocking those who make "a kind
of cult of the ineffable mysteries of this their Tuscan language"
(1.37), but when he confronts the ravages wreaked by time and
history, he feels nothing less than a kind of religious awe for
those past remains which, albeit in slightly changed form, have
nevertheless survived into the present. Castiglione's linguistic
preferences are thus both a matter of abstract, linguistic idealism and of preserving the precious heritage of a distant and
revered past.

   If Castiglione accepts the fact that men's lives, languages, and
history are caught up in the movement of time, ultimately subject to the power of fortune which lets few vestiges of the past
survive into the present, he does not stop yearning for some
way to transcend such realities. Symptomatic of this yearning,
the visions of Ottaviano and Bembo in book 4 can be construed
as attempts both to escape time and history and to raise man to
a position beyond the power of fortune to touch his individual
life. Castiglione's immediate problem in *Il Cortegiano*, however,
a problem that does not admit of such visionary solutions, is to
provide some sort of enduring monument for the court of
Urbino, whose most glorious epoch has already started slipping
away irrecoverably into the past. At the start of book 3 Castiglione specifically defines his task as a matter of vindicating
(*vendicar*), perhaps even rescuing or avenging, the brilliant
memory of the court in the face of mortal oblivion (3.1). His
terms here imply a significant struggle against time and fortune waged by the author, who himself thereby acquires an
almost heroic aura. In the letter to Don Michel de Silva, for

instance, Castiglione depicts himself as oppressed by fortune, which has prevented him over the years from completing his book and paying the enormous debt of gratitude he feels he owes. Nevertheless like the heroic lords and ladies of Urbino, Castiglione has indeed finally triumphed over fortune; in finishing his book, he pays his debt and erects a monument so that the image of Urbino may live again in the minds of posterity.

What exactly does Castiglione mean when he says that through his work Urbino will live again in the minds of posterity? In one sense he means obviously that his book will be read by future generations and that they will be prompted to dream up a court at least as great as the one Castiglione depicts. *Il Cortegiano* offers, however, in its style and language, themes and form, an even more significant illustration of what it means to have the past live again in the minds of posterity. In this case it shows how the *Roman* past is brought to life in the reader's mind through the pages of Castiglione's book. For if Castiglione feels nostalgia for Urbino, he shares with his Renaissance culture an all-embracing nostalgia for the classical past and a desire to resurrect it in the present.[13] Both Castiglione and his culture realized, to be sure, that a genuine recreation of that past was impossible. As early as the trecento, Petrarch wrote familiar letters to ancient authors, treating them thus as though friends and contemporaries, but he could not help noting that they lived before the advent of Christ, evoking in a word the immense temporal and spiritual distance of the Christian Middle Ages that separated him from them.[14] Castiglione does not contrast a Christian present with a pagan past but he does recognize that antiquity is irrecoverably past. For instance, in a well-known sonnet he laments that the arches and theaters and triumphal ceremonies of Rome have all turned to dust and that the city is now only a name attached to a collection of ruins ("Superbi colli, e voi sacre ruine"). In *Il Cortegiano* he stresses how the wars and devastations of Italy have destroyed and corrupted both Roman culture and its language. Moreover, he never speaks of the present equaling, let alone recreating, the past, for that was a time, quite simply, when men were greater than they are now (1.52). From Castiglione's perspective the cultural triumph of his own era, the court of Urbino, is named most felicitously, for the "little *urbs*" prompts both a recollection of and offers a direct contrast to the great *urbs* of antiquity, the *urbs romana*.

If one cannot literally become a Roman again, what one can do is to create a world here that in some measure integrates elements from the Latin past into the present. In Castiglione's case this means imitation: the fashioning of a text that gives the past a continuous, subterranean life as a kind of subtext within (or beneath) it. Castiglione achieves this goal as fully as any Renaissance artist ever did through a variety of means. Most generally, he models the structure, subject matter, and ideals of his *Cortegiano* on those of Cicero's *De oratore*. Although the resemblance was closer when *Il Cortegiano* had just three books, as it did at least through 1516, even in its final, four-book form, it still recalls its Roman original. Castiglione imitates Cicero by opening his last book with an extended elegiac passage, by discussing jokes and humor in the second half of book 2, and by assigning his ideal courtier qualities that replicate those desired by Cicero for his own ideal. Even more effective than such general parallels of structure and subject matter, Castiglione's direct imitation of passages from Cicero (and other ancient writers) brings the past vividly alive again in his book. During his courtiers' debate on language Castiglione has Count Ludovico define just what such imitation means. He rejects a slavish copying of the original and emphasizes instead the primacy of the imitator's own creativity and judgment as he chooses and adapts ancient writings to meet the requirements of his work and the nature of his language. Thus, putting his own theory into practice, when Castiglione imitates passages from Cicero's *Orator* at the start of book 1 or from his *De oratore* at the start of book 4, he does not follow Cicero's word order or repeat exactly his sentence architecture, because to do so would do violence to the structure of the vernacular.[15] Moreover, while he keeps the general order of thoughts in his model, he follows his own genius as he alters syntactic and logical connectives in order to make relations among the parts of his sentence as clear and explicit as possible.[16] Thus, the style of such imitated passages does not clash with that employed throughout Castiglione's work; like the style of an ideal courtier, it does not call attention to itself as a form of affectation, of deliberate artifice. Nevertheless, such passages allow the educated reader to perceive the Latin originals they are modeled on, to sense the ghostly presence of Cicero hovering just below the surface of Castiglione's text.

While Castiglione's imitation of specific passages from ancient authors remains intermittent in his *Cortegiano,* the continuous presence of antiquity as a subtext is ensured by two other means. First, Castiglione's syntax, especially in the narrative portions of the book, is characterized by a formality that directly evokes Latin style in general and Cicero in particular. Castiglione constructs long, elaborate sentences where main clauses are placed in the center, flanked on either side by lengthy subordinate ones,the whole suggesting the dense architecture of Latin prose. Like Cicero, Castiglione also favors coordinative (or binary) structures and the use of pleonasms. Even more important, however, in evoking the classical past is his rich, Latinate lexicon. Although he excuses himself for speaking Lombard dialect in *Il Cortegiano,* in fact the book has few Lombardisms or regionalisms. On the contrary, although Castiglione's basic lexicon is Tuscan, it is a Tuscan modified continually by his preference for Latin roots and orthographies. He even adopts familiar metaphors from Latin, speaking of the "sali" of jests (1.4) or the "odor" of Duke Guidobaldo's virtues (*Let.* 1.68). Vittorio Cian sees Castiglione's use of Latinisms as an act of homage to Rome:

> This cohort of Latinisms which is encamped in open order throughout the pages of *Il Cortegiano* represents not only the personal taste of this humanist author, but also the homage which he, interpreter of the sentiments of his finest contemporaries, intended to render to the revived spirit of Rome.[17]

More than an act of homage to a reborn Roman antiquity, Castiglione's Latinism are the *means* by which that rebirth, the reintegration of the past into the present, has been accomplished.

Fully aware of how the masterpieces of Roman antiquity had collapsed to the ground and of how many of them had recently been literally dug up from the earth and brought back to the light of day, Castiglione, like the rest of his culture, could hardly have avoided making the metaphor of resurrection a central one in his thinking on language, time, and history.[18] Throughout *Il Cortegiano* he takes that metaphor seriously and develops its implications in many directions. For instance, the worst crime Castiglione can conceive is to *bury beneath the ground* something good and humanly significant that deserves to live. In the passage mentioned above, where he attacks those who would reject Latinate words still in current use, he describes their sin as a wish to "sepelir vivi" (*Let.* 2.75) ("bury alive") words that have remained alive so many centuries. Moreover, the chief agent responsible for burying words, as well as their users, is, of course, fortune, and in a passage striking for its metaphors of raising up and burying, Gasparo Pallavicino denounces the whimsical way the wheel of fortune turns as it constructs social hierarchies in complete disregard for merit.

Ma delle diversità nostre e gradi d'altezza e di bassezza credo io che siano molte altre cause: tra le quali estimo la fortuna esser precipua, perché in tutte le cose mondane la veggiamo dominare e quasi pigliarsi a gioco d'alzar spesso fin al cielo chi par a lei senza merito alcuno, e sepellir nell'abisso i piú degni d'esser esaltati. (1.15)

[But I believe that there are many other causes of the differences and the various degrees of elevation and lowliness among us. Among which causes I judge Fortune to be foremost; because we see her hold sway over all the things of this world and, as it seems, amuse herself often in uplifting to the skies whom she pleases and in burying in the depths those most worthy of being exalted.]

Later, Gasparo will argue in consistent terms that self-praise is necessary for the ideal courtier, lest he lack recognition for his good deeds and his valor remain "sepulto" (1.18). Although Gasparo's vision may be somewhat darker than that of the other courtiers, all of them admit the arbitrary power of fortune and share Gasparo's desire to keep men, their honors, languages, and cultures out of the ground.

Opposed to fortune and its whimsical raising and burying of human achievements, Castiglione not only places "virtù," which manifests itself as the ability to survive in spite of fortune, but more significantly, art, which can allow men's achievements a more absolute form of triumph—resurrection throughout future ages. Art, of course, plays a major role in the development and growth of languages and cultures. According to Castiglione's linguistic history, Italian for a long time remained unshaped and variable because no one tried to write anything of substance in it, to give it grace and splendor, to *cultivate* it (1.32). Thanks to Dante, Petrarch, and Boccaccio, the flower of Italian took root and grew in Tuscany, and Castiglione insists that since then it has done so all over the peninsula. If art, especially the art of writing, thus proves indispensable so that the flower of language and culture may rise up out of the ground, then that art is even more important for its preservation beyond the brief span of life allotted to any flower. Writing is, as Count Ludovico observes, speech that remains (1.29). In the brief debate over arms and letters that surfaces in book 1, although Bembo first argues for the superiority of letters over arms on the basis that the spirit, to which letters are addressed, is superior to the body, he quickly changes his ground. He argues instead that letters are superior because they give men a blaze of glory and make their deed immortal (1.45). Count Ludovico then replies that letters would not confer immortality if their subject matter were vain and frivolous (1.46), but his reply, although placing the emphasis differently, actually concedes Bembo's point: Letters *are* essential if deeds are to be remembered. Bembo's and Ludovico's accord reveals just how important the immortality earned by art was to Castiglione and his culture. Of course, nature offers man a form of immortality through his children, as Castiglione's spokesman notes in passing in book 3 (14), but this argument is given little emphasis, for the kind of immortality really desired is not family continuity so much as individual preservation. What is wanted is what Ludovico calls "gloria," and he goes on to ask rhetorically: What man, having read of Caesar and Alexander, would not put off "this transitory life of a few days' span as less important, in order to win an almost eternal life of fame which, in spite of death, makes him live on in far greater glory than before" (1.43).

Only the arts can provide that sort of immortal glory by preserving the images of men and their cultures so that they can be resurrected by the future and integrated into its life, just as Castiglione has resurrected the Latin past and integrated it into the life of his book. It is fitting that he repeatedly ascribes to the arts a particularly memorialistic rather than a didactic or an aesthetic function. Both sculpture and painting, for instance, are defined as mimetic arts whose first, though admittedly not sole, function is to preserve the memory of the individual, the group, or the culture, and in the debate over the superiority of painting and sculpture, quite significantly Count Ludovico argues on behalf of the latter because stone is more durable than paint and wood or canvas (1.50). Literary works are similarly praised for the way they immortalize the deeds of famous men, and Castiglione defines his own purpose in writing, it must be remembered, as a desire to *preserve the memory* of his heroic little court for the sake of posterity. Actually, his memorialistic aim is not so different from a didactic one, for by preserving the image of Urbino and its courtiers for the future, he makes it possible for them to become a kind of moral subtext in the mind and art of posterity.

If the terms of the preceding discussion are reviewed, it should be apparent that, although Castiglione's work is quite thoroughly secular, its concerns are nevertheless frequently those of religion. Not only does the ideal courtier shape his activities for the sake of acquiring grace in his master's eyes, but grace is consistently presented as the goal toward which languages and the cultures they embrace also strive to move. To attain that grace, they must be cultivated by wise and thoughtful men, for all languages and cultures are brought to their maturity through the agency of human art. That same art is also responsible for resurrecting the past in the present and creating enduring images that will enable the present to be resurrected in the future. Thus, art makes it possible for languages and cultures to defeat fortune and gain some measure of eternal life in this world. And it is thus fitting that Castiglione, animated by fervent zeal, pursues his Christlike mission of saving Urbino's court from the envious jaws of death.

To describe Castiglione's goal as the achievement of some sort of eternity in the midst—and with the materials—of this life is to suggest how basically paradoxical his desire really is. Yet this is the very paradox of art, for the artwork, however enduring, is made of perishable materials and is wedded by its language, style, and contents to the fleeting, historical moment of its creation. In a sense Castiglione shows his awareness of the artwork's simultaneously time-bound and timeless qualities in the way that he conceives his book. Rather than fabricate a utopian "nowhere," he takes as his subject a real, historical court; he sets his dialogues in a specific place and time and gives them the movement of life; and he suggests here and there both something of the historical events transpiring about the court and its interaction with them. At the same time, Castiglione uses a most significant phrase to describe his aesthetic aim in writing; he says he will paint the "ritratto di pittura della corte d'Urbino" (*Let.* 1.71) ("portrait of the court of Urbino"). His metaphor here stresses the static and hence atemporal quality of the artwork he is producing. He thus suggests that his record of a living and changing court is also a fixed and unchanging image, just as his language, however much wedded to the specificities of its changing historical culture, is also, once it has been written down, fixed and unchanging as well.

This paradox of movement and stasis, history and eternity, action and image is made most beautifully apparent by the last page of Castiglione's work. There, Gasparo and Emilia Pia once again square off to fight the war between the sexes that has flared up so often in *Il Cortegiano*. Before they have really begun, however, Castiglione stops them in mid-career, postponing the continuation of their debate for some hypothetical tomorrow the reader will never see. Moreover, instead of then supplying a formal close to his book through a third-person narrative, Castiglione simply terminates it inconclusively with these last remarks of Gasparo and Emilia. The effect here is like that of a freeze-frame at the end of a film: his debaters are stopped right in the midst of their discussion, frozen in a final image. This effect calls attention to itself and to the paradoxical status of *Il Cortegiano* as both moving dialogue and static image, caught up in history and effectively timeless. Of course, what Castiglione achieves brilliantly on this last page is what he has achieved by means of his entire book, but with the addition that here the terms of that achievement call attention to themselves and underscore the paradoxical nature of art.

NOTES

1. On Bembo, see Bruno Migliorini, *Storia della lingua italiana*, 2d ed. (Florence, 1960), pp. 340–41, and B. T. Sozzi, *Aspetti e momenti della questione linguistica* (Padua, 1955), pp. 43–47.

2. For discussions of the "questione della lingua," see Migliorini, *Storia*, pp. 340–59; Sozzi, *Aspetti*, pp. 17–59; and Thérèse Labande-Jeanroy, *La Question de la langue en Italie* (Paris, 1925).

3. Labande-Jeanroy, *La Question*, pp. 73–77.

4. Vittorio Cian, *La lingua di Baldassare Castiglione* (Florence, 1942), p. 13.

5. "Baldassar Castiglione e la teoria cortegiana: ideologia di classe e dottrina critica," *Modern Language Notes*, 83 (1968), 16–66.

6. Ibid., pp. 16–19, 32–38.

7. Thomas G. Rosenmeyer, *The Green Cabinet: Theocritus and the European Pastoral Lyric* (Berkeley, 1969), pp. 19–23.

8. *Lettere del conte Baldesar Castiglione, ora per la prima volta date in luce . . . dall'Abate Pierantonio Serassi* (Padua, 1769–71), I, p. 71.

9. Vittorio Cian, "Religiosità di Baldassare Castiglione," *Convivium*, 22 (1950), 772–80.

10. Cf. Erich Loos, *Baldassare Castigliones "Libro del Cortegiano"* (*Analecta Romanica*, II: Frankfurt am Main, 1955), 154–55.

11. Cian, *La lingua*, pp. 67–81.

12. Labande-Jeanroy, *La Question*, pp. 86–87.

13. In this and subsequent paragraphs on the Renaissance's relationship to antiquity and the importance of its aesthetic of imitation, I am generally indebted to Thomas M. Greene, "Petrarch and the Humanist Hermeneutic," in *Italian Literature: Roots and Branches*, ed. Giose Rimanelli and Kenneth J. Atchity (New Haven, 1976), pp. 201–24.

14. Myron Gilmore, "The Renaissance Conception of the Lessons of History," in *Facets of the Renaissance*, ed. William Werkmeister (New York, 1963), pp. 83–84.

15. Maurizio Dardano, "L'arte del periodo nel Cortegiano," *Rassegna della letteratura italiana*, 67 (1963), 441–62.

16. Ibid., p. 444.

17. Cian, *La lingua*, p. 79.

18. Greene, "Petrarch," p. 207.

6

The Portrait, the Courtier, and Death

David Rosand

"I send you this book as a portrait of the Court of Urbino," Castiglione writes in his dedicatory letter to Don Michel de Silva—adding then, with the modesty required on such occasions, "not by the hand of Raphael or Michelangelo, but by that of a lowly painter and one who only knows how to draw the main lines, without adorning the truth with pretty colors or making, by perspective art, that which is not seem to be."[1]

I propose to take Castiglione's analogy seriously, that is, as more than a rhetorical figure, for the *Book of the Courtier* is indeed a portrait: a group portrait representing the image of a society described in all its complexity, with all its ambiguities and contradictions. As a portrait, the *Courtier* assumes its place securely within the development of the pictorial genre at a particular moment in its modern evolution; moreover, as in the case of so many themes treated by Castiglione, the book actually offers us the fullest and most satisfying articulation of the aims, ethical as well as aesthetic, and function of the art of portraiture. It does so, of course, by the ways in which it constantly defines the contexts of its operation, the dimensions of its own experience, the frames of its reference—by its keen awareness of the tension between the ideal and the real.

The court of Urbino under Guidobaldo da Montefeltro and Elisabetta Gonzaga, the subject of Castiglione's portrait, no

This text is dedicated to the memory of Willard Midgette, who in his life and by his death instructed me in the meanings of art.

longer existed when he decided to publish his work, a decision
taken precisely to preserve the record of a vanished world.
Over this vital image of court life, death already casts its shadow,
asserts itself as a basic reality in the world celebrated in the
Courtier. Castiglione's dedicatory letter opens on a morbid note:
"When signor Guidobaldo da Montefeltro, Duke of Urbino,
passed from this life. . . ." And this elegiac tone continues to
sound through the text. For even in life the duke carried the
signs of his mortality: terribly crippled by the gout, unable to
"stand upon his feet or move" (1.3), Guidobaldo never appears
in the *serate* of the *Courtier,* but his figure, sick and deformed,
lurks behind the scenes, a constant reminder of the cruelty of
envious Fortune, ever "the enemy of virtue."

We recall how frequently throughout the dialogues the participants respond, individually or collectively, with laughter
(*ridendo*). If, in book 2, man is defined as a "risible animal,"
we fully appreciate the desperateness of his plight: "whatever
moves to laughter," we read, "restores the spirit, gives pleasure,
and for the moment keeps one from remembering those vex-
ing troubles of which our life is full" (2.45). Reality in the
Courtier is too often the prey to cruel Fortune.

Castiglione declares that he wrote his book in order to com-
memorate the virtues of the duke and duchess and their court.
Then, upon rereading the text before sending it to press, he
confesses that he "was seized by no little sadness (which greatly
grew as I proceeded), when I remembered that the greater
part of those persons who are introduced in the conversations
were already dead." "And since, while they lived," he continues
to Don Michel, "you did not know the Duchess or the others
who are dead . . . , in order to make you acquainted with them,
in so far as I can, after their death, I send you this book as a
portrait."

Speaking to us with impressive feeling of the aims of portraiture, Castiglione dramatizes its function as a commemorative art that claims to evoke the dead, to substitute itself for life.
His appreciation of its power is perhaps most pointedly articulated elsewhere, when he writes of his own image, that most

1. Raphael, *Portrait of Baldesar Castiglione*. Paris, Musée du Louvre

famous portrait by Raphael (Fig. 1), underscoring the position of the effigy as a substitute for reality. I am referring to the "Elegy that Baldesar Castiglione pretends was written to him by his wife Ippolita." Within the complex fiction of this poem the

2. Bernardino Licinio, *Portrait of a Woman*. Milan, Castello Sforzesco

wife laments her absent husband: only the painted image re-
lieves her constant anguish. "I caress it," she writes, "laugh and
joke with it, speak to it as though it were itself capable of
speech; and often it seems almost to respond, to indicate a
desire to say something, to open its mouth and repeat to me
your words. Our child recognizes the father [in the painting]
and, babbling, he greets it: thus do I deceive the long days and
console myself."[2]

In Castiglione's poem the portrait participates in the life of
the family as a surrogate for the absent father, whose presence
it evokes. (A portrait by Bernardino Licinio of a woman hold-
ing a portrait [Fig. 2] and Castiglione's verse stand as mutual
commentary, their clear eloquence requiring no further ex-

plication.) Here the absence of the subject, Castiglione himself, is due to physical distance; inevitably, however, in the end, that absence will be due to time—that is, to death. Then, the memorial function of the portrait, like the *Book of the Courtier*, becomes in some way, however vain, a negation of death, a desperate gesture that must nevertheless acknowledge death's undeniable reality. If, like the *Courtier*, the painted portrait too seems an affirmation of life, it must, nonetheless, finally render homage to death.[3]

These values and terms had been clearly formulated by 1435, at the beginning of our tradition, in Leon Battista Alberti's little book *On Painting*: "The face of one already dead," he asserted with rhetorical purpose, "through painting lives a long life" ("Il viso di chi già sia morto, per la pittura vive lunga vita").[4] A generation later the Carmelite monk Ferabos will celebrate the portrait of Federico da Montefeltro (Fig. 3), father of Guidobaldo, in a poem in which "The Likeness of the Prince painted by Piero della Francesca addresses the Prince himself." Following a series of verses invoking the names of the most illustrious artists of antiquity—from Timanthes and Zeuxis to Phidias—the poem concludes with the following declaration:

> Piero has given me nerves and flesh and bone,
>> But thou, Prince, has supplied me with a soul from
>>> thy own divinity.
> Therefore, I live, and speak, and am able to move.
>> Thus does the glory of a King transcend the glory
>>> of the artist.[5]

The balance of these words, praising the noble subject of the portrait above its creator, will be more than redressed in later critical appreciation of the genre. For the moment I wish only to stress the theme that lies at the heart of the traditional rhetoric surrounding the art of the portrait: the conceit of the living image. To appreciate the moving eloquence of such rhetoric we might adduce Petrarch's Sonnet 58, on Simone Martini's portrait of Laura, which so frustrates the poet by its failure to respond to his words; he can only envy happy Pygmalion.[6]

3. Piero della Francesca, *Portrait of Federico da Montefeltro*. Florence, Gallerie degli Uffizi

The portrait's evocation of life, however, assumes its special urgency in the face of death, when the sitter "già sia morto." Then the portrait confers that "lunga vita" which is the afterlife of memory. Fully aware of its responsibility to posterity and proud of its commemorative function, the Renaissance portrait developed in a quite deliberately monumental mode; it found its inspiration and its formal conventions in the models of antiquity—even as it shaped that heritage into a still more feeling art of memory.

We can follow the development of the portrait's expressive mechanics, so to speak, by attending to a particular element in its tradition, a form at once compositional and symbolic: the parapet (Fig. 4). As a most precise reference, this ledge recalls the origins of the modern portrait in the funerary traditions of antiquity, especially when it carries a commemorative inscription. Perhaps no other example is more eloquent than the first modern portrait of this type, the first so knowingly to revive the ancient conventions; I refer, of course, to the "Tymotheos" that Jan van Eyck painted in 1432 (Fig. 5), the portrait of a musician, probably—a Timotheos redivivus, possibly Gilles Binchois, as Erwin Panofsky has suggested.[7] On a damaged parapet, whose distressed surface records the hard passage of time, are incised the words LEAL SOUVENIR, explicit testimony to the image's function and meaning.

This type of effigy, with the figure seen *en buste* behind a parapet would become a favorite model in Renaissance portraiture. Inspired by ancient Roman stele and tombstones (Fig. 6), the type itself assumes a particular value as a sign, complex but clear, of the commemorative context of the image. This signifying role of the parapet has been traced into religious imagery by Rona Goffen in a study of the half-length Madonnas of Giovanni Bellini (Fig. 7).[8] Goffen defined the double reference of these images, their dual function as both vision and portrait, and she isolated the special meaning of the half-length form, a resultant of the parapet, as a sign of "the commemoration of the individual, combined at its most basic level with the hope for eternal life." Thus, the parapet itself, deriv-

4. Titian, *Portrait of a Man.* London, National Gallery

ing from a dual tradition—that is, portrait and funerary—
could assume in a representation of the Madonna and Child a
specific referential value, signaling both the tomb and the altar
of Christ, while guaranteeing the likeness of the Virgin.

5. Jan van Eyck, *Portrait of a Man* ("Timotheos"). London, National Gallery

6. Roman Tombstone. Boston, Museum of Fine Arts

More strictly within the traditions of portraiture proper is an epigraphic formula frequently applied to portraits in the early sixteenth century (Fig. 8). This is the inscription "V.V." and its variants, for example, simply "V" or "V.V.O." These have occasionally been read as *Vanitas Vanitatum* or as *Virtus Vincit Omnia,* but recently Nancy Thomson de Grummond has suggested that all these initials probably abbreviate *Vivus Vivo* or

Vivens Vivo.[9] Such a reading gains a certain persuasiveness exactly within the memorial context of the portrait that is our concern. The declaration that the living created such an effigy for the living—an allusion, in an eternal present, to the moment

7. Giovanni Bellini, *Madonna and Child*. Venice, Gallerie dell'Accademia

8. Titian, *Portrait of a Young Man*. Berlin-Dahlem, Staatliche Gemäldegalerie

of construction of the monument—acknowledges, in effect, the inevitable death of the subject. With all its ambiguity, the inscription "V.V." refers to the passing of time and thereby directly confronts the fact of death. Once again the words of

9. Giovanni Bellini, *Portrait of Doge Leonardo Loredan*. London,
National Gallery

Alberti best summarize the situation: "Il viso di chi già sia morto, per la pittura vive lunga vita."

The parapet itself, as we have already noted, could assume full symbolic responsibility, serving as the clear sign of the portrait's memorial function, a reference to the funerary context of its origins. In its Renaissance development, however, the parapet becomes ever more conscious of itself and of its complex pictorial function: serving as a base for the figure and simultaneously identifying itself, at the very surface of the painting, with the frame—a barrier between sitter and spectator that is meant to be traversed. And the fundamental ambivalence of this structure is epitomized in the artist's signature, whether attached as a *cartellino* (Fig. 9) or cut directly into the face of the parapet. Affirming the existence of the artist—and therefore of the portrait as artificial creation—the signature adds a new dimension to the "Vivus" of the old inscription, insisting on the power of the painting—and therefore of the painter—to guarantee the "lunga vita."

This notion of art competing with time takes us naturally into the realm of the *paragone,* the comparison of the arts, that ever so fertile topos of Renaissance criticism. It is a notion that informs one of the most impressive portraits by the young Titian: the so-called "Schiavona" (Fig. 10). Here, not only does art compete with time but art with art. Every side or term of the paragone finds its voice in the competitive forum of this image. On a basic level, painting is set against sculpture. And because the painting itself does indeed represent more than one fixed view of the subject, thereby appropriating one of the virtues of sculpture, its multidimensionality, the art of the painter emerges victorious in this particular contest. Moreover, by its incorporation of a sculpted image within the image, painting implicitly lays claim to another virtue of its sister art: greater permanence. We may quote Count Ludovico da Canossa in the *Courtier* (1.50) on this topic: "Because statues are more durable, one might perhaps say they have a greater dignity; for, since they are made as memorials, they serve better than painting the purpose for which they are made."[10]

10. Titian, *Portrait of a Woman* ("La Schiavona"). London, National Gallery

Still, for all its structural conceit, Titian's "Schiavona" is not merely an aesthetic game; it is a portrait charged with all the expressive responsibilities and associations of such an image. If Titian has transformed the parapet, he has in no way abandoned its traditional value; indeed, he has imbued it with an

11. Titian, *Portrait of a Woman* (detail)

even greater and more complex significance. Rather than an inscription—the initials here surely stand as signature, "Titianus Vecellius"—it is the carved relief itself that enlarges the dimensions of experience of the image (Fig. 11). Sculpted in profile and representing the same sitter, this portrait presents itself *all'antica*, in the guise of a Roman matron. And by such stylistic allusion to the past the sculpture introduces a sense of time into our apprehension of the picture, and the function of the relief, so clearly monumental, reinforces this temporal significance.

The painting is constructed on the basis of a set of tensions, a fundamentally dialectical structure whose poles manifest themselves in several ways: painting and sculpture, flesh and marble, nature and artifice, present and past—and, by projection, future as well. Was "la Schiavona," whatever her real identity, already dead? Might she have died during the execution of her portrait? Might this have been the reason that Titian changed his original composition (as we know he did from X rays of the picture[11]), raising the parapet in order to add a monument to the deceased? Unfortunately, we are in no position to answer these questions. But the questions themselves, inspired directly by the picture, are important even if they must remain unanswered, for they involve on the level of historical reality all the values of the portrait and of its expressive significance.

Perhaps more than any other portrait of this period, Titian's "Schiavona" (normally dated about 1511 or 1512) reveals a very special awareness of the competition between nature and art, between life and death, between the lost past and living memory. Looking at the portrait of this woman posing alongside her own monument, we become conscious above all of the victory of painting, which does indeed confer a long life, Alberti's "lunga vita."

In the world of the paragone the most authoritative spokesman for the supremacy of painting was Leonardo da Vinci. Arguing the cause of painting in his notebooks, Leonardo consistently cites the mimetic power of his art, that power which would be epitomized later in the motto selected by Titian: *Natura potentior Ars* (Art more powerful than Nature).[12] Ironically, the painter of the ruinous *Last Supper* in Milan declared that one of the principal virtues of painting was its permanence. "Oh marvelous science," Leonardo exclaimed of painting, "which can preserve alive the transient beauty of mortals and endow it with a permanence greater than the works of nature; for these are subject to the continual changes of time, which leads them to inevitable old age."[13]

12. Leonardo da Vinci, *Study of Heads*. Windsor, Royal Library. Reproduced by Gracious Permission of Her Majesty Queen Elizabeth II

In the pages of his notebooks, in his drawings (Fig. 12), and in his paintings Leonardo reveals a preoccupation with the transience of things, with the ravages caused by time, in the macrocosm of the universe and in the microcosm of man. We find in his thought a tense dialectic between the vision of an ideal youthful beauty, on the one hand, and, on the other, the image, at times frightening, of devastated old age (Fig. 13). Leonardo betrays an almost morbid fear of aging, and painting seems to offer him one way of countering the destructive effects of time. And it is the human face itself, the portrait, that becomes the arena of this conflict.

Among his writings one particularly dramatic passage comes to mind, his paraphrase of lines from the fifteenth book of the *Metamorphoses*:

> Oh Time, who consumes all things! Oh envious age, you who destroy all things and devour all things with the hard teeth of the years, little by little, in slow death!
>
> Helen, when she looked in her mirror, seeing the withered wrinkles in her face made by old age, wept, and thought to herself, why ever had she been twice ravished.
>
> Oh Time, who consumes all things! Oh envious age, by whom all things are consumed![14]

Bearing in mind these words, at once bitter and terrible, I would like to propose a reading of the most famous and intriguing of Leonardo's images of feminine beauty (Fig. 14). Considering the degree to which this portrait has indeed suffered from the "hard teeth" of time and the oppressive weight of accumulated interpretations, it is not without some hesitation that I dare to add to her problems. Nevertheless, the *Mona Lisa*, the epitome of Leonardo's portrait art, stands as the fullest realization of his thoughts on the genre in its disturbing thematic richness.

The basic structure remains dialectical and the terms of confrontation the same: that is, art and nature, the ideal and the real, the beauty of youth and the destructiveness of time. In the *Mona Lisa* Leonardo created an image that contains and esca-

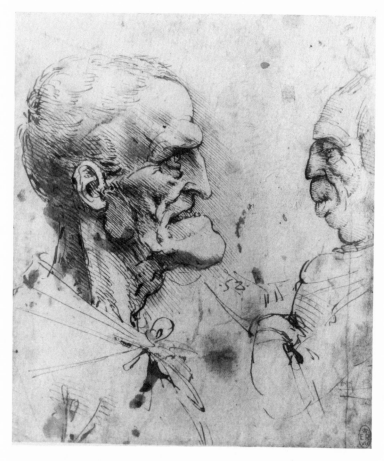

13. Leonardo da Vinci, *Profiles of an Old Man and an Old Woman*. Windsor, Royal Library. Reproduced by Gracious Permission of Her Majesty Queen Elizabeth II

lates all those values inherent in portraiture that we have been discussing; yet they are comprehended in a structure so subtly organic that we often forget that the picture belongs to a well-defined category.

14. Leonardo da Vinci, *Mona Lisa*. Paris, Musée du Louvre

Two elements constitute the essential compositional construct: the figure that dominates the foreground and the background landscape that sets it off. Between these two complementary terms, however, there exists that certain tension. The
smooth and perfect forms of the portrait proper—disturbed,
perhaps, only by the famously enigmatic smile—contrast with
those of the landscape, hard and rocky (Fig. 15). On one level
of interpretation we might read this neat contrast as a simple
binary structure: flesh and rock, soft and hard, feminine and
masculine. But the mind of Leonardo was rarely satisfied with
terms so rigidly determined and fixed; always more organic
and flexible, his art acknowledged instead relationships that
were more open, complex, and dynamic.

The landscape itself offers us such a complex spectacle of
change, a world containing its own internal conflicts. Through
this realm of mountains and denticulated rock the waters flow.
And it is water that actually dominates this landscape, water
that is the cause of the formations—or, better, deformations—
of this earth. Searching for the meaning of such natural opposition, we can do no better than return to Leonardo's own
words. From among his many observations on water, I need
cite but one: Water, he writes, "wears away the lofty summits of
the mountains. It lays bare and carries away the great rocks."
And then, in a marginal gloss on this passage, he adds: "With
time everything changes" ("Col tempo ogni cosa va variando").[15]
In Leonardo's thought, then, water is both the symbol and the
agent of time (Fig. 16).[16] Considered in this light, the landscape
of the *Mona Lisa* assumes its special meaning within the expressive traditions of the portrait that have been our theme.

In Leonardo's vision, water comes to be identified with the
basic forces of life, whether generative or destructive (Fig. 17).
Like the mountains and rocks of the background of the *Mona
Lisa*, life remains subject to time, which leads it to "inevitable
old age" and death. The landscape in this portrait of a beautiful woman emerges as a record of the brevity of "the works of
nature," a reminder of the transience of things. It thus com-

15. Leonardo da Vinci, *Mona Lisa* (detail)

ments on the image itself, on that beauty which must suffer the transformation of time, the "withered wrinkles" of old age.

Another portrait of the first decade of the cinquecento, of an old woman (Fig. 18), generally attributed to Giorgione,[17] may be considered a reverse of the medal to the *Mona-Lisa*. The message implicit in Leonardo's portrait is here fully realized in the

16. Leonardo da Vinci, *Old Man in Meditation and Studies of Water.* Windsor, Royal Library. Reproduced by Gracious Permission of Her Majesty Queen Elizabeth II

wrinkled face of *la vecchia,* who, with a gesture, seems to speak of herself, of the fate of aging. The significance of her discourse is explicitly articulated by the inscription she holds: COL TEMPO. Instead of youthful beauty, human and fragile, with its poignant poetry, we find ourselves now before an image that all too forcefully recalls to us our end. If not exactly a memento mori, *La Vecchia* stands nonetheless as a warning, evoking a tradition more openly moralizing and medieval: *vanitas vanitatum, et omnia vanitas.* Yet we must recognize the continuity of such traditions, of such preoccupations, which the poetry of humanism might treat in new ways but whose essential truth it could never deny. "Col tempo," as Leonardo noted, "ogni cosa va variando."

The poetry of the Renaissance portrait was predicated on a profound recognition of the absolute truth of death. From the conflict between the ideal and the real, the willed life of art and the accepted fact of death, derived the expressive power, the special pathos, of a pictorial form that insisted on realizing as fully as possible its potential vitality. Artists such as Leonardo, Giorgione, Raphael, and Titian pushed the mimetic limits of their art, activating its space so that it not only enlarged the physical movement of the sitter, creating new forms of active portraiture, but comprehended as well new dimensions of psychic experience (Fig. 19). Sitters assumed an increasingly active and profound engagement with the space about them—through their own movement as well as through the containing tonal ambience of the new *sfumato*—and with the confronting viewer.

17. Leonardo da Vinci, *Deluge*. Windsor, Royal Library. Reproduced by Gracious Permission of Her Majesty Queen Elizabeth II

18. Giorgione, *Old Woman.* Venice, Gallerie dell'Accademia

The effigy acquired implications of narrative motion and therefore of temporal extension; the portrait subject became a dramatis persona—thus, for example, Raphael's portrait of Tommaso Inghirami (Fig. 20) presents him as *vates,* as the inspired
writer, or, more accurately perhaps, the poet awaiting his muse's
intervention.[18] No longer content to describe the outer features

of physiognomy, the new portraiture—of Castiglione's generation—aimed at the revelation of an inner (or, at least, a com-
pleter) life.[19]

But painting, as the Renaissance artist well knew, is a fiction;

VERO RITRATTO DE GIORGONE DE CASTEL FRANCO
da luy fatto come lo celebra il libro del VASARI.

19. Giorgione, *Self-Portrait as David* (engraving by Wenceslas Hollar)

20. Raphael, *Portrait of Tommaso Inghirami*. Boston, Isabella Stewart Gardner Museum

21. Bernardino Licinio, *Portrait of a Young Man*. Oxford, Ashmolean Museum

the life of a portrait can be no more than a fictive life. Such an image can no more than evoke the memory of a reality that, inevitably, no longer exists. The affective portrait of the High Renaissance seems simultaneously to acknowledge and to challenge this fact. There often appears, in the allusive sentiment

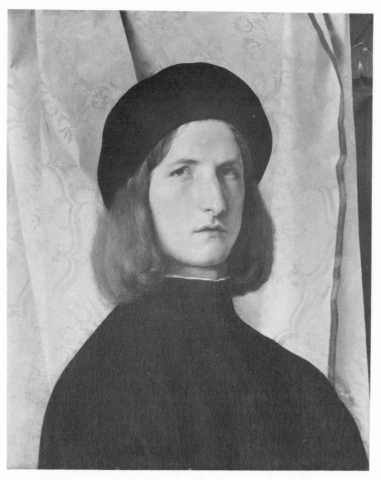

22. Lorenzo Lotto, *Portrait of a Young Man*. Vienna, Kunsthistorisches Museum

of many of these images—a sentiment that draws us so deeply into an interpretive relationship with the painted persona— a gentle, indeed melancholic awareness of the transience of things, of youth, of life itself—an awareness not always prod- ded by a reminder as obvious as a skull (Fig. 21).

How many of these Renaissance faces, whether proud in the vigor of their youth or wiser with the experience of age, are poignantly set off by some reminder of their mortality: the flickering candle behind the brilliant white curtain in Lorenzo Lotto's portrait of a young man (Fig. 22),[20] or the hourglass perched upon the rug-covered parapet in Moretto da Brescia's painting in the Metropolitan Museum (Fig. 23). Or, moving

23. Moretto da Brescia, *Portrait of a Man*. New York, Metropolitan Museum of Art (Rogers Fund, 1928)

24. Titian, *Portrait of a Knight of Malta*. Madrid, Museo del Prado

further into the sixteenth century—when the morality of the portrait had become somewhat compromised, in part, by the assertiveness of a more ambitious pictorial format and its affect diluted by an allegorizing impulse—Titian's portrait of a knight of Malta (Fig. 24) continues the earlier tradition. Without the

BILIBALDI·PIRKEYMHERI·EFFIGIES
·AETATIS·SVAE·ANNO·L·III·
VIVITVR·INGENIO·CAETERA·MORTIS·
·ERVNT·
·M·D·XX·IV·

25. Dürer, *Portrait of Willibald Pirckheimer* (engraving)

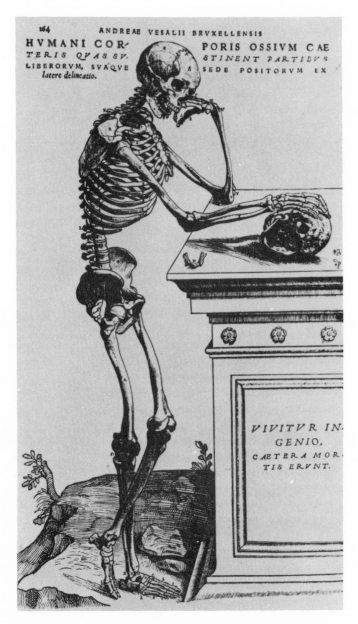

26. Illustration from Andreas Vesalius, *De humani corporis fabrica libri septem* (Basel, 1543)

least trace of rhetoric, the image presents in a straightforward manner a man, standing, with one hand touching a clock. The very understatement of its simple composition, chromatically so subtly muted, is the source of this portrait's moving affect: a man quite casually, almost absentmindedly, caressing the symbol of his mortality.[21] Titian's brush was celebrated for its power to endow its subjects with life, to challenge the claims of death, even by reviving the dead: "resuscita i morti in lo stile," in the explicit words of Pietro Aretino.[22] Deliberately extolling "the glory of the artist," Aretino speaks for an aesthetic enthusiasm quite different from the courtly response of a Ferabos. And yet, if Titian's portrait affirms that "lunga vita," it nonetheless carries with it the awareness of inevitable death; the very quiet of the image seems pervaded by the solemn tones of the *ars moriendi*. The affirmation of life implicates the recognition of death.

In the articulation of the great cycle of life, death, and the afterlife of memory the very concept of the portrait, as a commemorative image, came to play a central role. Its monumental function, emphasized by the prominent slab of the parapet, is clear in a portrait such as Dürer's of his friend Willibald Pirckheimer (Fig. 25). Here the inscription, adapted from a pseudo-Virgilian text (*Elegiae in Maecenatem* i, 37–38), most eloquently speaks to all that concerns us: "Vivitur ingenio, caetera mortis erunt"—we live through genius, all the rest belongs to death. Nearly two decades later the same text would find its meaning in a somewhat different graphic setting (Fig. 26), the seven books *De humani corporis fabrica* published by Andreas Vesalius in 1543.[23]

For the author the book is a monument through which he continues to live long after death. And, in turn, the example of Castiglione's *Book of the Courtier* reminds us of how deeply involved the portrait was with matters of life and death.

NOTES

1. Bruno Maier rightly called attention to this definition of the *Courtier* as a portrait; its suggestiveness, he found, encourages us to understand Castiglione's

book as something "figurative and representational rather than narrowly instructional" ("è assai suggestiva e ben giova a farci comprendere il carattere del libro castiglionesco, e cioè la sua fisionomia piuttosto figurativa e rappresentativa che angustamente didascalica") (*Il Cortegiano, con una scelta delle opere minori,* 2d ed. [Turin, 1964], p. 71, n. 25).

For the topos, cf. Lombardo della Seta's comment on his abridgement of Petrarch's *De viris illustribus:* "I shall draw and not paint the image of the subject so that the quality of the linear contours can be seen without an adumbration of the inward character" (trans. T. E. Mommsen, "Petrarch and the Sala Virorum Illustrium in Padua," *Art Bulletin,* 34 [1952], 106).

2. "Balthassaris Castilionis elegia qua fingit Hippolyten suam ad se ipsum scribentem": . . .

sola tuos vultus referens, Raphaelis imago
    picta manu curas allevat usque meas.
Huic ego delicias facio arrideoque iocorque
    alloquor et, tanquam reddere verba queat.
Assensu nutuque mihi saepe illa videtur
    dicere velle aliquid et tua verba loqui.
Agnoscit balboque patrem puer ore salutat:
    hoc solor longos decipioque dies.

(*Il Cortegiano, con una scelta delle opere minori,* ed. Maier, p. 598)

3. Erasmus, sending a portrait of himself to Thomas More in 1517, wrote: "I am sending you the portrait in order that we may be always with you, even when death shall have annihilated us" (quoted by William S. Heckscher, "Reflections on Seeing Holbein's Portrait of Erasmus at Longford Castle," in *Essays in the History of Art presented to Rudolf Wittkower* [London, 1967], pp. 144–45).

4. Leon Battista Alberti, *Della pittura,* in Alberti, *De Pictura,* ed. Cecil Grayson (Rome and Bari, 1975), ii.25, p. 44. Alberti's discourse in book 2 begins: "Tiene in sé la pittura forza divina non solo quanto si dice dell'amicizia, quale fa gli uomini assenti essere presenti, ma più i morti dopo molti secoli essere quasi vivi, tale che con molta ammirazione dell'artefice e con molta voluttà si riconoscono." Cf. Cicero, *De amicitia* 7.23.

A century after Alberti, Francisco de Hollanda (among many others) reiterated this theme in one of his dialogues, which seems almost to borrow its pathos from the model of Castiglione. Painting, Vittoria Colonna declares,

makes present to us men long dead, whose very bones have perished from off the face of the earth . . . and likewise the beauty of an unknown woman many leagues distant, as Pliny noticed in wonder. It prolongs for many years the life of one who dies, since his painted likeness remains; it consoles the widow, who sees the portrait of her dead husband daily before her; and the orphan children, when they grow up, are glad to have the presence and likeness of their father and are afraid to shame him.

Here the Signora Marchesa paused, almost in tears; and, in order to divert her sad thoughts and memories, Messer Lattanzio added. . . . (*Four Dialogues on Painting*, trans. A. F. G. Bell [London, 1928], pp. 25–26)

5. "Imago ejusdem principis a Pietro Burgensi picta alloquitur ipsum principem": . . .

Ast Petrus nervos mihi dat cum carnibus ossa,
   Das animam, Princeps, tu deitate tua;
Vivo igitur, loquor et scio per me posse moviri [*sic*];
   Gloria sic Regis praestat et artificis.

(Quoted from John Pope-Hennessy, *The Portrait in the Renaissance* [London and New York, 1966], p. 319, n. 8.)

6. Quando giunse a Simon l'alto concetto
   ch'a mio nome gli pose in man lo stile,
   s'avesse dato a l'opera gentile
   colla figura voce ed intelletto,

di sospir molti mi sgombrava il petto
   che ciò ch'altri à più caro a me fan vile,
   però che 'n vista ella si mostra umile
   promettendomi pace ne l'aspetto.

Ma poi ch'i vengo a ragionar con lei,
   benignamente assai par che m'ascolte:
   se risponder savesse a' detti miei!

Pigmalion, quanto lodar ti dei
   de l'imagine tua, se mille volte
   n'avesti quel ch'i' sol una vorrei!

7. Erwin Panofsky, "Who is Jan van Eyck's 'Tymotheos'?" *Journal of the Warburg and Courtauld Institutes*, 12 (1949), 80–90; idem, *Early Netherlandish Painting* (Cambridge, Mass., 1953), pp. 196–201. An alternative (although not fully persuasive) reading, identifying Timotheos as a sculptor, has recently been proposed by Wendy Wood, "A New Identification of the Sitter in Jan van Eyck's *Timotheos* Portrait," *Art Bulletin*, 60 (1978), 650–54.

8. Rona Goffen, "Icon and Vision: Giovanni Bellini's Half-Length Madonnas," *Art Bulletin*, 57 (1975), 487–514.

9. Nancy Thomson de Grummond, "VV and Related Inscriptions in Giorgione, Titian, and Dürer," *Art Bulletin*, 57 (1975), 346–56. (The Giustiniani portrait in Berlin, our Fig. 8, is generally attributed to Giorgione; for the arguments in favor of an attribution to Titian, see David Rosand, *Titian* [New York, 1978], p. 66.)

10. Cf. Benedetto Varchi, *Lezione nella quale si disputa della maggioranza delle arti e qual sia più nobile, la scultura o la pittura* (1547), ed. Paola Barocchi, in *Trattati d'arte del Cinquecento*, I (Bari, 1960). Still a most useful introduction to the topic is Irma A. Richter, ed., *Paragone: A Comparison of the Arts by Leonardo da Vinci* (London, New York, and Toronto, 1949).

11. See Cecil Gould, "New Light on Titian's 'Schiavona' Portrait," *Burlington Magazine*, 103 (1961), 335–40.

12. On Titian's impresa, see Hans Tietze, "Unknown Venetian Drawings in Swedish Collections," *Gazette des beaux-arts*, 35 (1949), 183–84; for further bibliography, cf. Arthur Henkel and Albrecht Schöne, *Emblemata: Handbuch zur Sinnbildkunst des XVI. und XVII. Jahrhunderts* (Stuttgart, 1967), col. 442. For a discussion of Titian's impresa in a larger context, see David Rosand, "Titian and the Critical Tradition," in *Titian: His World and His Legacy* (New York, 1982), pp. 1–39, esp. 16, 36–37.

13. Leonardo da Vinci, *Treatise on Painting [Codex Urbinas Latinus 1270]*, ed. A. Philip McMahon (Princeton, 1956), II, 16ᵛ; also in Richter, *Paragone*, p. 74.

14. *The Notebooks of Leonardo da Vinci*, ed. Edward MacCurdy (New York, 1958), p. 62 (Codex Atlanticus, 71ʳ).

15. Reale Commissione Vinciana, *I manoscritti e i disegni di Leonardo da Vinci* . . . , I. *Il codice Arundel 263*, i (Rome, 1923), p. 88. Cf. Ovid, *Ars amatoria*, 1.476: "Dura tamen molli saxa cavantur aqua." Also relevant to this discourse is a poem by Panfilo Sasso (d. 1527), cited, in a different context, by Ernst Robert Curtius, *European Literature and the Latin Middle Ages* (New York, 1953), pp. 289–90:

Col tempo el villanel al giogo mena
El tòr sí fiero e sí crudo animale;
Col tempo el falcon si usa a menar l'ale
E ritornar a te chiamato a pena.

Col tempo si domestica in catena
El bizzarro orso, e 'l feroce cinghiale;
Col tempo l' acqua, che è sí molle e frale,
Rompe el dur sasso, come el fosse arena.

Col tempo ogni robusto ardor cade;
Col tempo ogni alto monte si fa basso,
Ed io col tempo non posso a pietade

Mover un cor d' ogni dolcezza casso;
Onde avanza di orgoglio e crudeltade
Orso, toro, leon, falcone e sasso.

16. On these themes in the thought of Leonardo, see Joseph Gantner, *Leonardos Visionen von der Sintflut und vom Untergang der Welt* (Berne, 1958), pp. 62–71 ("Der Mikrocosmos und das Wasser"); V. P. Zubov, *Leonardo da Vinci* (Cambridge, Mass., 1968), pp. 221–63 ("Time"); and E. H. Gombrich, *The Heritage of Apelles* (Ithaca, New York, 1976), pp. 39–56 ("The Form of Movement in Water and Air"); also Jan Bialostocki, "Renaissance Artists as Philosophers in Meditation: Two Small Problems Concerning Two Great Masters," *Acta historiae artium*, 24 (1978), 207–10.

17. Terisio Pignatti, *Giorgione*, 2d ed. (Milan, 1978), cat. no. 29. The attribu-

tion of this picture, very likely that identified by Marcantonio Michiel as "il retrato della Madre de Zorzon de man de Zorzon . . . ," has been questioned—and not without stylistic reason—by Michelangelo Muraro, *Treasures of Venice* (Cleveland, 1963), pp. 168–69, and by Erwin Panofsky, *Problems in Titian, Mostly Iconographic* (New York, 1969), pp. 90–91—both of whom favor an attribution to Titian.

18. Although fully recognizing the "new type of active portrait" and adducing Raphael's likeness of Inghirami as "the first independent Renaissance portrait that is not psychologically self-contained," Pope-Hennessy offers an interpretation that may render rather too prosaic the conception of the image: "The sitter has been interrupted at his desk, and his attention is attracted by some unseen interlocutor" (*The Portrait in the Renaissance*, p. 117). Surely the portrait gains in resonance and affect when viewed in the tradition of images of inspired poets and evangelists; Inghirami's pen is poised in anticipation of the divine afflatus.

19. On this theme, in addition to the general observations of Pope-Hennessy, see especially Jaynie Anderson, "The Giorgionesque Portrait: From Likeness to Allegory," in *Giorgione: Atti del Convegno Internazionale di Studio per il 5° Centenario della Nascita* (Castelfranco Veneto, 1979), pp. 153–58; also Carlo Pedretti, "Ancora sul rapporto Giorgione–Leonardo e l'origine del ritratto di spalla," in ibid., pp. 181–85.

20. In T. S. Eliot's paraphrase, "The smoky candle end of time / Declines. . . ." Indeed, Eliot's "Burbank with a Baedeker: Bleistein with a Cigar" takes us directly back to the moralizing reminders of Renaissance imagery: its epigraph—*nil nis divinum stabile est; caetera fumus*—comes from Mantegna's Ca' d'Oro *St. Sebastian*, where the inscription winds around a smoking candle.

21. On the topic in general, see Panofsky, *Problems in Titian*, pp. 88–108 ("Reflections on Time"); cf. also the comments in my review of Harold E. Wethey, *Titian: The Portraits*, in *Renaissance Quarterly*, 26 (1973), 497–500.

22. Pietro Aretino, *Lettere sull'arte*, ed. Fidenzio Pertile and Ettore Camesasca (Milan, 1957–60), II, no. dcxliii. I have discussed this aspect of the rhetoric surrounding and informing Titian's art in "Titian and the Critical Tradition," and in "Alcuni pensieri sul ritratto e la morte," in *Giorgione e l'umanesimo veneziano*, ed. Rodolfo Pallucchini (Florence, 1981), pp. 293–308.

23. See David Rosand and Michelangelo Muraro, *Titian and the Venetian Woodcut* (Washington, D.C., 1976), pp. 223–24.

7
Castiglione's Verbal Portrait: Structures and Strategies

Robert W. Hanning

"And since, while they lived, you did not know the Duchess or the others who are dead, . . . in order to make you acquainted with them, in so far as I can, after their death, I send you this book as a portrait of the Court of Urbino." Castiglione's famous designation of his masterwork as a portrait appears in the dedicatory letter to Don Michel de Silva which he appended to the *Book of the Courtier* well after its completion. The intent of this essay is to explore, by means of textual analysis, the structures and strategies inherent in the work that led Castiglione to characterize it ex post facto as a portrait. The more carefully we scrutinize the text, the more apposite its author's suggestion of a *paragone* between his own art and that of Michelangelo or Raphael can be seen to be.[1]

Thanks to the research of Ghinassi and others, we can now trace the stages of evolution of the *Book of the Courtier* and watch the theme here under discussion taking shape. The letter to de Silva was composed so late that it appears for the first time in the first published edition of 1528, not in the Laurentian–Ashburnham manuscript on which that edition is otherwise based.[2] Neither of the two canceled beginnings of book 1 of the *Courtier,* printed two centuries ago by Serassi, manifests the elegiac note of the de Silva letter—not surprisingly, we might say, since presumably none of the participants in the dialogue had died, including Alfonso Ariosto, the initial dedicatee, when these early *proemi* were penned.[3] Instead, Castiglione's emphasis is on the ideality, not on the mimetic or memorial quality of his

131

work, and his focus is not a living court but rather the perfect
courtier, a paragon he never expects to see but useful as a
mark for all to shoot at, even if none can hit it.[4] In a sense, then,
Castiglione's announced intention for the *Book of the Courtier*
evolved from the creation of a personal ideal to the preservation of a social memory. An indication of the stages of this
evolution in his attitude toward his book can be gleaned from
prefatory remarks he makes in the *Courtier* elsewhere than at its
beginning.

First, in opening book 4 (which is, we recall, book 3 in the
earlier, "seconda redazione" of the *Courtier,* recently edited by
Ghinassi), Castiglione reflects on the untimely death of some of
the courtiers of Urbino whose words he has been recording,
and expresses to Alfonso Ariosto his profound sadness at these
losses.[5] Next, in the prefatory remarks to book 3, which were in
fact written later than those of book 4 (they are lacking in the
seconda redazione), Castiglione extols the court of Urbino and
confesses to Ariosto, "I consider myself obliged, as far as I can,
to make every effort to preserve this bright memory from mortal oblivion, and make it live in the mind of posterity through
my writing" (3.1). Here is an expression of art's power to defeat devouring time, a commonplace of Renaissance poets and
closely akin to Alberti's claim for painting as the giver of "lunga
vita," a claim quoted by David Rosand in his essay elsewhere in
this volume (see above, p. 95).[6]

The final step in the progression came in the letter to de
Silva, when Castiglione linked the fact of death's depredations
among the courtiers of Urbino to the goal of making the court
live on by his writing, using the metaphor of the portrait to
characterize what he had come to perceive as the major, commemorative function of the *Book of the Courtier.* But we must
beware of interpreting the portrait metaphor too narrowly or
univocally. Castiglione also uses it to evoke a paragone or rivalry between his verbal portrait and the paintings of Raphael
and Michelangelo, even as he ostensibly denies being their
equal—a fine demonstration of the courtly art of praising one-
self without appearing to do so, as recommended by Count

Ludovico da Canossa later in book 1.[7] There may already be an
element of paragone in the description of Raphael's portrait of
Castiglione that the latter included in the Latin elegy to which
Rosand has referred, a poem in the form of a supposed letter
sent to Castiglione in Rome by his wife Ippolita (see above,
pp. 92–95).[8] Castiglione's source for the passage of the elegy in
which his wife extols the mimetic power of the "Raphaelis imago
picta manu" (11.27–34) is in fact the thirteenth epistle of Ovid's
Heroides, in which Laodamia writes to her absent husband, Protesilaus: "While you, a soldier in the distant world, will be bearing arms, I keep a waxen image to give back your features to
my sight; it hears the caressing phrase, it hears the words of
love that are yours by right, and it receives my embrace. Believe me, the image is more than it appears; add but a voice to
the wax, Protesilaus it will be. On this I look, and hold it to my
heart in place of my real lord, and complain to it, as if it could
speak again."[9] Laodamia's *imago,* unlike Ippolita's, has no independent existence save in Ovid's words; here, as elsewhere in
the *Heroides,* Ovid uses the *ekphrasis* of an imago to call attention to the vividness of his verbal art, a vividness challenging
that of a painted or sculpted image, or of life itself.[10] So Castiglione, in describing how Raphael's portrait makes him present
to Ippolita even when he is physically absent, asks us, I believe,
to recognize how his word portrait makes Ippolita present to
him and to us, with all her concern for her faraway spouse and
advice about avoiding the dangers of Rome, through the power
of his art. Indeed, by imitating and updating the Ovidian genre
of the epistle by the left-behind wife or mistress, Castiglione
challenges Ovid even as he does Raphael.[11]

Can we say more precisely whether, and if so how, Castiglione incorporated rivalry with the painters in his greatest
work? Students of Castiglione have long recognized the inter-
twining in the *Book of the Courtier* of artistic theory and prescriptions for ideal courtly behavior. Castiglione innovates as much
in articulating the aesthetic of the perfect painting as in defining the excellence of the perfect courtier. In the remainder of
these remarks I want in part to fix on a particular topos of art

theory, already popularized by Alberti, namely, the painter's
duty to create an idealized yet mimetic art by imitating only the
most nearly perfect models.[12] The locus classicus of this topos is
the example of Zeuxis of Crotona, the ancient painter who
created a portrait of Aphrodite by combining features from the
five most beautiful women he could find.[13] Castiglione uses, in-
verts, and plays with the idea of the combinative element of an
ideal portrait; his manipulation of the topos functions as a key
part of a larger strategy in giving the *Book of the Courtier* a
design, a structure, analogous to and rivaling that of a certain
type of narrative painting (*istoria*) practiced by his contemporaries.[14] This strategy comprises establishing relationships among
the various levels of narrative or mimetic "reality" built into the
work, relationships that can in part be understood as a series
of interactions among artist, work of art, and audience. The
levels are distinguished, but not closed off, from one another
by framing devices, which, as Rosand has shown with respect to
the parapet motif, characterize and complicate High Renaissance portraits and other paintings (see above, pp. 97–104)[15] and
which, in the *Courtier*, contribute to the sense of human limits
which art attempts, however vainly, to transcend.[16]

At the center of Castiglione's book is the portrait, formed in
words, of the perfect courtier, who is both artist and his own
work of art. He must constantly create himself by incorporating
in his person the virtues of many men who excel in various
skills.

> Therefore, whoever would be a good pupil must not only do things
> well, but must always make every effort to resemble and, if that be
> possible, to transform himself into his master. And when he feels
> that he has made some progress, it is very profitable to observe
> different men of that profession; and, conducting himself with that
> good judgment which must always be his guide, go about choosing
> now this thing from one and that from another. And even as in
> green meadows the bee flits about among the grasses robbing the
> flowers, so our Courtier must steal this grace from those who seem
> to him to have it, taking from each the part that seems most worthy
> of praise. (1.26)[17]

The courtier is both Zeuxis *and* Zeuxis's portrait, forming one ideal from many fine parts, with the goal, as Castiglione tells Alfonso Ariosto, of "winning favor from [princes] and praise from others" (1.1). Like the painter Apelles, the courtier must also disguise the effort and artfulness that go into this living, idealized self-portrait. The courtier-as-masterpiece has two audiences: first, the other courtiers, who, like true connoisseurs, appreciate him because they thoroughly understand his art form; and second, the prince, who can reward the artist as well as enjoy the artwork.[18] The prince, in his special position vis-à-vis the courtier, resembles the ideally placed viewer of a perspective painting or theatrical set. We know, of course, that in Renaissance court theaters the prince's box was in fact placed precisely at the central point from which the perspective was to be viewed. And Alberti calls the ray going from the eye of such a viewer to the center of the picture plane the "princeps radiorum," or "principe de' razzi."[19]

But if the ideal courtier, performing for the prince and fellow courtiers, stands at the center of the courtly *teatrum mundi*, he stands in Castiglione's book at the center of a game played by "real" courtiers of Urbino; he is *their* work of art, the reflection of their skills, behavioral and verbal. Federico Fregoso, in suggesting that the game to be played that evening be the formation in words of the perfect courtier, declares that if there are good courtiers anywhere, they are here at Urbino, and that their idea of the good courtier can thus be used as a touchstone "to put down the many fools who in their presumption and ineptitude think to gain the name of good courtiers" (1.12). The ideal courtier, in other words, will be a translation into a word portrait of the behavioral patterns of Urbino's courtly paragons.

We can say then that there are two portraits of the court of Urbino existing in mutual tension in the *Book of the Courtier*: the ideal, timeless portrait of themselves that the courtiers of Urbino collectively fabricate, and the enveloping, commemorative portrait of them that Castiglione offers us in the face of time's deadly reality.[20] And this tension between portrait levels frames in turn a complementary tension. On the one hand, as a hypothetical persona, the exemplary courtier—the new Zeuxis, as it were—actively takes to himself, like a bee gathering honey, the excellences of other courtiers; on the other hand, as a verbal construct, that same courtier becomes the passive vessel into which his creators, the courtiers of Urbino, pour their own excellences. At this outer level, the creators of ideal courtly excellence are also its models—as though those five famous beauties of Crotona had agreed to depict Aphrodite by working as a committee and had thereby eliminated Zeuxis as an unnecessary middleman.

But of course, middlemen—and -women—are present in abundance at further framing levels of the *Book of the Courtier*. Each one contributes uniquely to the adornment of the portrait of Urbino and its denizens, but each also exemplifies the forces in life that oppose all human art and achievement. First, there is the duchess, Elisabetta Gonzaga, of whom Thomas Greene writes so movingly elsewhere in this volume (see above, p. 11). Her presence, we are told, functioned "as a chain that bound [the courtiers] all together in love." Such was her influence that "it seemed that she tempered us all to her own quality and fashion, wherefore each one strove to imitate her style, deriving, as it were, a rule of fine manners from the presence of so great and virtuous a lady." Castiglione's idiom here is Neoplatonic: The courtiers are, in effect, copies of the duchess's goodness, which she creates by the force of that goodness and binds together with a chain of love, like the divine demiurge of Plato's *Timaeus*. Yet even this godlike creature, Castiglione tells us, has, thanks to fortune, suffered "many adversities and stings of calamity" (1.4).

The courtiers also owe their existence to the duke of Urbino, who has surrounded himself with them. They are his prize works of art, the human analogues to the beautiful books in Greek, Latin, and Hebrew which his father, Duke Federico, collected and "adorned with gold and silver, deeming these to be the supreme excellence of his great palace" (1.2). Duke Guidobaldo is the raison d'être of his courtiers but also an emblem of their limits. Afflicted with gout and no longer able to perform deeds of chivalry, "he still took the greatest pleasure in seeing others so engaged; and by his words . . . he showed clearly how much judgment he had in such matters. Wherefore . . . in all exercises befitting noble cavaliers, everyone strove to show himself such as to deserve to be thought worthy of his noble company" (1.3). Guidobaldo has become a connoisseur of courtlinesss, which connoisseurship, combined with his political power, has made him the artist-creator of his superlative courtiers as well. Yet in the *Book of the Courtier* Guidobaldo is primarily important because of his absence. His infirmity forces him to retire early, clearing a play space for the courtiers' game of reproducing themselves as verbal, rather than living, works of art.[21] His absence reminds us, as would his presence, of the limits Fortune places on all *virtù*, and therefore on all art, visual or verbal, that celebrates heroic or strategic mastery.

There is, of course, another absent–present artist who creates and frames the *Book of the Courtier*, at once exalting and limiting its commemorative power. This is Castiglione himself, who forms the perfect courtier for Alfonso Ariosto by recapitulating conversations at which he was not present. He has received reports of the conversations from a friend and will recall them "in so far as my memory permits" (1.1)—and, we might add, insofar as the friend's memory permitted as well. The absence of Guidobaldo and Castiglione—the artist-creator and artist-commemorator of the court of Urbino, respectively—dramatizes the gap between potential and performance, ideal and blemished reality, in both life and art. The shining portraits of courtly perfection—a historical portrait framing an exemplary one—come to us framed with darker hues of human limitation, both permanent (the gouty duke) and temporary (the absent Castiglione). Wayne Rebhorn reminds us in his book that Castiglione was in fact in Urbino at the time he claims the dialogues took place.[22] The fictiveness of his absence argues all the more, I believe, for its function as part of a deliberate strategy of framing the ideal portrait.

If Castiglione's decision to call his book a portrait was in one

sense the product of an evolution in his ideas about what he
had accomplished in it, we can see that in another sense the
elements and tensions of High Renaissance portraiture were
structurally inherent in the *Book of the Courtier*. The portrait
designation has threefold significance: First, it reflects his desire to preserve the memory of a great, departed generation of
courtiers from time's oblivion; second, it signals his entrance
into rivalry with the great painters of his day for the laurels
owing to the most successful exponent of an aesthetic of mime-
sis, both idealized and challengingly complex in its techniques;
finally, it refers directly to the sophisticated interaction among
artist, work of art, and audience that is repeated in the *Book of
the Courtier* at several levels, each one enclosing and complicat-
ing the ones preceding it. The clarity and apparent simplicity
of the book's structure (it seems, at first reading, merely a
series of pleasant after-dinner discussions) constitute a triumph
of literary *sprezzatura*. Castiglione's structural model was the
multiple envelopes of reported discourse within which Plato
places Agathon's party in the *Symposium*. (The events of that
evening—at the center of which Socrates reports an earlier discourse by his teacher, Diotima of Mantinea—are reported to us
by Apollodorus, who received them from a friend, Aristodemus,
who had been present.) Some years ago Helen Bacon convincingly demonstrated the philosophical uses to which Plato put
the *Symposium*'s envelope structure;[23] alone, I suspect, of all his
contemporaries, Castiglione imitated this feature of the influential dialogue, but not because it exemplified the Platonic doctrine of recollection. Rather, in the form in which he adopted
it, it enabled him to build into his framed dialogue key elements of the theory and practice of High Renaissance portraiture.[24] At the theoretical level, Castiglione demonstrates the
power of his art, like that of the painters, to keep alive and
present those distant from us in time or space. At the practical
or technical level, Castiglione's verbal construct matches or sur-
passes the ability of a visual image to counterpoise the "real"
and the "ideal" at several temporal, spatial, moral, or philosophical planes. In sum, the more closely we study the *Book of*

the Courtier, the more revealing Castiglione's description of it as a *ritratto di pittura* becomes.

NOTES

1. On the subject of the *Book of the Courtier* as a portrait, see Wayne Rebhorn, *Courtly Performances: Masking and Festivity in Castiglione's* Book of the Courtier (Detroit, 1978), "A Portrait of Urbino," pp. 53–90, and the essays by Rebhorn and David Rosand in the present collection.

2. See Maier's edition, pp. 60–61.

3. See *Lettere del conte Baldesar Castiglione, ora per la prima volta date in luce . . . dall'Abate Pierantonio Serassi* (Padua, 1769), I, 181–86, 191–95. The latter of the two versions, headed by Serassi, "Altro proemio del Cortegiano, Tratto della prima bozza dell'Autore," makes no mention of Ariosto or any other dedicatee.

4. Serassi, p. 194: "Questa perfetta forma di Cortegiano, la quale io più presto spero poter dire che veder mai in alcuno. . . . La idea dunque di questo perfetto Cortegiano formaremo al meglio che si potrà, acciocchè chi in questa mirerà come buono arciero si sforzi di accostarsi al segno quanto l'occhio e il braccio suo gli comporterà."

5. See Ghino Ghinassi, ed., *La seconda redazione del "Cortegiano" di Baldassare Castiglione* (Florence, 1968), pp. 183–84. Cf. Maier, pp. 445–46.

6. Alberti, *De pictura,* ed. C. Grayson (Rome and Bari, 1975), ii.25 (p. 44): "E così certo il viso di chi già sia morto, per la pittura vive lunga vita."

7. *Courtier* 1.18: "In my opinion, the whole art consists in saying things in such a way that they do not appear to be spoken to that end, but are so very apropos that one cannot help saying them; and to seem always to avoid praising one's self, yet do so" ("Ma, al parer mio, il tutto consiste in dir le cose di modo, che paia che non si dicano a quel fine, ma che caggiano talmente a proposito, che non si posse restar di dirle, e sempre mostrando fuggir le proprie laudi, dirle pure"). For the text of Castiglione's self-deprecating comparison of his art with Raphael's and Michelangelo's, see the beginning of Rosand's essay, p. 91, above.

8. Maier prints the text, *Balthassaris Castilionis Elegia qua fingit Hippolyten suam ad se ipsum scribentem,* pp. 596–605, with an Italian translation by A. Bonaventura.

9. *Heroides* xiii.151–58, trans. Grant Showerman (Loeb Classical Library; London and Cambridge, Mass., 1914, repr. 1971). The Latin text is: "Dum tamen arma geres diverso miles in orbe, / quae referat vultus est mihi cera tuos; / illi blanditias, illi tibi debita verba / dicimus, amplexus accipit illa meos. / crede mihi, plus est, quam quod videatur, imago; / adde sonum cerae, protesilaus erit. / hanc specto teneoque sinu pro coniuge vero, / et, tamquam possit verba referre, queror." Hope P. Weissman, in a paper read before the Special Session on the Ovidian Legacy in medieval and Renaissance literature, Modern Language Association annual meeting, 1978, points out that Ovid here

adapts to his use the Pygmalion story. Interestingly, the fact that Laodamia's *imago* will shortly become a memorial image, after the death of Protesilaus, makes of the statue a proleptic parallel to the *Courtier* as portrait of the Urbino court.

10. See *Heroides* xi.3–5: "My right hand holds the pen, a drawn blade the other holds, and the paper lies unrolled in my lap. This is the picture of Aeolus' daughter writing to her brother" ("Dextra tenet calamum, strictum tenet altera ferrum, / et iacet in gremio charta soluto meo. / haec est Aeolidos fratri scribentis imago"). Cf. *Heroides* iv.175–76: "I mingle with these prayers my tears as well. The words of her who prays, you are reading; her tears, imagine you behold!" ("Addimus his precibus lacrimas quoque; verba precantis / perlegis et lacrimas finge videre meas!").

11. Maier's notes to the poem refer only to its similarities to and inspiration by Propertius, *Elegiae* iv.3, although in the introduction (p. 44), he says that Castiglione was thinking of the Propertius poem, "e, forse, delle *Eroidi* ovidiane." In addition to Castiglione's adaptation of the passage about Laodamia's wax statue, his poem also contains a reference in 1.45 to the *cultae puellae* of Rome—a key Ovidian phrase and concept from the *Ars amatoria*. No such locution occurs in Propertius iv.3.

12. Alberti, *De pictura* iii.55–56: "E di tutte le parti li piacerà non solo renderne similitudine, ma più aggiugnervi bellezza, però che nella pittura la vaghezza non meno è grata che richiesta. . . . Per questo sempre ciò che vorremo dipignere piglieremo dalla natura, e sempre torremo le cose più belle" ("But, considering all these parts, [the painter] should be attentive not only to the likeness of things but also and especially to beauty, for in painting beauty is as pleasing as it is necessary. . . . So, let us always take from Nature whatever we are about to paint, and let us always choose those things that are most beautiful and worthy") (trans. Cecil Grayson, in Leon Battista Alberti, *On Painting and On Sculpture* [London, 1972], pp. 99, 101).

13. Alberti, iii.56; the story is repeated in *Courtier* 1.53.

14. On the *istoria*, see Alberti, iii, and on Castiglione's conception of the *Courtier* as an istoria, see Rebhorn, *Courtly Performances*, p. 63.

15. One might fruitfully compare the secular, memorial use of the parapet motif in Renaissance painting with its ironically theological use by Dante in *Inferno* x.22–36, where Farinata, nonbeliever in eternal life, rises halfway from his tomb—becomes a memorial bust—to confront Dante and Vergil.

16. See Wayne Rebhorn's essay, pp. 86–87, above, for an astute analysis of how art, including Castiglione's art in the *Courtier*, works at this transcendence, especially in the face of time; Rebhorn also takes note of some of the paradoxes involved in the attempt.

17. Count Ludovico da Canossa is speaking (see p. 53 for original language). Cf. 1.25, where it is said of Galeazzo Sanseverino that "he has taken the greatest care to study with good masters and to have about him men who excel, *taking from each the best of what they know*" ("ha posto ogni studio d'imparare da

bon maestri ed aver sempre presso di sé omini eccelenti e *da ognun pigliar il meglio di ciò che sapevano*" [my emphasis]).

18. Cf. the comments of Eduardo Saccone, p. 49, above, on an analogous phenomenon in the *Book of the Courtier*: the double origin of *grazia*, which comes both in the "vertically directed lord–courtier relationship" and in "a horizontal dimension, . . . from the other members of the class to which the courtier belongs."

19. Alberti, *De pictura*, i.8.

20. The relationship between these portraits or levels is a good instance of what Louise George Clubb calls "the humanistic art [that] tries to reconcile in creative tension what is held to be unreconcilable," and "the art that sets out to have it both ways" (see below, p. 193).

21. See above, pp. 7, 11, where Greene makes this point about Guidobaldo's withdrawal creating a play space for the courtiers.

22. *Courtly Performances*, pp. 53–54. See also the Chronology above, p. xix.

23. "Socrates Crowned," *Virginia Quarterly Review* 35 (1959), 418–21.

24. Cf. Rebhorn, *Courtly Performances*, "Festive Symposium," pp. 151–76, for a wide-ranging discussion of the effect of Castiglione's adoption of the form of the *Symposium* for the *Book of the Courtier*. My comments here attempt to define only one small aspect of the process of adaptation.

8

Castiglione's Military Career

J. R. Hale

In 1942 the doyen of Castiglione studies, Vittorio Cian, re-marked that "one of the least studied aspects of Castiglione is his career as a soldier, as the courtier in arms taking his role in war seriously, suffering wounds and sickness and enduring hardships which came to weaken prematurely a constitution which was sound and hardy."[1] The challenge was not taken up. There is still no study of Castiglione's career as a soldier. In-stead, it has been taken for granted that this was a serious, even a distinguished one.

This is readily understandable. Just as the accessibility and appeal of the *Book of the Courtier,* then as now, reside in the sensitive re-pondering and the deft expression of *idées reçues,* so a group of idées reçues about Urbino and Castiglione himself strongly suggests that his military career must have been a no-table one. Through some quirk of the historiography of culture it is above all the court of Urbino, rather than that of Milan or Naples, Mantua or Ferrara, that has been identified with a genial fusion of the arts both of war and of peace. This view originates with one of the most engaging of Vespasiano's *Lives,* that of Federico da Montefeltro, ruler of Urbino from 1444 and its duke from 1474; with Federico's portrait by Justus of Ghent which shows him reading a manuscript while clad in armor; and with the spare harmonies of his palace, where the painting of Piero della Francesca lived in unjarring concord with relief sculptures displaying the weapons and trophies of war. Its vein of truthfulness was given a mythic dimension by

A version of this essay appeared in *Italian Studies,* 36 (1981).

Castiglione himself, who wrote of Urbino in the *Courtier* that "in all Italy it would perhaps be hard to find an equal number of cavaliers as outstanding and as excellent in different things, quite beyond their principal profession of chivalry, as are found here" (1.12). It is thanks to Castiglione that the arms versus letters debate—"a debate," as he acknowledges, "that has long been waged by very wise men" (1.45)—has become identified with Urbino and a society at once spirited, thoughtful, and learned. And it is he who, practically single-handed and against considerable evidential odds, clad Federico's successor Guidobaldo in his father's image: toughly professional in war, agreeable and scholarly in peace.

Artistically, such an image was necessary to his book; the portrait of a court of varied accomplishments required a prince of corresponding versatility. So although we learn from the conversations in the *Courtier* that not only was Guidobaldo absent from them because he was in an invalid's bed but that he had long been impotent,[2] the work begins with a character sketch of Guidobaldo that explains its happy unity of mood, for "everyone strove to show himself such as to deserve to be thought worthy of his noble company" (1.3).

This sketch, however, is only the residue of the extended biographical eulogy of Guidobaldo which Castiglione had written before his vision of the *Courtier* had matured, the letter to Henry VII of England *De Guidobaldo Urbini Duce*. Although not published until 1513, this must have been written soon after the duke's death in 1508 and may have incorporated material from an oration delivered in 1506, when Castiglione went to Windsor to be installed, as Guidobaldo's proxy, as a Knight of the Garter.[3] It shows how deeply attracted Castiglione was to the ideal of the career that combined arms with letters. The duke is shown as precociously gifted in both areas from boyhood. Then the theme of arms is developed: Guidobaldo's passion for knightly exercise, his heroic appearance armed and mounted, the gallantry and fearlessness of what was, in fact, a somewhat sorry as well as a short military career.[4] There follows a long section on not only his knowledge of the Greek and Latin classics but also his feeling for them. His favorite works in both languages are listed and Castiglione concludes with a splendidly eloquent description of the rhetorical skills that flowed from this reading, the perfect adjustment of matter and manner to all occasions, whether grave affairs of state or lighthearted domestic conversation.

This noble description of the balanced personality, which progresses from sport to prowess in war and from study to eloquence, has become part of posterity's vision of Urbino. It was first applied to Castiglione himself in the grant enfeoffing him in 1513 with the castle and lands of Novillara, near Pesaro. The grant, made by Guidobaldo's successor and Castiglione's next master, Francesco Maria della Rovere, explains that it is a reward for "vigils, toils, lengthy and innumerable journeys, and dangers undergone by day and night on our behalf" and opens with words that must have afforded him the greatest pleasure: "Your noble ancestry, loyalty, and honorable service, the elegance of the languages in which you excel, your expertise in war and peace."[5] And the conjunction arms–letters was picked up in Leo X's confirmation of the grant in the following year: "And thus, since we ourselves knew that, even when a minor, you were excellently adorned with those qualities suited to the formation of a distinguished man, since you were born from most honorable stock, and excel in the study of letters, and have obtained a not undistinguished reputation of military worth" (ibid., p. 122).

Whether or not Castiglione was consulted as to the wording of these documents, he applied the arms–letters formula to his own person not long afterward. In December 1515, as Duke Francesco Maria's envoy, he met King Francis I at Bologna.[6] It was about this time that he composed an early version of the first book of the *Courtier*.[7] Here he expresses the earnest wish that the young king would undertake a crusade to drive the Turks from Greece and the Holy Places of Asia. In this event, nothing would please him more than serving with the Most Christian King and "seeing such glorious deeds with my own eyes and perhaps writing of some part of them, and accom-

panying your Highness in arms. . . . And though I am very
sure that neither with pen nor arms could I embellish such
renown [*accrescer laude a tanta laude*] yet as little rivers add water
to the sea I think that my good intent should merit commenda-
tion, for God is as pleased with a coin offered from the heart
by a poor beggar as with a great treasure by a rich lord" (ibid.,
pp. 185–86).

That the long discussion of arms and letters in the *Courtier*
is so particularly accomplished in style and tone owes something, then, to Castiglione's habit of associating the theme with
Urbino and with himself. And what he did for himself during
his lifetime his friends did for him after his death. He was
"learned in Greek and Latin and Tuscan letters and himself a
poet," Bembo wrote for the epitaph on his tomb; "he received
the castle of Novillara . . . in reward for his military services."[8]
Jacopo Sadoleto marveled at the way in which a man trained
for war had mastered all the liberal arts.[9] Among the obituary
tributes printed by Antonio Beffa Negrini, his first biographer,
in 1606 was Tasso's "pen and arms have won you equal esteem."[10] The author himself, after referring to Castiglione's
youthful study of Latin and Greek, went on to say that "he then
became so expert and understanding in the weapons both of
foot and horse that in various exercises and trials of arms in
different places he left men doubtful of whether he was more
outstanding in these or in letters, in wisdom or in strength."[11]

This, then, is the tradition that has led to Castiglione's military career being taken for granted, to Cian's describing him
"suffering wounds" when "taking his role in war seriously"
while presumably well aware that the only wounds Castiglione
is known to have suffered were a cut in the hand received in a
joust in 1511[12] and a foot crushed when the mule he was riding
to his lodgings in Cesena fell on it during the papal campaign
in the Romagna in the summer of 1504.[13] We know about the
Castiglione of the pen; what can be learned about the Castiglione of the sword?

Castiglione's grandfather and his father, Christoforo, held
important commands under successive marquises of Mantua;

Christoforo had been wounded at the battle of Fornovo (1495), at which the forces of the League of Venice, led by Francesco II Gonzaga, had attempted to cut off the army of Charles VIII as it withdrew from the conquest of Naples, and it was his death in 1499 that called his twenty-one-year-old son from Milan to support his mother in her bereavement. Of the military context of Castiglione's youth we are left entirely to surmise based on his status as the heir to generations of reasonably prosperous landed gentry in the Mantovano and on the assumption in his future correspondence that his mother was thoroughly versed in the niceties of horse breeding and a man's need for good arms and armor, and on his being well thought of by a society—the one surrounding Lodovico Sforza in Milan—that valued spirit as well as cultivation.[14]

For the next few years information remains vague. From his estates at Casàtico, eighteen kilometers west of Mantua, he offered his services to the marquis and was appointed to a junior inspectorship in the garrisoned area of the northern Mantovano, as much an administrative as a military post.[15] When in the autumn of 1503 the marquis was appointed commander-in-chief of the French army against Naples, Castiglione was summoned to join his own contingent, in what capacity is unclear. A letter he wrote to the marquis on 4 October from Rome, eloquent as to his desire to put his life at Francesco's disposal, explains that he can not do that yet; it has taken a long time to find a good horse, and "the roads are so insecure that we are sure to be plundered if we start without a really large escort."[16] And although Beffa Negrini wrote of his conduct during the moves leading to the French defeat on the Garigliano in December that "it caused particular satisfaction to the Marquis who seemed to see the father in the son,"[17] the only evidence for his presence in this campaign is contained in his sonnet *Cesare mio. . . .* Starting with what seems to be a clear reference to the contested port of Gaeta, he exclaims that

> Tra foco, flamme, stridi orrendi e feri,
>   fame, roine e martial furore,
>   meno mia vita in duri aspri sentieri.

[Amid fire, flames, horrible and fierce cries,
    hunger, ruins, and the furor of war,
    I lead my life on hard, rugged paths.]

This leaves his experience of actual combat in doubt but begins a series of comments that are to reveal a growing distaste for war.[18]

Information that can be relied on begins only with the acquaintance Castiglione made with another ruler, Guidobaldo of Urbino. On 24 May 1504 Guidobaldo was formally invested by Pope Julius II as captain general of the forces of the Church on condition that he raise companies totaling four hundred men-at-arms, and three days later he wrote to the marquis of Mantua that "having to raise a company of men-at-arms . . . I am moved to write to beg Your Excellency that . . . you may be content to allow Baldassare da Castiglione to enter my service."[19] The marquis's favorable reply was as prompt as it was short, and when Guidobaldo's force set out to reduce to papal obedience the Romagnol towns that, after the now discredited Cesare Borgia's conquest of them, chose to claim their independence, Castiglione was with it. But again, not in action. Early in August he wrote to his mother from Cesena, which had surrendered without a fight. He appears to have had a triumphal return to Urbino in mind and asked for a helmet, which was to be covered in black velvet, his fine lance that was in the hands of "maestro Raphaello the painter" and was to be gilded and burnished and wrapped above the grip-guard (*ferro*) with "some beautiful silk that suits your taste," and a surcoat of gold brocade. At the moment he was in bed. On arriving in Cesena on 4 August he had lunched with the duke and with Cesare Gonzaga and Ludovico da Canossa (both to figure in the *Courtier*) and then, going to his quarters, his mule had fallen and hurt his foot.[20] He was nevertheless able to move on to the army's next objective, Forlì, whose citadel proved more recalcitrant. "This cursed attempt on the *rocca*" was how he put it, writing to his mother again on 12 August, and the impact of licentious soldiery on a poor countryside appears to have struck him with a novel force: "It is a grievous thing to see." He adds that the fall of his mule "made me see stars by daylight" ["m'ha fatto veder le stelle de' mezzo dì"], and in the same letter we learn for the first time about the conditions of his employment. "I have a personal salary [*provvisione*] from the Most Illustrious Duke of four hundred ducats and the command of fifty men-at-arms [shared] with a colleague who I think will be Cesare [Gonzaga]."[21] The campaign was short. Forlì surrendered and Castiglione was delighted to be back in Urbino in the first week of September (ibid., 6 Sept.).

A command of fifty men-at-arms meant the responsibility of raising and leading fifty heavy cavalry "lances," each lance comprising four men: the man-at-arms himself, fully armored in plate on a barded horse, two others more lightly armored and armed either with lance or crossbow on unbarded horses, and a groom or squire riding a baggage animal. As well as his personal salary the condottiere received a *caposaldo,* or bonus fund, which he distributed among his under-officers: lieutenant, ensign, and trumpeter. These sums, plus the one hundred ducats (less stoppages, paymasters' fees, and loan repayments) due to each man-at-arms, were disbursed quarterly, as were the fodder and stabling allowances called "tasse." Castiglione had neither the time nor the resources to raise a body of two hundred men, there is no suggestion that he was to take over a corps of "free-lances," men detached from other commands or previously leaderless. He mentions no one in his employ save two messengers and a groom.[22] His provvisione was clearly a device to enable him to live as a ducal aide and did no more than imply that military service could be expected of him. And it looks as though part of this sum was to enable his contemporary and friend Cesare Gonzaga to perform the same function.

That Castiglione saw his role at court as drawing more on his tact and eloquence than on his potential military talents is suggested by a letter to his mother written in March 1505, when Guidobaldo was considering sending someone to act as his proxy for the Garter installation ceremony. "Looking through the gentlemen in his suite and the duties of each of them, it is

not difficult for me to see that the journey falls to my lot. . . .
The mission calls for the sending of a man of standing and
great gravity and acceptable to His Majesty the King." It is
something of a relief to find the twenty-seven-year-old courtier
adding, "Though the journey is somewhat on the long side it is
an agreeable one,"[23] and again, a few days later, that he is looking forward first to serving his prince but also "to seeing a wide
extent of country" (ibid., 3 March). In April he expressed the
belief that to add weight to his mission "the Pope will make me
a knight on Easter Day" (ibid., p. 21, 23 April).

In fact the journey was postponed until the late summer of
1506. During the rest of 1505, which Castiglione spent with the
duke in Rome, the only military event was the preparation for
a general muster of the duke's forces in July. For this Castiglione spent an advance on his salary and wrote to his mother
highly satisfied by the part he had played—again, clearly as an
individual, not a company commander—in what had been "a
very fine parade" (p. 23, 3 and 30 July). And it may be noted
that when Castiglione was detached from the court for the
mission to England it was at the very time when Guidobaldo's
army was mobilized for Julius II's operation against the rulers
of Perugia and Bologna. At some point before his departure
it seems probable that he was made by Julius a Knight of
the Golden Spur,[24] an order with no specifically military con-
notations but which enabled him to be received in England as
"eques"[25] and to feature in the grant of 1513 making him count
of Novillara as "equestris ordinis splendore decoratum."

In the summer of 1507 Castiglione was sent to Milan to pay
Guidobaldo's formal respects to Louis XII.[26] In the following
April the duke died. Without an heir he was, by his wish, succeeded by his nephew Francesco Maria della Rovere. Castiglione, beset by debts he was finding it impossible to pay from
his provvisione, was nevertheless rightly optimistic that he and
Cesare Gonzaga would be kept on, and in August he was complaining that his plans to visit his family were likely to be ruined
by Julius's demand for a general muster of the troops whom

the new duke, like his uncle, was to bring to the service of the papacy (ibid., I, 44).

Unlike his predecessor who, as his epitaph put it, "cultivated letters instead of arms [and] protected men of general eminence instead of mere military adventurers,"[27] the new captain general of the Church was not only physically fit but a keen, though cultivated soldier. Moreover, events were moving toward the involvement of the papal army in the campaign waged by the allies of Cambrai against the possessions, including those in the Romagna, of Venice. A full mobilization was ordered for March 1509. Although so unprepared as to be ill-mounted and short of equipment, Castiglione was spared the full implications of his conditions of employment. Large as they were, the family estates around Casàtico could not have afforded the men or capital to enable him to muster his fifty "lances," and there is no suggestion that he received a loan from the duke or was deputed to command troops already in being. His correspondence still shows concern only for his own preparedness and that of his servitors.[28]

From letters to his mother we learn that in early May Castiglione was with the army besieging the citadel of Brisighella. "This," he wrote on 1 May, "has now been taken. . . . Before long I think we shall march on Faenza and, I hope, with God's help, soon gain fresh glory." From Faenza and its outlying strongpoint, Granarolo, which were both taken, the army moved to Russi. Here, he wrote on 18 May, the enemy made a diversionary sally from Ravenna—the most heavily garrisoned of Venice's Romagnol possessions. "We pursued the enemy and though they were in very strong position, attacked them so furiously that we broke their ranks, and some of our cavalry rode right into Ravenna. We made three hundred foot and fifty horse prisoners, as well as taking much cattle, and won a great victory, much to the honour of our most illustrious Signore."[29] How far "we" included Castiglione himself, especially during the dash into Ravenna, must remain open to doubt. If he had been actually in the shock of combat the account, given his normal readiness to share his experiences with his mother, is curiously impersonal. On 31 May he reported the fall of Rimini and expressed the hope that he would soon be back in Urbino. And referring, with the same sensitivity that he had expressed in 1504, to the havoc wreaked by the papal troops in the countryside, he commented: "I have done as little harm as I could; it's clear that everyone has made a profit except myself—which I do not regret."[30] This, to all intents and purposes, was the end of the 1509 phase of the papal campaign. By the end of June Castiglione was in Urbino, exhausted from the unaccustomed trials of campaigning. He was still weak in mid-September (ibid., I, 51).

The next phase began in August 1510. By this time Julius had concluded peace negotiations with Venice, and his force's target was the duke of Ferrara, who remained stubbornly attached to the pope's ex-allies of Cambrai. Castiglione, who had been used again as an ambassador, this time to Naples in April,[31] was once more indisposed, with fever, and was delayed in joining Francesco Maria's forces until 31 August.[32] He wrote on 16 October from Modena that "we often see the enemy; still, fighting for the Church we hope that God will be on our side" (ibid., p. 55). Neither side was eager to come to blows, however, and he remained in Modena until mid-December, when—while the army set off to beseige Mirandola—he was taken by the duke to Bologna to have consultations with the pope (ibid., p. 56). Whether or not he was present at the wintry siege of Mirandola, made memorable by the pope's own presence within cannon shot of the frozen moat, is uncertain but likely. Certainly his Latin poem on the distressful feelings of Mirandola's recently slain lord, *Prosopopoeja Ludovici Pici,* portrays the stricken town with something like an eyewitness's clarity—and much less than the professional soldier's usual unconcern for suffering. In the spirit of previous comments of his own, he makes the ghost of Pico say:

> Aspice captivis vacuos cultoribus agros,
>   Abductas pecudes, agricolasque boves,

Disjectasque domos passim, populataque raptis
   Arboribus late, et frugibus arva suis. (ibid., II, p. 295)

[Behold the empty fields, their cultivators
      now taken captive;
[Behold] flocks stolen, farmers and oxen;
Houses destroyed everywhere,
Trees laid waste all over, fields ravaged
                    of their fruits.]

Mirandola capitulated on 20 January. Thereafter, with the arrival of French reinforcements for the duke of Ferrara and
the loss of Bologna, the duke's outnumbered forces withdrew.
Castiglione's letters contain references only to the threadbare
and hungry state of himself and his little staff and to requests
for cloth, food, fodder for their horses, and, as usual, money
(ibid., I, pp. 57–58). After the fall of Mirandola the duke had
sent him to present his congratulations to Julius, and a plea to
be sent some blue satin suggests that, once again, Castiglione
was serving primarily not as a condottiere but as an equerry.
He was back in Urbino by the first of June.

   The petering out of the campaign against Ferrara was followed by nearly twelve months of inactivity for Francesco Maria
and his forces. It was not until May 1512, after the dramatic
engagement between the papal and Spanish army and that of
the French at Ravenna on 11 April, that Castiglione had to ride
off to war again. The loss of Bologna and the duke's consequent retreat had been blamed by Cardinal Alidosi, the pope's
legate in Bologna, on Francesco Maria's cowardice and con-
nivance with the French. The duke hotly rebutted both charges
and, meeting the cardinal on 24 May 1511 in Ravenna, stabbed
him to death. This appalling crime was all the more shocking
for being committed practically in the presence of Julius II himself. It was followed, after the duke's hasty return to Urbino,
by his dismissal from the post of captain general and, in July,
by a summons to Rome to answer a charge of murder. Enough
evidence of Alidosi's own treachery was produced to secure an
acquittal, but not until December. Even then, the duke's rein-
statement in his command did not cancel the lively suspicions

he and Julius entertained about each other. Thus there were no forces from Urbino at the battle of Ravenna.[33]

It was not until May 1512 that Francesco Maria took part in the third phase of Julius's campaign to quash insurgency in the Romagna and force Alfonso I of Ferrara to come to terms. Ravenna had left the French mauled rather than defeated, but the death of their general, Gaston de Foix, and the arrival of Swiss troops in papal service led to their army's retreat across the Alps; bereft of allies, the rebel cities of Romagna and Alfonso did little more than cry mercy when Francesco Maria's forces leaned on them. All the same, it was not until August—a month better remembered for the result of the activities of the main body of Julius's troops: the sack of Prato and the subsequent surrender of the republican Florence of Machiavelli and Soderini—that operations were concluded. Castiglione was only with the duke in the field during May, complaining of being "completely unequipped," a reference to the nondelivery of the fine German armor he had craved for years and had ordered from the great arms maker and dealer Bernardino Missaglia. By 6 June he was back in Urbino,[34] whence he wrote to his mother asking for a campaign tent, green-gray and tawny in color, that would, together with its poles, be an easy burden for a mule (ibid., p. 67). This anticipation of a renewed bout of active service was unnecessary. Although Francesco Maria's troops were kept in service, this was partly because Julius claimed to be unable to pay them off and partly because their presence added cogency to the pope's determination that the Church's suzerainty not only over the Romagnol cities and Bologna but also over Parma, Piacenza, and Reggio should be recognized. Castiglione was with the duke in Ravenna and Bologna in September and was sent in October to Modena to speak with the Emperor Maximilian's representative, Matteus Lang. The only moment during which he may have been with the army when it was actually fighting was later in October, when the duke was sent by Julius to expel Galeazzo Sforza from Pesaro. This operation was of lasting significance to Castiglione. To seal his reconciliation with his nephew Francesco

Maria—and to compensate him for heavy arrears of pay—Julius made Pesaro and its hinterland over to the duke. As soon as he was aware that this might happen, the duke offered Castiglione the castle of Ginistreto and accepted Castiglione's countersuggestion that he should be enfoeffed instead with Novillara, which he reckoned would yield him the same sum, about two hundred ducats a year (ibid., pp. 68–73). Castiglione may well have helped bring the reconciliation about. If so, Novillara (which he was able to enjoy only until Francesco Maria's expulsion by Lorenzo de' Medici in 1516) was earned more by his skill as a diplomat than as a soldier. And this is what we might expect from what we have seen of his career, flawed as our vision must be by the fragmented nature of the evidence. During the ten years 1503 to 1512 Castiglione was in the field for only eighteen months, and although danger and hardship played their part (he was seriously ill again for several months after the 1510–11 campaign against Ferrara [ibid., pp. 60–62]) he cannot be shown to have struck a blow in action. Although technically a condottiere there is no evidence to suggest that he functioned as one: not a word in his correspondence about a commitment so demanding in terms of men, subordinate officers, weapons, horses, and pay, no mention of the sort of agent other condottieri found it necessary to employ to recruit and to help with administration and accounting. An inventory of arms stored at Novillara in 1515 lists complete suits of armor for one man-at-arms and one light cavalryman: for Castiglione and his squire.[35] The mention of twenty-two cuirasses and a miscellany of other portions of armor need not change the picture; castle armories often stocked equipment for tenants and local militiamen. The reason why contemporary historians never refer to him as a soldier but only as a diplomatic emissary, why Julius II suspected him of being Francesco Maria's political agent (as Leo X was to do when trumping up charges for the excommunication and expulsion of the duke), is surely that although as aid or equerry, Castiglione may have cut, as he wished to do, the figure of a soldier, his other qualities made him too valuable to be used as one.

Castiglione did not take his place in an army again until 1523. By then nearly everything concerning arms and war that appeared in the printed version of the *Courtier* had already been drafted. All the same, before looking at the relevance of his experience to his writing about these themes, it will be worth rounding out our sketch of his military career.

We must pass quickly over years that are in any case among the cloudiest of a man who has never been accorded an adequate biography. Castiglione was fully involved as a diplomat in trying to ward off Leo X's determination to supplant Francesco Maria with his own nephew, Lorenzo de' Medici. The attempt failed in 1516. So did Francesco Maria's counterattack in 1517. Between the two, late in 1516 Castiglione went to Mantua; he married a girl from the Mantovano, Ippolita Torelli; his first son was born in August 1517, and until the spring of 1519 he divided his life between his home at Casàtico and the court of Isabella and Francesco Gonzaga. He wrote the extended second draft of the *Courtier*. He kept in touch with the exiled family of Urbino. But he had reverted to being a Mantuan. And on Francesco's death in March 1515, he obeyed Isabella's request that he should be the representative in Rome of the marquis's young successor, Federico, first for a few months and then, from July 1520 to the autumn of 1524, when he set off as papal nuncio to Spain, more or less permanently.

His greatest diplomatic coup was his persuading Leo X to make Federico captain general of the Church. The appointment was formalized on 1 July 1521. Only three weeks earlier another, private negotiation had been completed when Castiglione obtained a papal bull granting him clerical status and its symbol, the tonsure.[36] This step presaged a career in the Church similar to those of his close and nonmilitant friends, Bembo and Bibbiena, but was probably prompted too by the tragically early death of his wife in the previous year. Thus when Federico wrote at the time of his appointment to offer Castiglione a company of fifty men-at-arms, which, unlike the previous military commission, was conceived as a fully professional contract, Castiglione's first reaction was to refuse it. He explained to his mother that although this was a "great honor" he had seen by now "what a troublesome thing it is to have the command of troops" and how very expensive it could prove. And, besides, "I am no longer a child and hardships oppress me more than they used to do." So he arranged a compromise whereby he accepted the command on condition that while he remained Federico's representative in Rome the running of the company would be deputed to a lieutenant.[37] He nominated the Mantuan Capino da Capo, a man well-known to the marquess and to whose son Castiglione had stood godfather in the previous year, and the nomination was accepted (ibid., pp. 22–55). The only snag about this arrangement was that Capino himself came to be used by Federico as a diplomatic agent. In July 1522, for instance, when the marquess's uncle, the professional soldier Giovanni Gonzaga, wanted Castiglione's company to garrison Forlì, Capino was only just back from a mission to Spain. In a letter begging Giovanni to put one of the under-officers in charge if necessary, Castiglione characteristically urged that his men should be warned not to ill-treat the town's inhabitants.[38]

Generally, however, apart from the usual struggle to see that his men were not forced to desert for lack of pay (ibid., I, pp. 87–88), he was able to devote himself to Federico's affairs, which with the full mobilization of the papal–imperial–Florentine league against France in the summer of 1521 became predominantly military. It became Castiglione's task to gouge money for the marquess's troops out of the College of Cardinals, as represented by their chamberlain Cardinal Armellino of Perugia (ibid., I, 10–11); to keep him in touch with the overall military and political situation as it appeared from a Rome uniquely rich in news and rumors; to justify his strategic and logistic decisions and report on local criticisms of them; and to warn him of the inner contradictions concealed in the orders he received from Leo X and his successor from January 1522, Adrian VI, "for you must not think that there is less fighting among the cardinals [*questi Signori*] than there is in Lombardy" (ibid., I, 20).[39]

Although Castiglione possessed a remarkable degree of self-imposed equanimity, these Roman years, heralded by the death of wife and close friends—Raphael and Bibbiena—and punctuated by wars inefficiently conducted and with a toll of misery uncompensated by an unhesitating ideology, represent if not a psychological turning point at lest a consolidation of strands of inherent pessimism. As agent for the Church's captain general he worked diligently, but whether or not the barber chopped the tonsure into his hair, his correspondence shows no enthusiasm for the captain general's wars. As if in compensation it reveals a love of horseflesh—touchstone of aristocratic status as much in peace as in war—whether his own or his master's.[40] In one of the carnival horseraces in Rome in 1521 the jockey of a mare owned by the marquess was just about to snatch up the "prize" pole at the end of the course when he was startled aside by a lunge from one of the crossbowmen belonging to the force that policed the crowds, and the man riding second, on a horse owned by the archbishop of Nicosia, grabbed it instead and was judged the victor. Castiglione complained to the manager of the course. Rebuffed, he obtained from the pope the judgment that although the archbishop was entitled to the purse he must compensate the marquess with an equivalent value in cash. This was not enough for Castiglione. The offender was already imprisoned, he wrote to Federico, "but I wanted him to be hanged, or at least given four or five hoists with the rope[41] before being then condemned to the galleys."[42] Even allowing for his wish to please one of the premier horse breeders of Europe, this language is strikingly at odds with Castiglione's sympathy for those who got in the way of a horseman in wartime.

In September 1523 came his last, brief personal experience of war. Why he had been summoned to serve is unclear. The French, cleared from the Milanese by the league, had mounted a fresh invasion. In opposition were not only the papal troops under Federico and Charles V's forces but also those of Venice —commanded by none other than Francesco Maria, who had been restored to the Duchy of Urbino in the peceding year. On 13 September Castiglione was in Mantua, where he drew up his will.[43] On 24 September he told his mother that from Lodi the troops he was with had fallen back in forced marches, especially by night, toward the Venetian fortified town of Pontevico, and he asked for a waterproof cape cut in the Spanish style.[44] As the campaign slowed and the French went into winter quarters he wrote on 9 November of his hopes to spend some time in Milan and asked for the formal clothes he had left at Casàtico (ibid., I, 85). But Federico fell ill (or, out of jealousy of the imperial commander, Lannoy, feigned to fall ill) and Castiglione returned with him to Mantua. Once more he had served as an aide rather than as a soldier, and when the news arrived of Adrian VI's death and his succession by Clement VII on 18 November he was sent to Rome to convey Federico's congratulations. And once there he resumed his functions as the marquess's diplomatic and military agent. On 10 January he asked to be relieved of his military command altogether, suggesting that it be given to Capino. And although he added that "though no longer in arms I shall endeavor not to be a useless servant of Your Excellency,"[45] he was thankfully ridding himself of a position that might call him again into the field. Thereafter he moved closer to employment by a new master, the pope who would send him to Spain, closer to the final revision of the 1524 manuscript of the *Courtier,* and closer to his death.

In his book Castiglione selects only those military topics that would concern the civilian. Living in a generation that saw and discussed rapid changes in weapons, tactics, brigading, siegecraft, and the design of fortifications, he ignores them. He says nothing, either, about the officer class to which, contractually, he belonged, nothing about the campaigns—and there were so many of them!—in which they fought. There is no treatment of the art of war in the *Courtier.* From the martial skills required of the individual even in peacetime he jumps to the notion of war itself and its moral significance; the assumption here is that although noble qualities can be shown in it, war is "bad in itself" (4.27). We are listening to a well-horsed and expensively armored man of peace.

The description of the courtier's martial accomplishments is put by Castiglione into the mouth of a future bishop, Ludovico da Canossa. He is to be thoroughly versed in the handling of all weapons, whether of horse or foot, and in this connection more emphasis is placed on the duel than on war (1.20). He must be a judge of horses and a rider so accomplished that to skill must be added a grace that will arouse admiration in those who watch him (1.21). Though fierce in combat he must leave his deeds behind him on the battlefield lest he prove crass and tedious company in peace. And not only must his bravery be combined with modesty and social tact, but he does not have to be an actual student of war: "I do not deem it necessary," Canossa says, "that he have the perfect knowledge of things and the other qualities that befit a commander" (1.17). And he expressly declines to enter·upon the subject of what constitutes a great captain as irrelevant. And this avoidance of not only the character but also the function of the career soldier is emphasized when Federico Fregoso returns to the topic in book 2 and claims that "whenever the Courtier chances to be engaged in a skirmish or an action or a battle in the field . . . he should discreetly withdraw from the crowd, and do the outstanding and daring things that he has to do in as small a company as possible and in the sight of all the noblest and most respected men in the army, and especially in the presence of and, if possible, before the very eyes of his king or the prince he is serving" (2.8). For the courtier war was, and in Canossa's eyes should be, an occasion for personal glory and advancement, whereas "whosoever is moved thereto for gain or any other motive . . . deserves to be called not a gentleman, but a base merchant" (I.43).

Now Castiglione and his interlocutors were well aware (as were their contemporaries Machiavelli and Guicciardini) of the savage paradox whereby the Italians, most cultivated of European peoples and uniquely the direct descendants of the all-conquering Romans, were regularly being thwacked in battle by the "barbarian" nations they still affected to despise. This is acknowledged by Canossa. He refers to those who allege "that for all their knowledge of letters the Italians have shown

little worth in arms for some time now" and flinches from the
subject with the remark that "it is better to pass over in silence
what cannot be remembered without pain" (I.43). In book 3
Cesare Gonzaga, movingly commemorated by Castiglione for
his prowess in arms and letters alike, refers to the treachery
of Italian castellans who recently betrayed their trust: "Would
to God there were such a dearth of this kind of men in our
day" (3.46). In book 4 Ottaviano Fregoso attacks a courtiership
merely of effeminating externals: "whence it comes about that
the Italian name is reduced to opprobrium, and there are but
few who dare, I will not say to die, but even to risk any danger"
(4.4).[46]

The feebleness of the connection between war conceived as a
form of tournament and a moralizing analysis of the cause of
Italian defeats being due to supercivilization or faults of character was lessened in Castiglione's mind by the condemnation
of war itself. In antiquity war had been necessary to bring
civilization and order but the process could not go on forever,
because it was "wanting in reason according to the law of nature which will not let us be pleased with that in others which
displeases us in ourselves" (4.27). There is no longer any justification for a ruler to try to usurp the lands of others; war, as
we have seen, is now intrinsically evil. But what, then, is to be
done with the qualities of rulers born as fit for war as for
peace, especially with those three princes, the future Francis I,
Henry VIII, and Charles V, made by God "to resemble one
another, in youth, in military power, in state, in bodily beauty,
and constitution?" (4.39). Why, "leaving aside the ancients,
what more noble, glorious, and profitable undertaking could
there be than for Christians to direct their efforts to subjugat-
ing the infidels?" (4.38).

We are not, of course, to expect a formal treatise on the art
of war within the manuscript so dear to Vittoria Colonna and
whose publication was so much desired by Matteo Bandello as a
salutary lesson to those who professed to be courtiers but were
so only in name.[47] But given the widespread interest in war and
in the reform of military institutions that characterized the pe-

riod, an interest shown not only by lettered commanders such as Bartolomeo d'Alviano and amateur military buffs such as Machiavelli but by such thoroughgoing civilians as the Venetian diarist Priuli, Castiglione's treatment of the subject—even allowing for its fragmentary form and the different points of view attributed to those who discuss it—is as naive as it is incomplete. There were many well-educated Italians who in the spirit of the *Courtier* fought as well as they wrote. The chivalrous Vicentine, Luigi da Porto, was only one of those who preferred "splendid skirmishes" where a man's deeds could be noted to the anonymous shove and hack of battle.[48] But it is still disconcerting to find Castiglione failing to bridge the logical gap—the only such gap in the book—between personal valor and corporate defeat. It was a gap not to be filled by still more valor on the part of individuals but by better conditions of service for the ordinary soldier and a more dogged and knowledgeable and unselfish professionalism among the officer class.

For all his cult of effortless superiority and his consequent scorn of professionalism of any sort, we might have expected Castiglione to see and say something on these lines—but only if we continue to think of him as a seasoned and widely competent campaigner. Having reviewed his short and restricted career of active service, we can see that the lack of logic was based on a lack of experience. And in watching his temperamental reactions to the *vita activa* at its most active, we have perhaps acquired an additional clue as to why he came to reshape his book in a steadily more contemplative mold.

NOTES

1. *Nel mondo di Baldassare Castiglione. Documenti illustrati* (Milan, 1942), p. 64.

2. "Our Duchess who has lived with her husband for fifteen years like a widow" (3.49).

3. Guido La Rocca, *Storia dell'epistola di Baldassare Castiglione al re Enrico VII d'Inghilterra. Il reperimento del testo ufficiale* (Mantua, 1972).

4. From the age of twenty he became increasingly incapacitated by what Castiglione always describes as *podagra*, or gout.

5. Matteo Castiglione, *De origine, rebus gestis, ac privilegiis gentis castilioneae . . . commentaria* (Venice, 1596), pp. 120–21.

6. For the significance of this meeting, see Cecil H. Clough, "Francis I and the Courtiers of Castiglione's *Courtier*," *European Studies*, 8 (1978), 23–70.

7. Printed in P. A. Serassi, *Lettere del conte Baldessar Castiglione* (Padua, 1769–71), I, 181–86.

8. Translated in Julia Cartwright, *Baldassare Castiglione. The Perfect Courtier. His Life and Letters 1478–1529* (London, 1908), II, 429–30.

9. Vittorio Cian, *Un illustre nunzio pontificio del Rinascimento: Baldassare Castiglione* (Vatican City, 1951), p. 78.

10. Antonio Beffa Negrini, *Elogi historici di alcuni personaggi della famiglia Castigliona* (Mantua, 1606), p. 461. For other tributes, see Serassi, II, 238–43.

11. Beffa Negrini, pp. 407–08.

12. Cian, *Un illustre nunzio*, p. 36.

13. G. Gorni, *Baldassar Castiglione. Lettere inedite o rare* (Milan and Naples, 1969), p. 9.

14. In a letter of 8 October 1499 he described the entry of Louis XII and his forces into Milan and remarked that the French knights "had good horses but handled them badly" (Cartwright, I, 18–22).

15. Cian, *Un illustre nunzio*, p. 18.

16. C. Martinati, *Notizie storico-biografiche intorno al conte Baldassare Castiglione con documenti inediti* (Florence, 1890), p. 76.

17. Beffa Negrini, p. 414.

18. Carlo Dionisotti, review article on Cian's *Un illustre nunzio*, in *Giornale storico della letteratura italiana*, 129 (1952), 43–44.

19. Martinati, p. 76.

20. Gorni, pp. 9–10.

21. Serassi, I, 7.

22. Gorni, pp. 9, 11.

23. Serassi, I, 17, 3 March.

24. La Rocca, p. 107, n. 57.

25. Interestingly, Polydore Vergil, the Urbinate chronicler who was then resident in England refers to him in the 1512–13 MS. version of his *Anglica Historia* as "natione mantuanum equitem tam doctrina quam bellica virtute praestantem" but in the printed version of 1534 simply as "Mantuanum equitem honestum ac nobilem."

26. Serassi, I, 38, 39.

27. J. Dennistoun, *Memoirs of the Dukes of Urbino* (London, 1909), II, 85.

28. Serassi, I, 47, 16 March; Cartwright, I, 265–70.

29. Serassi, I, 48, 49; Cartwright, I, 267, 268–69.

30. Serassi, I, 50.

31. Cian, *Un illustre nunzio*, p. 35.

32. Serassi, I, 53.

33. Dennistoun, II, 335–45.

34. Serassi, I, 65–66.

35. Cian, *Nel mondo di Baldassare Castiglione*, pp. 64–65.

36. Cian, *Un illustre nunzio,* p. 93.

37. Gorni, pp. 19–21.

38. Serassi, I, 84–85.

39. For a particularly illuminating example of Castiglione's defense of his master (Federico's demand for more troops for the recapture of Rimini from Sigismondo Malatesta), see ibid., p. 50.

40. Gorni, pp. 15–16.

41. Tortured by being lifted up with a rope tying his hands behind his back.

42. Antonenrico Mortara, *Lettera di Baldassare Castiglione a Federico Gonzaga . . .* (Casalmaggiore, 1854), pp. 10–11. No provenance is given.

43. Cian, *Nel mondo di Baldassare Castiglione,* pp. 83–87.

44. Serassi, I, 85.

45. Cian, *Un illustre nunzio,* p. 103, note.

46. In the second redaction the blame for this lack of character was laid upon the trivializing influence of women, and Ottaviano asked whether it would not be better if "young men devoted themselves to a more praiseworthy object and paid regard to arms with which to defend their countries [*patrie*], their honor and the repute of Italy"? See Ghino Ghinassi, *La seconda redazione del "Cortegiano" [1518–20]* (Florence, 1968), p. 280. This rhetorical question was dropped in the final revision of the book.

47. *Novelle,* 2.57, epistle.

48. *Lettere storiche,* ed. B. Bressan (Florence, 1857), p. 191; cf. pp. 164, 177.

9

The Courtier as Musician: Castiglione's View of the Science and Art of Music

James Haar

For "science and art" in the title of this paper one could almost substitute the words "theory and practice." Almost, but not quite. Castiglione gives no evidence that he knew more than the rudiments of musical theory—either the classical science of harmonics or the subjects of *musica theorica* and *musica practica,* its twofold Renaissance descendants—and his remarks on the actual musical practice of his time are concerned as much with the performer's attitude as with the act of singing or playing.

Passages in the *Cortegiano* dealing with classical anecdote about the power of music will here be grouped with what little Castiglione has to say about the theoretical foundations of sixteenth-century music, the two topics combining to give us an idea of his grasp of music as received knowledge. In this field, loosely defined as musical science, Castiglione has nothing new to say and is not concerned to make his presentation in any way complete or systematic. Nonetheless, it seems important that in the *Cortegiano,* as rarely or perhaps never before in the educational treatises of the Renaissance, there is a genuine mixture of ancient and modern ideas on the nature of music.

Musical performance, as Castiglione understood it from his own experience and his observation of contemporary Italy, had no body of descriptive literature—ancient or modern—on which he could draw.[1] It is not then surprising that he should be more original here, and one wishes he had said much more, so illuminating are his remarks on the music and musicians of his time. Just as ancient and modern doctrine about music are found in mingled bits and pieces in the *Cortegiano*, so theory and practice mix easily in its pages. The result is a sparely drawn but convincingly real picture of how music, and talk about music, figured in the lives of Castiglione's peers. There are other sixteenth-century accounts of music in social context, such as Antonfrancesco Doni's *Dialogo della musica* or even Luis Milán's *El Cortesano*, a work written in emulation of Castiglione, and there are plenty of humanistic treatises that repeat classical injunctions about the ideal cultivation of music.[2] In modernizing this ideal and making it comprehensible in terms of contemporary musical sound, Castiglione performed a notable service, helping to bring into modern life the dead language of ancient musical thought. That this was no mean feat may be seen if one compares his work to the lumbering classicistic jargon on the subject of music in the work of his older contemporary Paolo Cortese.[3]

In the first book of the *Cortegiano* Count Ludovico da Canossa, here Castiglione's spokesman, turns from literature to music, saying that his courtier should be able to read music (and thus to sing) and to play various instruments since there is nothing better than music for filling moments of leisure and for pleasing women—who in both ancient and modern times have been strongly inclined toward this art. Stung by Gaspare's rejoinder that music is an art suitable only to women and to effeminate men,[4] Ludovico turns from the present to the past and launches into a "gran pelago" of praises of music (1.47; see the appendix to this paper, no. 1). This is a sea the waters of which were much traveled in antiquity and in humanistic writings of the fifteenth and sixteenth centuries. The *laus musicae* is found, among classical writings, with particular frequency in treatises on rhetoric, a prime example being Quintilian's *Institutio Oratoria*; it also occurs in works dealing with education in a general sense, an example being the closing section of Aristotle's *Politics*.

No subjects were dearer to, or more closely related for, humanistic writers than rhetoric and education, and they repeated whatever they could find in classical literature on these subjects. Greek anecdotes on the power of music had been retold in the Middle Ages in encyclopedic treatises and in the writings of musical theorists. Musical pedagogues of the fifteenth and sixteenth centuries continued to cite them, sometimes as in the case of Gafori profiting from humanistic scholarship to increase their stock of such references.[5] The encyclopedic tradition was carried on by scholars such as Giorgio Valla, who compiled an enormous jumble of examples.[6] Humanistic rhetoricians used the topic of laus musicae as had Quintilian, in service of their subject, and writers on education did the same.

It is not clear whether Castiglione drew the material for the passage in question directly from classical sources or from fifteenth-century writings on education and rhetoric. He had doubtless read Quintilian;[7] but although more than half the material in his musical encomium may be found in the *Institutio*,[8] by no means all of it comes from Quintilian. For example, the closing section, on music in divine worship and as a solace to all classes and all ages of man, is drawn, directly or from some intermediary source, from St. John Chrysostom's commentary on Psalm 41.[9] Single anecdotes might have stuck in Castiglione's mind from passages in Plato, Aristotle, and Plutarch. Or he may have remembered these things through their citation elsewhere. One possibility is the laus musicae in Beroaldo's *Oratio . . . in enarrationem Quaestionum Tusculanarum et Horatio flaccii,* which has half a dozen of the instances cited by Castiglione.[10] Other possible sources are fifteenth-century treatises on education. The relationship of the *Cortegiano* to these treatises is a subject I do not feel competent to discuss; I do not even know if Castiglione read any of them.[11] If he had looked at Aeneas Silvius Piccolomini's *De liberorum educatione* he would have seen some of the same anecdotes he used.[12] Others are given in Pietro Paolo Vergerio's *De ingenuis moribus* in a passage that would have struck Castiglione if he had read it because it appears to cite, uncharacteristically for the humanists, examples (admittedly so vague that one cannot be sure of their meaning) from modern music.[13]

Castiglione's laus musicae may be his own compilation but all its contents are very well known and had been widely cited. His list of these anecdotes is one of the duller pages of the *Cortegiano* (though it is more interesting than such listings are in most other writers). Why is it included? Count Ludovico did not mean to show off his erudition, surely; that would have been graceless affectation on his part. I suggest that the laus musicae, a topic emphasizing the extraordinary power of music over human emotions, is included because it represents, in the aggregate, idealized music, an archetypal force that stands behind the practical art. Thus the courtier should be a musician not merely in order to entertain ladies but also to help him reach toward the balance and harmony of spirit that is his highest aim. Renaissance musicians could not find classical models for their art, but they could try, helped by Platonic and Pythagorean doctrine, for audible representation of ideal form, less tangible than as depicted in the visual arts but with a mysterious power all its own. Castiglione is not, as far as music is concerned, an ardent Neoplatonist, but in this passage he alludes, in his own way, to the ideal in music. What sets him apart from doctrinaire humanists on the subject is that he does not stop here as they did.

Castiglione's one reference to the practical musical theory current in his own time is his citation of the rule forbidding successive perfect consonances (1.28; see appendix, no. 2). Anyone trained in the rudiments of composition knew this prohibition by heart, and no one theorist need be cited as Castiglione's source. He might indeed have done well to read up on this negative rule in a theorist such as Gafori before writing the passage. Here are rules 2 and 3 of Gafori's celebrated eight rules of counterpoint, from the *Practica musice* of 1496:

> The second rule states that two perfect consonances of the same size cannot immediately follow each other in parallel motion, as two unisons, octaves, fifteenths, or also two fifths and two twelfths. . . .

> The third rule states that between two perfect consonances of the same size, ascending or descending in parallel or contrary motion, at least one imperfect consonance, as a third, sixth, or the like, should intervene. . . .
>
> A counterpoint containing a single dissonance, as a second, fourth, or seventh, between two perfect consonances of the same size in ascending or descending parallel motion is not allowed . . . for if a clearly heard dissonance is unsuitable in counterpoint, it cannot take the place of and substitute for an imperfect consonance.[14]

The layman's version of these rules, as given in the *Cortegiano* by Giuliano de' Medici, omits two important points: the forbidden perfect consonances are only those in parallel motion, and they must be punctuated by imperfect consonances rather than solely by dissonances.

There is of course no reason to tax Castiglione for imprecise language; he was after all using this detail of music theory merely as illustration of a larger point, the achievement of grace through avoidance of affectation in every courtly activity. Nonetheless the passage is, as Cian has remarked, not very clear;[15] or rather, the illustration seems not a very apt one. Correctly used, imperfect consonances and dissonances are an integral part of the musical fabric; a piece made up entirely of perfect consonances is not so much "affected" as it is unthinkable. The easy grace that is opposed to affected pedantry in music is much better illustrated by Count Ludovico's remark, in the discussion following the passage in question, that a musician who ends a phrase with an easily tossed-off vocal ornament shows that he knows the art and could do more if he chose.[16]

If Giuliano's little excursus into music theory refers less to rules of composition—musical science—than to a manner of performance—musical art—in which dissonance is freely introduced and resolution artfully delayed, the passage makes better sense. More than that, it is historically important. Music making of this kind would then be an example, given along with others in speaking, dancing, riding, and bearing arms, of the courtier's important and, alas, untranslatable quality of *sprezzatura*.[17] This word is familiar to historians of music in its use by Giulio

Caccini at the turn of the seventeenth century. Caccini mentions the word in his preface to *L'Euridice* (1600), in his *Nuove musiche* of 1602, and most tellingly in the preface to *Nuove musiche e nuova maniera di scriverle* (1614), where he defines it thus:

> *Sprezzatura* is that charm lent to a song by a few dissonant short notes over various bass notes that they are paired with; these relieve the song of a certain restricted narrowness and dryness and make it pleasant, free, and tuneful [*arioso*], just as in everyday speech eloquence and facility make pleasant and sweet the matters being spoken of. And to the figures of speech and the rhetorical flourishes in such eloquence correspond the *passaggi*, tremolos, and other such [musical] ornaments, which may occasionally be introduced with discretion in music of any mood.[18]

One can see that Caccini took more than the word *sprezzatura* from Castiglione; different as was the music the two men had in mind, Caccini borrowed two specifically musical meanings of the term, one implied and one clearly stated, from the *Cortegiano* to justify his own practice—a practice aimed, as he says, at achieving an effect of "total grace" (*intera grazia*) in music.[19]

Turning in the second book to the practice of music, Castiglione has his spokesman Federico Fregoso begin by emphasizing that the courtier must perform only when urged; if he is too quick to sing or play he wll seem like a professional musician instead of one who makes music "per passar tempo." Because professional musicians were pretty low in the social order of Castiglione's world, this warning was to be taken seriously. But we must not blame Castiglione for the lowly stature of musicians; also we should not think of the *Cortegiano* as a work unfriendly to the practice of music. On the contrary its influence could only have been in the direction of elevating the place of music in the life of the educated classes all over Europe. For example, we tend to think of the English upper classes in the past as having been traditionally philistine about music, made so by their education if not their temperament. This generalization is least applicable, however, for the couple of generations of Englishmen who first read Castiglione in Sir

Thomas Hoby's translation, published in 1561. We should also consider that whereas humanistic treatises on education tended to appropriate Plato's distaste for the music of his own time— thus Sassuolo da Prato, a pupil of Vittorino da Feltre, dismissed the (secular) music of the mid-fifteenth century as "inquinata, impudens, corrupta atque corruptrix"[20]—Castiglione on the contrary implies in his work that music such as that performed in Urbino in the early sixteenth century or Rome fifteen years later was worth an educated person's notice, and we know from his letters that he was fond of performing it himself.

The insistence that professionalism in music be avoided was as old as Aristotle's *Politics,* if not older.[21] Aeneas Silvius, among other fifteenth-century humanists, echoed this sentiment;[22] Maffeo Vegio said of an educated young woman that she should not "sing and dance more elegantly than necessary";[23] and it may be recalled that Leon Battista Alberti excelled in music without any training and, it appears, without much practice.[24] Here of course Castiglione's courtier would apply sprezzatura; feigning a slight acquaintance with the art, he would nonetheless take care to give a pretty good account of himself whenever he did perform.

On being asked what kinds of music were best suited to cultivated tastes, Federico gives an interesting and surprisingly systematic list (2.13; appendix, no. 3). First comes the ability to sing well from notated music (*cantar bene a libro*), securely and *con bella maniera,* in other words, to read well and with a good sense of style at sight.[25] The music that Castiglione refers to could include motets and other sacred polyphony and French chansons, but above all he was thinking of the North Italian *frottola,* in vogue when he began his book, and the Florentine– Roman madrigal coming into fashion when he completed it. Much of this music was still circulating in manuscript copies, collections, or single pieces; an example of the latter is the *barzelletta Essi Diva Diana,* which Castiglione asked to have sent to him, "el canto e le parole," in a letter of 1504.[26] But during the first decade of the sixteenth century the bulk of the repertory of the frottola as we know it was coming out in the beautifully printed volumes published by Ottaviano de' Petrucci in Venice. Petrucci was a native of Fossombrone, a town in the duchy of Urbino and at times a retreat for the ducal family, and there is reason to think that his early career was supported by the duke and even that he may have been educated at Urbino.[27] In 1511 he returned from Venice to Fossombrone, and in the years 1518–20 he visited Rome to intercede for his city at the papal court; whether at any of these times he came in contact with Castiglione is not known.[28] At any rate we can be sure that Petrucci's elegant little books of *frottole* and other part music were well known to Castiglione and his friends.

In saying that the courtier should be able to sing at sight not only securely but "con bella maniera" Castiglione introduces his favorite notion of stylish grace as part of musical performance. How much he meant to imply here by use of the word *maniera* I do not know, although in other contexts he meant a good deal by it.[29] But it is worth noting that recognizably individual style in musical performance was a sought-after and talked-about thing in late fifteenth-century Italy (only in the mid-sixteenth century did the concept of individual maniera begin to be spoken of with regard to music itself). *Improvvisatori* such as Chariteo and, above all, Serafino Aquilano were famous not only for their facility but also for their stylish manner of performance.[30] In the circle of the *Cortegiano* one would expect that l'Unico Aretino, Cristoforo Romano, Giacomo di San Secundo, and especially Terpandro might have been possessed of such skill, although it would have been demonstrated primarily in improvised singing, what Castiglione calls "cantare alla viola per recitare."[31]

During the fifteenth century skill in reading the mensural notation of polyphonic music, once the exclusive property of ecclesiastical singers, came to be taught to laymen as well although it was probably not part of any severely humanistic program of studies.[32] Thus Isabella d'Este studied music with the Franco–Flemish polyphonist Johannes Martini; the children of Lorenzo de' Medici are said to have been instructed in music by the great Henrich Isaac. If textbooks on polyphonic music, such as those prepared by Tinctoris for his royal pupil in Naples,[33] are any indication, correctness rather than bella maniera was the primary aim of such teaching. Improvised singing (what Ficino and other humanists called "cantare ad lyram") must have required more attention to style, but the professionalism of the improvvisatori, dangerously close perhaps to the popular street art of the *cantimbanchi* of Florence and the North Italian cities, was surely a thing to be avoided.

At the turn of the century things seem to have changed somewhat. The art of the improvvisatori, much admired in Ferrara and in the Mantua and Milan of Castiglione's youth, was so popular in courtly circles that the poets, some of them aristocrats, and the musicians, some of them professional polyphonists, came to share in it. Thus Marchetto Cara, one of Isabella d'Este's favorite composers, was sent to Venice in 1503, along with a Ferrarese gentlewoman whom he later married, to entertain the exiled Elisabetta of Urbino; their style of singing was reported to be better than anything the Venetians were accustomed to.[34]

All the frottolists must have been good at improvising; the formulaic nature of their written music suggests this, and in spite of their careful printing Petrucci's collections of *barzellette*, *strambotti*, and the like are better guides for free, semi-improvisatory performance than for literal rendition of the contents of the written page.[35] Castiglione in associating bella maniera with the art of reading music is, I think, recognizing just this state of affairs; the blending of improvisatory skills with the learned science of mensural polyphony, the products of which were now becoming widely available in print; and the leveling of social distinctions in musical performance, with the aristocratic courtier doing very much the same thing, albeit with more sprezzatura and less professionalism, as the scholastically trained singer or the self-taught *improvvisatore*.[36] The appearance of the cultivated amateur on the musical scene in the early cinquecento is an important landmark in the history of music, and Castiglione seems to have been its first chronicler.[37]

In *cantar a libro* as Castiglione defines it, all parts of a polyphonic piece are sung. "Bella musica," but more beautiful still is "il cantar alla viola," or solo singing to instrumental accompaniment, for two reasons. First, one can attend more closely to the "bel modo e l'aria," and second, small errors are easy to detect since the aid and comfort given by singers to each other are lacking here. To those who believe that under differences of circumstance and detail people remain fundamentally the same it will come as pleasant confirmation to hear that sixteenth-century choral singers fudged through pieces by covering each others' mistakes much as they still do today. Yet Castiglione's second reason for preferring solo song seems odd in the ambience of sprezzatura; perhaps the latter quality did not extend to the making of audible mistakes. In the first reason there are two interesting words, *modo* and *aria*. The latter may be taken to mean melody, or more specifically the fusion of text and music; implied here is the necessity for correct and effective fitting together of words and melody, a union that surely existed in Castiglione's time but one that could not yet be taken for granted. *Aria* may also mean "air" in the sense of an individual manner of singing melodies. *Modo* does not mean "mode" in the technical musical sense but must here be used approximately in the way Petrucci was using it for paradigmatic pieces in his frottola collections ("modo di dir sonetti," a piece designed to serve any sonnet of orthodox design, for example). One could, in other words, hear the formal or poetic structure more clearly in solo singing. Or, *modo* could be taken to mean the result of *maniera*, the kind of music produced by the individual style of the performer; thus it would be a synonym for *aria*.[38]

Whether Castiglione meant by *viola* a single instrument or an instrumental family (perhaps including the *lira da braccio*) or instead used the word to indicate any instrument suitable for accompaniment (the phrase *cantare alla viola* thus being a kind of synecdoche) I am not sure. If he meant *viola*, the newly fashionable gamba or a *viola da braccio*, literally, this was one term that his translators changed.[39] Both the early French and German versions of the *Cortegiano* substitute lute for viol, and

so does Hoby;[40] the lute, already an instrument in prominent use
when Castiglione began his work, was by mid-century regarded
as the aristocratic accompanying instrument par excellence
(and thus again perhaps serving as a generic term).[41] Castiglione
himself owned viols and was fond of playing them; he wrote
twice to his mother from Rome, at just the time he was completing the second redaction of the *Cortegiano,* asking for his "beloved" instrument to be sent to him.[42] Isabella d'Este, that paragon of musical as well as of all other courtly virtues, learned
to play the viol, remarking in a letter of 1499 that she was
practicing in order to be able to accompany her brother Alfonso when she next visited Ferrara.[43] If, by the way, the future
Alfonso I d'Este could take time off from his artillery to sing
alla viola, it seems that one has sufficient proof of the realism of
Castiglione's remarks about aristocratic practice of music.

Federico, in ranking modes of performance, gives highest
praise to what he calls "il cantare alla viola per recitare." By this
Castiglione means improvised song or declamatory speech-song
over instrumental accompaniment. This was the art for which
Serafino Aquilano and his peers were famous; by means of it the
sonnets and *canzoni* of Petrarch and of late fifteenth- and early
sixteenth-century *petrarchisti* were performed before courtly
audiences. At a lower literary level the same improvisers, and
humbler poet-musicians as well, declaimed strambotti by this
method. Chains of ottava rima stanzas, such as those written by
Bembo for the carnival at Urbino in 1506, must also have been
occasionally performed in this way, and Castiglione's stanzas
for *Tirsi* might at some point, if not on the occasion for which
they were written, have been sung. The frontispiece to an early
edition of Pulci's *Morgante* shows an improvvisatore declaiming,
lira da braccio in hand, to an attentive audience.[44] It would have
been easy to do the same thing with other epic poetry of the
time, including part of Boiardo's *Orlando innamorato,* and it is
known that Ariosto's *Orlando furioso* later enjoyed great popu-
larity, both in the poet's own stanzas and in numerous popularized arrangements, performed in this way.[45] What is surprising
in this context is that the art of improvised song-and-accom-

paniment, which appears to have been the domain of profes-
sionals—not always of very exalted status even within their
class—is grouped with the other musical accomplishments suitable to the courtier. On the other hand, we hear of aristocratic
men of genius who are said to have excelled in just this pursuit;
Lorenzo de' Medici, despite his bad voice, was said to be one.[46]
Here, then, Castiglione might be referring to the kind of performance a humanistically trained person of talent would give.
Still, one suspects that in his mind this performance was not so
distant from the art of the *strambottisto* as pure humanists could
have wished.

In mentioning other instruments Gaspare singles out the keyboard family (perhaps including by implication the lute), useful for the full chords ("le consonanzie molto perfette") they
can produce and the ease with which they can produce a variety of effects. A consort of four bowed viols is praised for its
sweetness and artifice; this ensemble was perhaps not so common in the early sixteenth century as it later became, but there
is contemporary evidence of its use (Castiglione's specification
of "da arco" may support the notion that his earlier talk about
viola referred mainly to a plucked instrument).[47] Only the wind
instruments, outlawed to men of good standing since they had
been scorned in antiquity by Alcibiades and by the goddess
Athena,[48] are excluded, presumably because in playing them one
gave up the use of one's voice; also, they distorted one's face,
preventing one from making a *bella figura*.

In all this singing and playing, we are reminded, it is enough
to be acquainted with the art; but after this dutifully humanistic
phrase Castiglione adds, "But the better skilled you are, the
better for you." The discreet courtier will choose the right time
to perform, at the bidding of a company of friends and equals
and especially in the presence of women. He will attend not
only to the time of day but also to his time of life; music making, so often the accompaniment of amorous poetry, is suitable
only to the young.

On Giuliano de' Medici (hardly a graybeard in 1506) protest-
ing that the *poveri vecchi* should not be deprived of the pleasure

of music, Federico replies that he agrees; old men should indeed continue to cantare alla viola if they wish but in private and as solace for the unhappiness and troubles that fill their lives. This seems, if one remembers Castiglione's lifelong love for the viola and the melancholy of his later years, a touchingly personal remark.[49]

The long passage on music (not all of it is given here) ends with the acute observation that those who have performed music with some skill, even if in mature years they no longer do so, will enjoy it more than nonmusicians, who hear music as passing sounds that do not really enter their souls and who are affected by it in much the same way dumb beasts are.[50] By blending the Ficinian notion of music's effect on the *spiritus*[51] with that of the usefulness of technical and intellectual grasp of the art, Castiglione comes as close as anyone in his century to presenting a rounded aesthetic ideal for music.

In book 3 (8) music is briefly mentioned among the accomplishments suitable for women. The passage is chiefly negative in tone: Women should approach musical performance, or dancing, with "una certa timidità," should thus avoid brazen professionalism even more than men. They should shun instruments such as drums, pipes, and trumpets (but, we remember, so should male courtiers). In playing instruments suitable to them women should not make use of elaborate ornaments and fast repeated notes ("quelli diminuzioni forti e replicate") that would draw attention to their skill rather than their sweetness of execution. All Castiglione seems to be saying here is that things he advises against in the musical performance of the courtier are really forbidden in that of the lady of the court. In all other respects, it seems, women are free to take part in music as much as men—allowing for the limitation that much of the *poesia per musica* of the time was addressed to women and so meant primarily for them to listen to. The role of women in aristocratic and indeed in semiprofessional music making at this time is of course well documented.

In addition to the set speeches on music in the *Cortegiano* there are a few scattered allusions, interesting in themselves

and valuable in showing the role of music in some approxima-
tion of the everyday life of the cultivated society it depicts. The
most important of these may be described briefly in their order
of occurrence in the work.

1. In the midst of the long discussion of the use of language
in book 1, Count Ludovico speaks (37) of the differing types of
musical usage he has observed, contrasting the brilliant style of
singing exemplified by Bidon with the softer, sweeter style of
Marchetto Cara (appendix, no. 4). Bidon, a French-born singer
from Ferrara who joined the court of Leo X in the latter years
of his reign, was mentioned for his stylish singing by Folengo
and others.[52] Cara, the well-known composer of frottole at the
Mantuan court, has already been cited for his skill as a performer.[53] Castiglione had certainly heard Cara sing at some point
near the beginning of his work on the *Cortegiano,* and he must
have known Cara's setting of his sonnet *Cantai mentre nel cor
lieto fioria,* published in 1513.[54] Bidon's singing he came to know
at a later point; in the second redaction of the *Cortegiano* the
very words used to describe this musician were used, in the
same spot, for Alexander Agricola, a Flemish musician who
had been at Milan in the 1470s, had later spent some time in
Naples and Florence, but who had left Italy in 1493 and had
died, in the service of the Habsburg court in Spain, in 1506.[55]
The change of name is an interesting example of Castiglione's
effort to update his work even if it bespeaks a certain insensi-
tivity about the personal maniera of musicians.[56]

2. At the end of book 1 there is music and dancing, occur-
ring in a way reminiscent of the *Decameron,* performed at the
order of the duchess. Two ladies dance, to the music of the
accomplished musician-dancer Barletta, a *bassa* and a *roegarze.*
Barletta, who is also mentioned in the first book as a professional dancer, was apparently a favorite at the court of Urbino;
he is the subject of a letter of 1507 from Castiglione to Ippolito d'Este.[57] The *bassa danza* was a well-known Italian court
dance, under changing guises, from the mid-fifteenth century;[58]
about the roegarze we know only that it was one of the dances
performed at a wedding banquet for Ercole II of Ferrara in

1529, mentioned in the celebrated description of Cristoforo di Messisbugo.[59]

3. Early in the second book Federico, when speaking of the gentleman's need to choose carefully the time and place for display of his accomplishments, criticizes the music lover who fills every conversational pause with singing sotto voce. In the second redaction Castiglione had written "sotto voce a cantare ut re mi fa sol la" to emphasize the inanity of such musical interpolations.[60]

4. In emphasizing that the courtier should select and cleave to one friend, Federico cites as proverbial wisdom the fact that it is more difficult to tune together three instruments than two (2.30), a metaphor for human conduct prophetic of Elizabethan usage.

5. Federico, in a conversation on the force of opinion and prejudice (2.35; appendix, no. 5), illustrates with two anecdotes: in the first some verses thought to be by Sannazaro were acclaimed as excellent but when found to be by another poet were sunk in popular judgment to mediocrity;[61] in the second a motet sung in the presence of the duchess was not judged either good or pleasing until it was revealed to be by Josquin des Prez, whereupon it rose immediately in stature. As the only debunking statement about the great composer known to me, this remark has a certain perverse appeal.[62]

6. In illustration of the notion that the cobbler should stick to his last Federico speaks of a certain musician who gave up his art to write verses that he thought excellent but that everyone else laughed at (2.39); now he has lost even his musical skills. As Cian remarks, we will never know who this was, much as we would like to.[63]

7. Among the *facezie* in book 2 is an account (52) by Cesare Gonzaga of a Brescian bumpkin who watched the festivities in Venice on Assumption Day. Asked what part of the ceremonial music he most admired, he replied that the marvel of a strange trumpet that the player half swallowed, then regurgitated, pleased him most. The courtier, though he disdained playing it, was clearly expected to know about an instrument like the

slide trumpet or trombone (and we now know that these were used, in addition to the famous long trumpets, in Venetian festival music).

8. In the fourth book the irrepressible Gaspare remarks (48) that the courtier must be something special if Plato and Aristotle are his constant companions; still, he ventures to say that he finds it hard to believe that either of these ancient worthies ever danced or made music.

9. As part of Bembo's description of ideal love (4.62) there occurs what I would call a prose madrigal, surely written during the first flush of enthusiasm for this new poetic-musical genre.

> Therefore let him keep aloof from the blind judgment of sense, and with his eyes enjoy the radiance of his Lady, her grace, her amorous sparkle, the smiles, the manners and all the other pleasant ornaments of her beauty. Likewise, with his hearing let him enjoy the sweetness of her voice, the modulation of her words, the harmony of her music (if his lady love be a musician). Thus, he will feed his soul on the sweetest food by means of these two senses—which partake little of the corporeal, and are reason's ministers—without passing to any unchaste appetite through desire for the body.[64]

On this note, with Castiglione characteristically recognizing the real even while emphasizing the ideal, these remarks may end.

APPENDIX: PASSAGES DEALING WITH
MUSIC IN THE *CORTEGIANO*

1. 1.47: Non dite,—rispose il Conte;—perch'io v'entrarò in un gran pelago di laude della musica; e ricordarò quanto sempre appresso gli antichi sia stata celebrata e tenuta per cosa sacra, e sia stato opinione di sapientissimi filosofi il mondo esser composto di musica e i cieli nel moversi far armonia, e l'anima nostra pur con la medesima ragion esser formata, e però destarsi e quasi vivificar le sue virtù per la musica. Per il che se scrive Alessandro alcuna volta esser stato da quella così ardentemente incitato, che quasi contra sua voglia gli bisognava levarsi dai convivii e correre all'arme; poi, mutando il musico la sorte del suono, mitigarsi e tornar dall'arme ai convivii. E dirovvi il severo Socrate, gia vecchissimo, aver imparato a sonare la citara. E

ricordomi aver già inteso che Platone ed Aristotele vogliono che l'om bene instituito sia ancor musico, e con infinite ragioni mostrano la forza della musica in noi essere grandissima, e per molte cause, che or saria lungo a dir, doversi necessariamente imparar da puerizia; non tanto per quella superficial melodia che si sente, ma per esser sufficiente ad indur in noi un novo abito bono ed un costume tendente alla virtù, il qual fa l'animo più capace di felicità, secondo che lo esercizio corporale fa il corpo più gagliardo; e non solamente non nocere alle cose civili e della guerra, ma loro giovar sommamente. Licurgo ancora nelle severe sue leggi la musica approvò. E leggesi i Lacedemonii bellicosissimi ed i Cretensi aver usato nelle battaglie citare ed altri instrumenti molli; e molti eccellentissimi capitani antichi, come Epaminonda, aver dato opera alla musica; e quelli che non ne sapeano, come Temistocle, esser stati molto meno apprezzati. Non avete voi letto che delle prime discipline che insegnò il bon vecchio Chirone nella tenera età ad Achille, il quale egli nutrì dallo latte e dalla culla, fu la musica; e volse il savio maestro che le mani, che aveano a sparger tanto sangue troiano, fossero spesso occupate nel suono del citara? Qual soldato adunque sarà che si vergogni d'imitar Achille, lasciando molti altri famosi capitani ch'io potrei addurre? Però non vogliate voi privar il nostro cortegiano della musica, la qual non solamente gli animi umani indolcisce, ma spesso le fiere fa diventar mansuete; e chi non la gusta si po tener per certo ch'abbia i spiriti discordanti l'un dall'altro. Eccovi quanto essa po, che già trasse un pesce a lassarsi cavalcar da un omo per mezzo il procelloso mare. Questa veggiamo operarsi ne' sacri tempii nello rendere laude e grazie a Dio; e credibil cosa è che ella grata a lui sia ed egli a noi data l'abbia per dolcissimo alleviamento delle fatiche e fastidi nostri. Onde spesso i duri lavoratori de' campi sotto l'ardente sole ingannano la lor noia col rozzo ed agreste cantare. Con questo la inculta contadinella, che inanzi al giorno a filare o a tessere si lieva, dal sonno si diffende e la sua fatica fa piacevole; questo è iocundissimo trastullo dopo le piogge, i venti e le tempeste ai miseri marinari; con questo consolansi i stanchi peregrini dei noiosi e lunghi viaggi e spesso gli afflitti prigionieri delle catene e ceppi. Così, per maggiore argumento che d'ogni fatica e molestia umana la modulazione, benchè inculta, sia grandissimo refrigerio, para che la natura alle nutrici insegnata l'abbia per rimedio precipuo del pianto continuo de' teneri fanculli; i quali al suon di tal voce s'inducono a riposato e placido sonno, scordandosi le lacrime così proprie, ed a noi per presagio del rimanente della nostra vita in quella etá da natura date.

2. 1.28: Allora il signor Magnifico,—Questo ancor,—disse,—si verifica nella musica, nella quale è vicio grandissimo far due consonanzie perfette l'una dopo l'altra; tal che il medesimo sentimento dell'audito nostro l'aborrisce e spesso ama una seconda o settima, che in sè è dissonanzia aspera ed intollerabile; e ciò procede che quel continuare nelle perfette genera sazietà e dimostra una troppo affettata armonia; il che mescolando le imperfette si fugge, col far quasi un paragone, donde più le orecchie nostre stanno suspese e più avidamente attendono e gustano le perfette, e dilettansi talor di quella dissonanzia della seconda o settima, come di cosa sprezzata. . . . Un musico, se nel cantar pronunzia una sola voce terminata con suave accento in un groppetto duplicato, con tal facilità che paia che così gli venga fatto a caso, con quel punto solo fa conoscere che sa molto più di quello che fa.

3. 2.13: Bella musica,—rispose messer Federico,—parmi il cantar bene a libro sicuramente e con bella maniera; ma ancor molto più il cantare alla viola perchè tutta la dolcezza consiste quasi in un solo, e con molto maggior attenzion si nota ed intende il bel modo e l'aria non essendo occupate le orecchie in più che in una sol voce, e meglio ancor vi si discerne ogni piccolo errore; il che non accade cantando in compagnia perchè l'uno aiuta l'altro. Ma sopra tutto parmi gratissimo il cantare alla viola per recitar; il che tanto di venustà ed efficacia aggiunge alle parole, che è gran maraviglia. Sono ancor armoniosi tutti gli instrumenti da tasti, perchè hanno le consonanzie molto perfette e con facilità vi si possono far molte cose che empiono l'animo di musicale dolcezza. E non meno diletta la musica delle quattro viole da arco, la quale è soavissima ed artificiosa. Dà ornamento e grazia assai la voce umana a tutti questi instrumenti, de' quali voglio che al nostro cortegian basti aver notizia; e quanto più però in essi sarà eccellente, tanto sarà meglio, senza impacciarsi molto di quelli che Minerva refiutò ed Alcibiade, perchè pare che abbiano del schifo.

4. 1.37: Vedete la musica, le armonie della quale or son gravi e tarde, or velocissime e di novi modi e vie; nientedimeno tutte dilettano, ma per diverse cause, come si comprende nella maniera del cantare di Bidon, la qual è tanto artificiosa, pronta, veemente, concitata e de così varie melodie, che i spirti di chi ode tutti si commoveno e s'infiammano e cosí sospesi par che si levino insino al cielo. Nè men commove nel suo cantar il nostro Marchetto Cara, ma con più molle armonia; ché per una via placida e piena di flebile dolcezza intenerisce e penetra le anime, imprimendo in esse soavemente una dilettevole passione.

5. 2.35: E cantandosi pur in presenza della signora Duchessa un mottetto, non piacque mai né fu estimato per bono, fin che non si seppe che quella era composizion di Josquin de Pris.

NOTES

1. The *Deipnosophists* of Athenaeus, although it could hardly be described as a model for Castiglione, does give a good deal of space to accounts of musical performance, Greek and Roman. For a view of the *Cortegiano* as a symposium (the category to which Athenaeus's work belongs), see Wayne A. Rebhorn, *Courtly Performances: Masking and Festivity in Castiglione's* Book of the Courtier (Detroit, 1978), chap. 5.

2. On Doni's work, see James Haar, "Notes on the 'Dialogo della musica' of Antonfrancesco Doni," *Music & Letters*, 47 (1966), 198–224, and the literature cited there. For Milán's work, see below, n. 38.

3. The remarks on music in Cortese's *De Cardinalatu* (1510) are discussed in Nino Pirrotta, "Music and Cultural Tendencies in 15th-Century Italy," *Journal of the American Musicological Society*, 19 (1966), 142–61.

4. This rejoinder is given to Ottaviano Fregoso in the second redaction of the *Cortegiano*, Castiglione having not yet settled the roles his interlocutors were to play. See *La seconda redazione del 'Cortegiano' di Baldassare Castiglione*, ed. Ghino Ghinassi (Florence, 1968), p. 64.

5. See *Franchini Gafuri Theorica Musicae* [Milan, 1492], facs. ed. Gaetano Cesari (Rome, 1934). The first chapter of this treatise, "De effectibus et comendatione musice," was, in the first edition of 1480, comparatively short (it is given in Cesari's volume, pp. 41–43). By 1492 Gafori had learned so much about the subject that he could rewrite this chapter, now called "De Musicis et effectibus atque comendatione musice discipline," at more than five times its original length and with a vastly increased number of references. Gafori was so eager to gain knowledge of classical sources on music that he commissioned translations of Ptolemy and other Greek authors. See F. Alberto Gallo, "Le traduzioni dal greco per Franchino Gaffurio," *Acta musicologica*, 35 (1963), 172–74. It is conceivable that Castiglione could have known Gafori in Milan. However, Gafori's writings seem not to be a direct source for what Castiglione has to say about music.

6. Giorgio Valla, *De Musica libri V*, in *De expetendis et fugiendis rebus opus* (Venice, 1501). Valla was also an active translator of Greek treatises on music. For another, earlier example of humanistic literature in which the *laus musicae* figures, see Conrad H. Rawski, "Petrarch's Dialogue on Music," *Speculum*, 46 (1971), 302–17.

7. Apart from the general safety of the assumption that every educated sixteenth-century man read Quintilian, one might cite Castiglione's expressed desire that his son be taught Greek before Latin since the latter was closer to the vernacular and would be learned in the normal course of an educated

man's life; see Julia Cartwright, *The Perfect Courtier: Baldassare Castiglione*, 2 vols. (London, 1927; first publ. 1908), ii, 171; and compare Quintilian, *Institutio Oratoria*, trans. H. E. Butler, 4 vols. (London, 1921), I, i, 12: "A sermone Graeco puerum incipere malo, quia Latinum, qui pluribus in usu est, vel nobis nolentibus perbibit."

8. I, x, 9–34.

9. For an English translation of the passage in question, see Oliver Strunk, *Source Readings in Music History* (New York, 1950), pp. 67–68. I am grateful to John Wendland for calling this passage to my attention.

10. See *Varia Philippi Beroaldi opuscula* (Basel, 1513), fols. 12^v–14^v. The "Oratio habita in enarrationem Quaestionum Tusculanarum et Horatii flacii continens laudem musices" was first published in 1491. Castiglione may have studied briefly with Beroaldo (see C. Martinati, *Notizie storico-biografiche intorno al Conte Baldassare Castiglione con documenti inediti* [Florence, 1890], p. 9).

11. Some connection between the court of Urbino and the mainstream of Italian humanist educators is provided by the fact that Federico da Montefeltro had studied as a boy with Vittorino da Feltre at Mantua (see William H. Woodward, *Vittorino da Feltre and Other Humanist Educators* [Cambridge, 1897; repr. New York, 1963], p. 30). What kind of instruction in the humanist approach to music Castiglione received is unknown to me.

12. For the text, accompanied by an English translation, of Aeneas Silvius's treatise, see *Aeneae Silvii De liberorum educatione*, trans. J. S. Nelson, Catholic University Studies in Medieval and Renaissance Latin Language and Literature, 12 (Washington, D.C., 1940).

13. See Woodward, *Vittorino da Feltre*, pp. 93–118, esp. pp. 107, 108, 117.

14. Franchinus Gaffurius, *Practica musicae*, trans. Clement A. Miller (American Institute of Musicology, 1968), pp. 125–26.

15. *Il Cortegiano del Conte Baldesar Castiglione*, ed. Vittorio Cian, 3d ed. (Florence, 1929), p. 67n.

16. 1.28. This passage is not in the second redaction of the *Cortegiano*; it might have been prompted by Castiglione's hearing of expert singing, such as that of the Roman singer Bidon, whom he praises in another passage of the final version (see below and n. 52), at some point after 1520. *Groppetto*, a word in this passage that has caused Castiglione's translators some trouble, probably refers to a short trill; see the discussion in Walter H. Kemp, "Some Notes on Music in Castiglione's *Il Libro del Cortegiano*," in *Cultural Aspects of the Italian Renaissance: Essays in Honour of Paul Oskar Kristeller*, ed. Cecil H. Clough (New York, 1976), p. 355.

17. English translations of this word range from the literal but most unsatisfactory "disgracing" of Hoby to the sympathetic but rather free "nonchalance" of Singleton. In the *seconda redazione* of his work Castiglione says that the term had been in current usage "da noi," but its origin is unknown and it is not to be found in the first edition of the *Vocabolario della Crusca*. For a recent discussion of the term see Rebhorn, *Courtly Performances*, pp. 33–39.

18. For the Italian text, see Giulio Caccini, *Le nuove musiche*, ed. H. Wiley Hitchcock (Madison, Wisc., 1970), p. 45n. My translation differs in detail from that given by Hitchcock.

19. Caccini's borrowing thus seems to be directly from Castiglione, not through an intermediary such as Lodovico Dolce. The closeness of the borrowing is pointed out, although only for one of the two passages in question, by Hitchcock, p. 44n. Jacopo Peri also made use of the term; see Nino Pirrotta, "Early Opera and Aria," in *New Looks at Italian Opera: Essays in Honor of Donald J. Grout,* ed. William W. Austin (Ithaca, N.Y., 1968), p. 53.

20. Cesare Cuasti, *Intorno alla vita e all' insegnamento di Vittorino da Feltre. Lettere di Sassolo Pratesi volgarizzate* (Florence, 1869), p. 69.

21. *Politics* 8.5.1339b. Plato's opposition to virtuosic professionalism in music (expressed in book 3 of the *Republic,* among other places) was of course well known to humanists.

22. See Woodward, *Vittorino,* p. 240.

23. Ibid.

24. Nanie Bridgman, *La vie musicale au quattrocento* (Paris, 1964), pp. 80, 105.

25. Cf. 1.47, where Count Ludovico says he is not content with the courtier as a musician unless the latter can "intendere ed esser sicuro a libro." This phrase is not to be confused with the technique of improvising counterpoint from the "sight" of a notated voice, called by fifteenth-century theorists "cantare supra librum."

26. See Cartwright, *The Perfect Courtier,* pp. 46–47, and Cian, *Il Cortegiano,* p. 116n. This piece is unfortunately not to be found in Knud Jeppesen's catalogue of the frottola repertory (*La Frottola,* 3 vols. [Copenhagen, 1968–70]).

27. Claudio Sartori, *Bibliografia delle opere musicali stampate da Ottaviano Petrucci* (Florence, 1948), p. 13. In 1504 Guidobaldo appointed Petrucci to the town council of Fossombrone, and in succeeding years the printer held a number of civic offices (see ibid., pp. 17, 20–21).

28. In 1513 Petrucci printed, in Fossombrone, the letter of Castiglione to Henry VII of England (*Baldhasaris Castilionei ad Henricum Angliae Regem Epistola de vita et gestis Guidobaldi Urbini Ducis*) as an act of homage to the late Duke Guidobaldo. See Augusto Vernarecci, *Ottaviano de' Petrucci da Fossombrone* (Fossombrone, 1881), pp. 111–12.

29. Cf. the letter of Castiglione and Raphael on Roman architecture, cited among other places in John Shearman, *Mannerism* (Harmondsworth, 1967), p. 17. Other early uses of the term *maniera,* with meanings allied to social deportment, are given by Shearman.

30. See E. Percopo, *Le rime di Benedetto Gareth* (Naples, 1892); "Vita del facondo poeta vulgare Seraphino Aquilano per Vincentio Calmeta composta" (1504), in Mario Menghini, ed., *Le rime di Serafino de' Ciminelli dell' Aquila* (Bologna, 1894).

31. These are men spoken of in the *Cortegiano* for their skill as musicians. All but San Secondo are introduced in the first book (5); l'Unico Aretino (Ber-

nardo Accolti) takes some part in the dialogues. Terpandro was a friend of Castiglione (see Cian, *Cortegiano,* pp. 532–33). San Secondo was also a personal friend, and Castiglione made efforts on his behalf at the end of the singer's career (see Cian, pp. 205–06n). San Secondo was apparently a virtuoso performer (see 2.45): "come soglio maravigliarmi dell'audacia di color che osano cantar alla viola in presenzia del nostro Jacomo Sansecondo." He is mentioned as a "cantore al liuto" in Pietro Aaron, *Lucidario in musica* (Venice, 1545), iv, fol. 31ᵛ.

32. See Pirrotta, "Music and Cultural Tendencies," pp. 137–38, on the aversion of some humanists toward, and the ignorance of others about, the polyphonic art they associated with scholasticism.

33. Tinctoris dedicated several of his treatises to Beatrice of Aragon, daughter of Ferdinand I; see Heinrich Hüschen, "Tinctoris," *Die Musik in Geschichte und Gegenwart,* XIII (1966), col. 419. Further information on the relation of Tinctoris to the Neapolitan court may be found in Leeman L. Perkins and Howard Garey, eds., *The Mellon. Chansonnier,* 2 vols. (New Haven, 1979), I, 17–22.

34. See Alfred Einstein, *The Italian Madrigal* (Princeton, 1949), p. 52. The letter recording this is transcribed in William F. Prizer, "Marchetto Cara and the North Italian Frottola," Diss., University of North Carolina, 1974, II, 282, doc. 13.

35. From literal reading of what Petrucci gives, many pieces cannot in fact be performed correctly, their musical and poetic form jibing.

36. It is an interesting sign of the changed cultural climate of the end of the sixteenth century that Caccini associates the quality of sprezzatura with the art of the professional singer.

37. The importance of the musically literate amateur in sixteenth-century culture is stressed by Manfred F. Bukofzer, "The Book of the Courtier on Music," *Volume of Proceedings of the Music Teachers National Association,* 38 (1944), 232–35.

38. On early uses and meanings of the word *aria* see Pirrotta, "Early Opera and Aria," pp. 57–60.

39. Kemp, "Some Notes on Music," p. 358, thinks the passage refers to the plucked *viola da mano,* a guitar-like instrument much used in informal music making in the early sixteenth century. A bowed *lira da braccio* would be a possible alternative.

40. See *Les quatres livres du Courtisan du Conte Baltazar de Castillon. Reduyct de langue Ytalicque en Francoys* (Paris [1637]), fols. 41ᵛ–42ʳ: "Chanter sur le livre semble ugne belle musicque pourveu que ce soit personne quil' le sache bien faire & en bonne mode mais encores plus chanter sur le luc . . ."; cf. Hoby: "Me thinke then answered Sir Fredericke, pricksong is a faire musicke, so it be done upon the booke surely and after a good sorte. But to sing to the lute is much better." Hoby translates *cantare alla viola per recitare* as "singing to the lute with

the dittie," this being one of the idiosyncrasies (to use the kind view taken by Bukofzer," Book of the Courtier on Music," pp. 230, 234) of his version.

The Spanish version by Juan Boscan (1534) uses *vihuela*, which could refer, like Castiglione's *viola*, either to that instrument or to string instruments in general (see *El Cortesano, traducción de Juan Boscan* [Madrid, 1942], p. 123). The great Spanish vihuelist Luis Milán wrote a work called *El Cortesano* in emulation of Castiglione but closer in spirit to dialogues of Doni, Aretino, Dolce, and others; in this work music is often mentioned in passing but the musical topics treated by Castiglione are not taken up. See Luis Milán, *Libro intitulado El Cortesano* [Valencia 1561], Coleccion de libros españoles raros ó curiosos, tomo séptimo (Madrid, 1874).

For the use of lute in place of viol in the German translation of 1565, see Robert Haas, *Aufführungspraxis der Musik* (Wildpark-Potsdam, 1931), p. 131.

41. Both lira da braccio and lute are among the instruments depicted in the studiolo of Federico da Montefeltro. See Edmund A. Bowles, *Musikleben im 15. Jahrhundert*. Musikgeschichte in Bildern, III, 8 (Leipzig, 1977), illus. 79. On the studiolo see F. Remington, "The Private Study of Federigo da Montefeltro," *Metropolitan Museum of Art Bulletin*, 36 (1941), 3–13.

42. See *Baldassar Castiglione. Lettere inedite e rare*, ed. Guglielmo Corni (Milan, 1969), pp. 26, 38, letters dated 24 August 1521 and 18 March 1522.

43. See Prizer, "Marchetto Cara," p. 28.

44. See illus. 83 in Walter Salmen, *Musikleben im 16. Jahrhundert*, Musikgeschichte in Bildern, III, 9 (Leipzig, 1976). L'Unico Aretino was referred to by Paolo Cortese as a great improviser on the "lyre" (see Pirrotta, "Music and Cultural Tendencies," p. 161). It is said that when he sang in Rome the shops closed and large crowds gathered (see Bianca Becherini, "Il 'Cortegiano' e la musica," *La Bibliofilia*, 45 [1943], 86).

45. See Vittorio Rossi, "Di un cantastorie ferrarese del secolo XVI," *Rassegna emiliana di storia, letteratura ed arte*, 2 (1889–90), 435–46, and Giuseppina Fumagalli, "La fortuna dell' Orlando furioso in Italia nel secolo xvi," *Atti e memorie della deputazione ferrarese di storia patria*, 20 (1912), 397.

46. Luigi Parigi, *Laurentiana: Lorenzo dei Medici cultore della musica* (Florence, 1954), pp. 12–15. For reference to other aristocratic performers see Bridgman, *La vie musicale*, pp. 73–76.

47. Five viols were heard in consort at the Ferrarese banquet of 20 May 1529 described by Messisbugo. See Howard Mayer Brown, "A Cook's Tour of Ferrara in 1529," *Rivista italiana di musicologia*, 10 (1975), 234, 238 (see also Brown's remarks about the common Ferrarese practice of doubling voices with viols). For other references to viol consorts in the first half of the sixteenth century, see Haas, *Aufführungspraxis*, pp. 133–34.

48. For Alcibiades and the "flute," see Plutarch's *Life of Alcibiades*, trans. Bernadotte Perrin (Cambridge, Mass., 1916), 2.4–5, pp. 7–9, where it is said that Alcibiades not only disliked contorting his handsome face but hated the

aulos because he could not talk or sing while playing it. Minerva's hatred for the aulos is described, among other places, in Athenaeus, *The Deipnosophists*, xiv, 616 (vol. VI, pp. 321 ff., in the translation of C. G. Gulick [Cambridge, Mass., 1937]); see also Rawski, "Petrarch's Dialogue," p. 314n.

49. Cf., however, Aristotle, *Politics* 8.6.1340b, where it is said that older people may drop musical practice but remain judges of the art.

50. See n. 49.

51. On Ficino's view of music and the *spiritus*, see D. P. Walker, *Spiritual and Demonic Music from Ficino to Campanella* (London, 1958), pp. 3–11.

52. Bidon [Antonio Collebaudi] was at the court of Alfonso I of Ferrara in 1506. In 1511 he visited Mantua, and by 1519 he was a member of the papal chapel, described as such in a letter from Leo X to Alfonso I. See Hermann-Walther Frey, "Regesten zur päpstlichen Kapelle unter Leo X, and zu seiner Privatkapelle," *Die Musikforschung*, 8 (1955), 62; Anne-Marie Bautier-Regnier, "Jachet de Mantoue (Jacobus Collebaudi), v. 1500–1559; Contribution à l'étude du problème des Jachet au xvi^c siècle," *Revue belge de musicologie*, 6 (1952), 101–02; and William F. Prizer, "La cappella di Francesco II Gonzaga e la musica sacra a Mantova nel primo ventennio del cinquecento," *Mantova e i Gonzaga nella civiltà del Rinascimento* (Segrate, 1978), pp. 269–70. Folengo's mention of Bidon is on fol. 196 of the *Opus Merlin Cocaii macaronicorum . . .* (1521). Bidon is also mentioned by Cosimo Bartoli (see Bautier-Regnier, "Jachet de Mantoue," p. 102). His singing was held by the Ferrarese to by synonymous with a standard of excellence against which other musicians could be judged; see Lewis Lockwood, "Jean Mouton and Jean Michel: French Music and Musicians in Italy, 1505–1520," *Journal of the American Musicological Society*, 32 (1979), 218–19.

53. See above and n. 34. The fullest account of Cara's career is to be seen in Prizer, "Marchetto Cara."

54. It appeared in the *Canzoni Sonetti Strambotti et Frottole Liber Tertio* of Andrea Antico. A letter from Cesare Gonzaga to Isabella d'Este, dated 2 December 1510, asked for Cara's musical setting of an unnamed *madrigaletto* and also for "quella aria del sonetto Cantai" (see Prizer, "Marchetto Cara," II, 300, doc. 28). Cara's setting of this text is a schematic one with much repetition; it is really a "modo di dir sonetti" and as such would suit Castiglione's category of *cantar alla viola* very well. The work was popular enough to have been intabulated for keyboard performance; see Dragan Plamenac, "The Recently Discovered Complete Copy of A. Antico's *Frottole Intabulate* (1517)," in *Aspects of Medieval and Renaissance Music: A Birthday Offering to Gustave Reese*, ed. Jan LaRue (New York, 1966), pp. 683–92, with a facsimile and a transcription of *Cantai mentre nel core. Cantai* appears in modern edition in Alfred Einstein, ed., *Canzoni . . . Libro Tertio*, Smith College Music Archives, 4 (Northampton, 1941).

The only other poem by Castiglione known to have been set to music during his lifetime is *Queste lacrime mie questi suspiri*, a text written for the 1506 carnival at Urbino. The piece, by Bartolomeo Tromboncino, appears in book 11 of

Petrucci's *Frottole* (1514). If this setting was written for the 1506 festivities Castiglione may have had some personal contact with Tromboncino; but he does not mention the latter in the *Cortegiano*.

55. On Agricola, see Allan W. Atlas, "Alexander Agricola and Ferrante I of Naples," *Journal of the American Musicological Society*, 30 (1977), 313–19, and the articles by Martin Picker and Edward R. Lerner cited there (p. 313n).

56. Bidon and Cara were together in Mantua in 1511, and Bidon was allowed to prolong his visit, partly because the Ferrarese chapel had been temporarily disbanded (see Bautier-Regnier, "Jachet de Mantoue," p. 101). Castiglione could possibly have heard both of them, or heard about this visit, at this time. Bidon appears to have stayed about four months in Mantua (see Prizer, "La cappella di Francesco II," pp. 269–70).

57. See Cian, *Cortegiano*, pp. 134, 506.

58. On the basse danse see Frederick Crane, *Materials for the Study of the Fifteenth Century Basse Danse* (Brooklyn, 1968); cf. Daniel Heartz, "The Basse Danse, Its Evolution circa 1450–1500," *Annales musicologiques*, 6 (1958–63), 287–340. In the second redaction of the *Cortegiano* the ladies performed two *basses danses*.

59. See Cian, *Cortegiano*, p. 134; Brown, "Cook's Tour," p. 227n (where the French translator's version of this dance, "rovergoìse," is given).

60. *Seconda redazione*, p. 92.

61. 2.35. In the second redaction the poet was Pontano rather than Sannazaro.

62. It is not cited among the sixteenth-century anecdotes about Josquin in Helmut Osthoff, *Josquin des Prez* (Tutzing, 1962).

63. *Cortegiano*, p. 197.

64. A madrigal text of a similar nature is *Quando col dolce suono / s'accordon le dolcissime parole* (speaking of the Florentine–Venetian musician Polissena Pecorina), set by Jacques Arcadelt ca. 1530 and printed in his *Primo libro* (1538? earliest surviving edition Venice, 1539). See *Jacobi Arcadelt Opera Omnia*, ed. Albert Seay, II (American Institute of Musicology, 1970), 99.

10

Castiglione's Humanistic Art and Renaissance Drama

Louise George Clubb

In an eighty-year-old number of PMLA there is to be found an earnestly argued claim that in *Much Ado About Nothing* Shakespeare is indebted to Castiglione for the characters of Beatrice and Benedick, having adapted the merry war between Emilia Pia and Gaspare Pallavicino as it reached England in Hoby's translation, *The Book of the Courtyer*.[1] The argument smacks of that desperation which is an occupational hazard to source hunters, especially Shakespearean ones.

But if, after acknowledging the dangers of that chase, we look back across the years that separate Shakespeare's plays from Castiglione's nontheatrical (but hardly undramatic) work, we see a century that coincides with the coming of age of Italian Renaissance drama, a process that long preceded equivalent events in other countries. And thinking about Beatrice and Benedick in Anglicized Messina and about Emilia Pia and Gaspare Pallavicino in idealized Urbino leads to some thoughts, of the kind comparatists think, about Castiglione in relation to drama. For the *Courtier*, its growth, publication, and even its fictional time belong to the period when modern vernacular genres were finally established onstage. Castiglione himself had written the dramatic eclogue *Tirsi* in 1506, and the founding fathers of the cinquecento theater were his contemporaries, some his acquaintances, some his friends.

Until fairly recently it has been thought that Castiglione wrote the prologue for Cardinal Bibbiena's comedy *La Calandria*.[2] Of Bibbiena and Bembo, Mario Baratto has said that they are

in the *Courtier* "two faces of a single culture."[3] Agreeing with
Baratto, I would emphasize "in the *Courtier*," for it is what Castiglione does with these two figures that is relevant to the view I
am taking of cinquecento humanistic art.

As an interlocutor in dialogues set in the fictionally recreated
year 1507 but composed long after *Calandria*'s premiere in
1513, Bibbiena was to Castiglione, as to all playgoers and pa-
trons by the 1520s, an Olympian of the drama, author of the
commedia erudita most exemplary of the genre and most likely to
succeed forever, an expectation abundantly fulfilled throughout the sixteenth century and after that hardly at all. In the
Courtier, book 2, however, Bibbiena is assigned a task not un-
suited to the author of *Calandria* but restricted so that he talks
about some of the matters of commedia but not about the form
or the principles of their combination. The brief discourse on
the risible with which he begins retraces the opening of Gaius
Julius Caesar's speech in the *De oratore*, book 2. Bibbiena's ostensible function is primarily that of raconteur and anchorman for
a panel on jests. In his analysis of *facezie* there is the merest
gesture at the genre of comedy, and the playwright is not immediately visible. The "lower face" of Renaissance civilization
that Baratto finds characterized by Bibbiena as a witty imitator
of daily life is very much in evidence. A closer look, however,
shows that even in what Bibbiena is allowed to *tell* there is more
than the underside of the Renaissance. The concerns of the
serious dramatist are sketched: the theoretical in the discussion of what is laughable; the substantial in the kinds and examples of comic *narrazioni* (*festività, urbanità*), *detti*, and *burle*;
and the tonal—surprisingly moral—in the concluding judgments on tricks such as the substitution of bodies in dark bed-
rooms which were staples of the *novellieri* and would be of
the *commediografi*. The structural and technical concerns of the
dramatist are not absent from the *Courtier* either, but instead of
being discussed by Bibbiena they are demonstrated, later, by
Castiglione.

Bembo is Baratto's upper side of the Renaissance by virtue of
his solemn soaring into the disquisition on progressively ideal-

ized love in book 4. As everyone knows, his, the most influential voice on the vexed old *questione della lingua,* is not heard in the debate on language in book 1. Despite an earlier intention of involving Bembo in the linguistic section, Castiglione chose to hold him in reserve as the exponent of a Neoplatonism that, despite the pedagogical orderliness of its exposition, leads to a rapture of the kind associated rather with Ficinian Platonism than with the Ciceronian variety described by Giancarlo Mazzacurati[4] and of a kind quite alien to the unecstatic climax of Bembo's own Platonic dialogues, *Gli Asolani.*

Polarizations—Baratto's two faces of the Renaissance, Mazzacurati's two Platonisms, the active versus the contemplative strains in humanism, the ideal and the real in Castiglione's vision of the world—are essential to organizing our thinking and teaching about the Renaissance. But in this essay I prefer to comment on the unitary thrust discernible in the art often polarized, the single aim that required polarizable issues and that was an ideal held in common by Bibbiena, Bembo, and Castiglione. It was, moreover, common to the art of the first contemporary names that come to mind—Ariosto, Rabelais, Machiavelli—I would say to the vernacular humanists of the early cinquecento, except that I would not wish to exclude the neo-Latinists Erasmus and More.

What I am calling humanistic art is the art that sets out to have it both ways, an art that rests on principles of imitation and of contamination of plural elements, not merely in the Terentian sense of fusing two plots but in that of seeking out opposites for the *contaminatio.* This is different from the hybridism present to some degree in almost any art, different too from medieval syntheses of invitingly reconcilable traditions or figures, and different even from quattrocento humanistic syncretism. The humanistic art I mean tries to reconcile in creative tension what is held to be unreconcilable, a self-conscious dandified art that plunges at challenge, sets out to square the circle, and tries to do it all: to be old while new, dark while light, ideal while real, *grave* while *piacevole.* An art for which Neoplatonic phrases like *discordia concors* and *serio ludere* could serve as mottoes, though many practitioners of it were only armchair Neoplatonists, if at all.

In the *Courtier* this intention transpires in Castiglione's choices of matter and in his techniques of disposition. A similar goal was set for regular drama when the vernacular humanists and humanist sympathizers took to it, and it remained in diminishing force into the seicento, ossifying with time into schemata and fragments.

One reason that for centuries no one challenged Castiglione's authorship of the prologue to Bibbiena's *Calandria* was undoubtedly the harmony between the statement made there and the premises on which the *Courtier* rests. "Una nova commedia," the prologue announces,

> in prosa, non in versi; moderna, non antiqua; vulgare, non latina . . . Calandria detta è da Calandro el quale voi troverrete sì sciocco che forse difficil vi fia di credere che Natura omo sì sciocco creasse già mai. Ma, se viste o udite avete le cose di molti simili, e precipue quelle di Martino da Amelia (el quale crede la stella Diana essere suo' moglie, lui essere lo Amen, diventare donna, Dio, pesce ed arbore a posta sua), maraviglia non vi fia che Calandro creda e faccia le sciocchezze che vedrete.

> [A new comedy, in prose, not verse; modern, not ancient; vernacular, not Latin . . . is called *Calandria* from Calandro, whom you will find so foolish that you may find it hard to believe Nature ever created so foolish a man. But, if you have seen or heard of similar things, especially as those of Martino da Amelia (who believes the star Diana to be his wife, himself to be the end all, woman, God, fish and tree as he pleases), marvel not that Calandro believes in and does the foolishness that you will see.]

Using the vernacular is justified thus:

> La lingua che Dio e Natura ci ha data non deve, appresso di noi, essere di manco estimazione né di minor grazia che la latina, la greca e la ebraica: alle quali la nostra non saria forse punto inferiore se la esaltassimo, la osservassimo, la polissimo con quella diligente cura che li greci e altri ferno la loro.

> [The language that God and Nature have given us must not, once learned by us, be held in less esteem or of less grace than Latin,

Greek, or Hebrew, to which our language would be in no way inferior if we praised it, maintained it, and polished it with that diligent care which the Greeks and others lavished upon theirs.][5]

Note the procedure. The *prologo* sets up opposites and declares for one of them—*vulgare* as opposed to *latina*—but then explains the choice in such a way as to associate the vulgare not only with latina but with all three of the ancient languages supporting Renaissance civilization, not to contrast it with them but to make it more like them by according it the treatment they have received. The program is that of European vernacular humanists in general, *l'illustration de la langue*. The presentation is playful. Such legerdemain of argumentation is used also with regard to the title of the play itself and the content it indicates: Calandro from the Decameronian figure who was a byword for foolishness. In other words the fiction is derived from fiction, the art from art, ostentatiously borrowed and expanded (for Boccaccio's Calandrino is different in character and situation from Bibbiena's Calandro), but the extreme artfulness, the very *maraviglia* of Calandro's silliness, which is opposed to nature, is deftly defended by recourse to nature and to real examples from popular knowledge.

Finally the pretense of opting for the modern instead of the ancient is contradicted doubly by introducing the charge of those "who will accuse the author of being a great thief of Plautus" and fending it off with a brazen assurance that "he has not robbed him," the doubter being urged "to seek how much Plautus has and he will find that nothing is missing."

The comedy brings together an expanded cast of stock characters from Roman comedy with Decameronian figures in a stream of all three kinds of facezie discussed in the *Courtier*, book 2. But Bibbiena the *commediografo*, albeit unremittingly making fun, hilariously or ironically, is not concerned with *piacevolezza* to the exclusion of *gravità*. His seriousness resides not in the matter—for all its potentially bitter aftertaste, *Calandria* is laughing comedy—but in his disposition of it. In a balancing act Bibbiena performs a gravely humanistic exercise of uniting disparate things without canceling the disparity. Consider how he sets up the basic *intreccio*. He takes twins from Roman comedy, makes one of them a girl disguised as a boy (a device of the novella tradition), gives them Greek nationality, and leads them to a new life in Rome, a Rome peopled by types from Plautus, from Boccaccio, and from the sixteenth-century streets of the city under Leo X. He conducts the intrigue in Tuscan and causes it to culminate in a reconciliation of two families—and of more than two cultural and generic lines. The most authoritative character of the play says portentously at the very end that the Greeks will be better off in Rome than at home, as much better as Italy is better than Greece, as Rome is worthier than Methone (the Greek city from which they came), and as two fortunes are worth more than one. Etc. *Valete et plaudite.* "*As two fortunes are worth more than one*"—there's the paydirt. The final result is not better because of compromise or substitution of the worthier for the less worthy but because both are to be kept, nothing lost. I think this concluding speech is a humanistic signpost planted to point out the aim and the achievement of the vernacular humanists' activity in the recreation of the comic genre. It is one with the tenets and with the jesting method of the prologue, which also has serious aesthetic and structural aims.

The movement of the new, consciously unmedieval vernacular drama was a movement toward mixture. This was so, paradoxically, even at the time when the forms of "pure" comedy and "pure" tragedy were being recovered. The supposed restoration of authentic Greek tragedy by Trissino in *Sofonisba* can be identified more readily as a reconciling contaminatio of Euripides, Sophocles, Seneca, Petrarch, and Roman and sixteenth-century history with Aristotle—in principle comparable with the comic enterprise of Bibbiena.

Almost simultaneously with segregating the matters appropriate to the two primary dramatic genres—the public, state and court, for tragedy; the domestic, urban society for comedy—came recognition that the formulation was inadequate. There was no genre that could concern itself directly with the individual self, the heart or the soul, in a nonsocietal privacy. Eventually the best vehicle for this third matter turned out to be pastoral tragicomedy. But long before that genre assumed regular shape, the humanistic art of creative contamination was feeling its way toward something of the kind.

If few would wish to attach to the *Courtier* the label of pastoral, notwithstanding the link between the figure of the courtier and that of the shepherd so often made in Renaissance poetry, there can be little argument that Castiglione tacitly introduces the idea of tragicomedy into his work and that his art of contaminatio reconciling opposed forces employs, among other techniques, those of comic dramaturgy. Richard Cody sees Ficinian Platonism as dominant in the *Courtier,* love as the central subject and force, Signor Morello as a pastoral satyr[6]— tantalizing perceptions that leave out of consideration most of the work other than its spirit of serio ludere. The humanistic art that Castiglione shared with contemporary playwrights may be seen better in his primary formal and substantial contaminatio, of Cicero's *De oratore* with Plato's *Symposium* (not ignoring Ficino, Mario Equicola, or Leone Ebreo), in which the subjects of rhetoric, political duty, social responsibility, and self-cultivation, discussed as both ideal and practical, are joined with the subject of love, moving from the real to the abstract to the ideal. Ciceronian pedagogical Platonism *and* Florentine hermetic or rapturous Platonism are introduced. The tour de force of humanistically artful reconciliation is accomplished by continual practice of the very principle that Castiglione defines as the key to success in all undertakings: *difficile* and *onesta mediocrità.*

It is perhaps coincidence that the matters distinguished for the regular drama from this time forward through the sixteenth century should be those among which Castiglione works his integration—that of tragedy: the state, its government, the primary duty of the courtier to counsel the prince and bear arms in his cause; that of comedy: society, its relationships, styles of communication, amusements, groupings, and its give-and-take. The casting of the interlocutors as well as their subjects frequently derives from the sources used by dramatists, especially commediografi. Morello is less a satyr than a *vecchio amoroso*, younger lovers are present as topics of discussion and their behavior is adumbrated in the courteous bantering of the *urbinati* courtiers, braggarts and pedants are not only described but also quoted, in lines that could serve in *commedie*. The discourse on love, of course, contains the issues and the levels of loving that were to be established after mid-century as standard features of the regular tragicomedy.

All of these are held together by timing and by the famous moderation of tone and balance between threatening extremes, but also by the use of interlocutors in unexpected ways and by constant recourse to comic surprise and dialogue in ways surpassing anything similar in the sources. Book 1 opens with a dramatized act of choice which both introduces and rejects the subject of love as treated in the social pastime of *questioni d'amore* and settles on the task of forming a courtier, thereby announcing by association the Ciceronian model of *De oratore* and the Castiglionian variations and departures to come. Shortly thereafter it launches into a conspicuously long excursus on imitation—ostensibly restricted to the question of language and introducing points from Cicero but in the spirit of the art that tries to have it both ways; Mazzacurati calls the *Cortegiano* "an imitation of Cicero that stands opposed to *ciceronismo*."[7]

At the other end, Bembo is made to imitate Socrates from the *Symposium* in a climactic moment of book 4, not the first or the last Renaissance dialogue to conclude with an imitation of the Platonic crescendo. But what Castiglione's Bembo does specifically is to quote Socrates, imitate him by his stance and subject, expound it in the rational manner of the Ciceronian Platonists, and propel himself into an ecstasy at the end that, on the other hand, invokes the spirit of the Florentine Platonists. This is accomplished by soliloquy with narrated stage directions aiding the reader to envisage the climax: Bembo sitting there in rapt silence, interrupting the verbal flow. The pause, furthermore, invites the reader to remember the end of the *Symposium*, when after Socrates' discourse and Alcibiades' praise of him, everyone falls asleep until at dawn there are only Aristophanes and Agathon drowsily listening to Socrates as he holds forth to these comic and tragic playwrights on the common source of the two genres—the tragicomic principle, we might call it. It is a joke, of course, one made of serious stuff. Serio ludere. However, Bembo finishes his discourse and sits mute until he is physically roused by a theatrical gesture and a theatrical line changing pace and subject, delivered by Emilia Pia as she pulls him by "the hem of his robe and, shaking him a little, said: 'Take care messer Pietro, that with these thoughts your soul, too, does not forsake your body'" (4.71). The moment is one of stage timing, stage contrast, gesture, and dialogue, and it both recalls and reconciles the contradictory sources, moods, and kinds of human experience and works of art it conjoins. Too, Bembo was a spokesman for a combination of gravità and piacevolezza in art, although he is usually thought of as gravity incarnate; Piero Floriani has remarked that Bembo could only preach the equilibrium of the two that Castiglione could achieve.[8] It is important, nevertheless, that Bembo did preach this balance of opposites and was associated with it in the minds of his contemporaries. Moreover, although Bembo is kept out of the discussion of language, where it would have been natural to give him a leading role, in the *Courtier* he is not exclusively the instructive and rapturous Neoplatonist of book 4. His assignment there is exceedingly grave, but in book 2, in the witty discussion of wit, Bembo and Bibbiena jocosely fight a round of chauvinistic insult. Castiglione makes Bembo not only piacevole but even, briefly, funny. Altogether, Castiglione's handling of Bembo as an interlocutor typifies his procedures: assigning to Bembo the most gravely spiritual portion of the entire *convegno* while also depicting him in a comic *battuta* with Bibbiena (where, to add to the *ridiculum*, Bembo supports the Venetians against Bibbiena's Tuscans—a natural regional partisanship, were it not for Bembo's known views on the language). Castiglione uses a friend whose views were well known, uses, therefore, his reality as a datum, sets him in an ideal structure of triumphantly triple origin—Ciceronian dialogue,

Platonic dialogue, and Renaissance humanistic dialogue cum courtly pastime—and causes him to display the extremes of piacevolezza and gravità. Castiglione's theatrical finesse is furthermore illustrated by his modulating from Bembo's almost inaudibly high solo ascent into a harmonious tutti by his everyone-onstage-for-the-last-scene technique of assigning speeches in the finale. Everyone already *is* onstage, as it were, but following Emilia Pia's physical gesture of pulling Bembo's clothes and her jesting to retrieve him from his rapture, there comes a spate of interjections from various members of the group— seven speakers in eighty-four lines, back and forth rapidly. More people are talking at once in a short space than is usual in the *Courtier* as the conversation moves away from Platonism back toward sexual sparring, disjunctions preliminary to disbanding, description of the dawn signifying the natural end of the discussion as well as the unnatural length of it, with further joys promised in the near future. The culmination is a ceremonious yet lighthearted withdrawal punctuated by a laughing curtain line: "On condition that if signor Gasparo wishes to accuse and slander women . . . let him give bond to stand trial, for I cite him as a suspect and fugitive" (4.73). An ending looking toward happily-ever-after. A tragicomic ending, for the author has repeatedly reminded us in his own voice, in this imitating Cicero, as in the ending at dawn and the double tone he has imitated Plato, that death has swept it all away. The finale of the *Courtier,* more than those of its main sources, has a predominantly theatrical aspect—its gestures, general movement and number of speakers, its windup at once conclusive and promising for the future, are all redolent of the stage. The ending is a primarily happy one, even with its tragic undercurrent. As was graphically documented later in the century, when illustrations of stage sets with actors in place were often printed, comic final scenes, in contrast to those preceding them, were densely populated—commedia visibly pulls together the society and its members proceed together to future happiness, to feasting, to marriage, to bed, to life going on. Moreover, a pattern that became fashionable for both comedy and tragicomedy was that of the night piece, with action that involves grave troubles in the dark and turns out well and pleasantly when the sun comes up.

As for the theater proper, Italian regular drama in its century-long development that fertilized and marked the European stage in general, in its proliferation and diversification continued to be spurred by the humanistic hope of reaching two goals in one movement. So many Italian scholars from the ottocento on have tried variously to get away from the humanism of vernacular Renaissance drama, emphasizing everything that conceivably can be considered nonclassical, nonimitative, and irregular, that the originality of the dramatists' aims has often been denied or misunderstood. This originality consists in Renaissance *imitatio* of the classical genres, in searching for rules and in pushing incessantly toward mixed forms that would be simultaneously ideal/universal and real/Italian cinquecento. The great challenge was to mix tragedy and comedy. Preregular vernacular plays in which it was doubtful where one genre left off and another began were followed by the establishment of distinct commedia and *tragedia*, but very soon the germs of the one in the other began to be cultivated toward a regular third genre. From as early as the 1530s the comedies of the Intronati of Siena were freighted increasingly with the psychology of feeling, with suffering and pathos, and through the century a certain kind of gravity became their trademark, extending beyond personal emotion to cautious indication of social problems and propaganda for religious reform.

Especially after the Council of Trent got under way did the substance of comedies comprehend the potentially tragic. This included not only promotions in rank for some characters from burghers to aristocrats but also such grave matters as madness (temporary), death (supposed), and bloody feuds (threatened). But although such weighty substance is juxtaposed with facezie of all sorts, the mixing is accomplished not only by alternation of heavy and light but also by involving the serious characters in the laughter, as instigators or butts, and by letting the clowns sometimes brush up against tragedy. That the yoked and blended contraries were not fortuitous but corresponded to a principle both humanistic and purposefully contaminating is attested by many prefaces, such as Alessandro Centio's to his commedia *Il padre afflitto* of 1578.[9] He boasts that he has achieved the piacevolezza of Plautus with the *honesta gravità* of Terence, has imitated them both à la Bibbiena and Ariosto, and has added borrowings from Alessandro Piccolomini, the leading dramatist of the Sienese Intronati.

Another approach to the double goal was from the direction of tragedy, lightening its gravity and adducing in justification Aristotle, Euripides, and even Plautus's *Amphitruo*. When Giraldi Cinthio distinguishes in the *Discorsi* (1554) between "unhappy tragedies . . . like the *Iliad*" and "happy ones like the *Odyssey*,"[10] he is citing classical authority for the different kinds he wrote himself: the bloodbath type of *Orbecche*, which leaves almost no one alive but the chorus, and the *tragedia di fin lieto*, such as *Altile*, in which the good characters end up with thrones and marriages and the villains just end. But the spirit of serio ludere and even the discordia concors have departed from this phase of humanistic dramatic art. The unanswerable injustice of true tragedy has been excised to permit the simple concord of a justice calculated to the last *centesimo*. The opposites of tragedy and comedy are reconciled not by tension but by distribution along dual tracks.

Other dramatists tried other combinations, bold, often bizarre—or as bizarre as was consonant with the neoclassical essentials they held in common. Not relaxing their grip on unities, five-act structure, touchstones of decorum, and the like, they produced experimental contaminations labeled *tragedia sacra, commedia spirituale* (*spirituale* not synonymous with *spiritosa*), *tragicommedia* (with various modifiers, *pastorale* or *boscareccia, marittima* or *pescatoria*), *commedia pastorale* and *tragedia pastorale*, both different mixtures from those justified as *tragicommedie*. I have read an *Arcicommedia capriciosa morale*,[11] which is an allegory about the Patriarch of Venice, no less, and a fascinating play by G. B. Leoni described as *tragisatiricomica*.[12]

The reconciling of opposites became more and more a question of joining genres. In tragedy classical and medieval subjects were added to others from modern history, sad novellas and epic romance; courtly love conflicts, warrior maidens in armor, and episodes from Dante were grafted onto Senecan and Sophoclean plots. So-called comedies often headed straight for tragic endings, swerving aside at the eleventh hour, i.e., the fifth act, and built to a crescendo of solemn, sometimes religious thanksgiving, on the rapturous side, in group finales brought back to earth with quips, invitations to wedding feasts, and future revels.

One of the most articulate voices in the later phase of humanistic art in drama was heard in the duchy of Urbino thirty years after Castiglione's death and until the end of the cinquecento. It was that of Bernardino Pino from nearby Cagli, whose ecclesiastical career did not interfere with his theatrical writing, which included a treatise on comedy and a group of plays with happy endings and various generic subtitles. His *Ingiusti sdegni*, one of the most successful comedies of the time, was introduced by a typical prologue boast of being both grave and piacevole without diminution of either quality. Torquato Tasso's often-quoted sonnet congratulating Pino on having brought comedy and tragedy together is a demonstration of contemporary critical regard for contaminatio by one who knew something about its difficulties.[13]

Pino drew, as many other regular playwrights had done, on the *trattatistica d'amore* and the by-then vast dialogue literature for types of scenes but really preferred that his comedies be called *ragionamenti*. The printer suppressed that subtitle in issuing the celebrated *Falsi sospetti* as simply commedia but several of Pino's other plays were published—and performed—as ragionamenti.

Gli affetti, written in 1566 and played several times in Pesaro, is called *ragionamenti famigliari*, and although less philosophical, is as full of discourses on abstractions as the nontheatrical works of Ficino, Leone Ebreo, or Castiglione. But *Gli affetti* is also an intrigue comedy and Pino makes clear his determined development of the genre and its range of contaminatio. His dedication of the play to "Guido Baldo Feltrio della Rovere Duca quarto d'Urbino" defines comedy as *conversation* and, varying the pseudo-Ciceronian *speculum consuetudinis* and *imitatio vitae,* he calls it a mirror of *thought* and an imitation of Idea. The plot, too, has been Neoplatonized. The comic twist of the go-between who falls for his friend's girl is here charged with significance when a courtier woos a beautiful widow with the help of a half-blind intermediary who cannot see her but falls in love with "the Idea of her beauty" (2.i). The resolution that disposes of several different sorts of couples in marriages all round achieves the standard piacevolezza of commedia with philosophical gravità—the fiction illustrates the movement of the soul toward beauty and love and its ascent to the various levels familiar to armchair Neoplatonists. The resolution is described metaphorically in terms of the discordia concors which was the password of Neoplatonic mystery and an ideal of humanistic art: "From a discordant tone, by the work of an able musician is born sweet harmony" (5.iv).

In *L'Evragia,* another of his five-act ragionamenti famigliari, Pino makes the discourses on various topics almost detachable from the context, yet he maintains the comic intreccio plot while constantly emphasizing the ideality of his enterprise and employs all the features that the essentially realistic commedia erudita had acquired in several decades.

Castiglione had achieved precarious contaminatio of the ideal and the real partly by intensifying the reality and the lively dramatic quality of theoretical dialogues among idealized interlocutors on abstract subjects. Pino, the lesser and later frequenter of the court of Urbino, intensifies the ideal and introduces the abstract as much as possible into a primarily theatrical and, in intention, realistic genre. Despite the abyss that lies between the two in the matter of quality, they share the principle of maintaining a genre in form while expanding it to the extreme of its recognizability and contaminating it not only with other material but also with other genres to multiply and to unify simultaneously.

The crisis of the cinquecento fever to bond contraries was

reached in the 1580s and 1590s, when *Il pastor fido* and the polemic surrounding it emphasized homogenizing as the method for making tragicomedy, as represented by Guarini's blend of blunted general tragic and comic features with particular ingredients from Sophocles, Seneca, *commedia grave*, Tasso, and both the Old and New Testaments of the Bible in meticulously neoclassical structure (the straight way from humanism to baroque).

The breakdown of structures was also in process, however, especially at the hands of the *comici dell'arte*, whose proficiency in improvising has been blamed for the withering up of regular comedy in the seicento. But in the late cinquecento the *commedia dell'arte* was still much involved with the regular literary drama, never more than in the first period of its adulthood, which was marked by the successes of the great troupes, the Gelosi, the Confidenti, and others, and culminating in the early seventeenth century with Flamminio Scala's publication of fifty ideal scenarios.

Scala and colleagues such as the Andreini were not limited to improvising. They also performed, as written, literary plays of all genres and sometimes wrote them themselves. A few who were famous for the learning that went into their improvisations also published their star turns. After Isabella Andreini's death, her husband brought out a volume called *Fragmenti*,[14] including many *contrasti amorosi* composed by both of them for her use onstage in almost any scenario. Such documents from a unique moment in theater history suggest another kind of contaminatio, that of the reality of craft and performance with the literary idea of genre. These contrasti amorosi give us a taste of what was actually said in the tonier of the "improvised" comedies and a glimpse of how much they retained of the literary drama that had been fueled for over a century by the aims of humanistic art. The range of subjects is wide. There are, for instance, contrasti on the passion of hate and love, on being a courtier, on doctors and lawyers, on the death of love, on vows, on tragedy and epic poetry, and on comedy.

Under the last heading the *innamorati* Ersilia and Diomede

discuss the arrival in their city of "actors who daily recite comedies in public" (ibid., p. 58). They criticize the sloppiness and
irrelevance of the pieces often presented by the worst companies and they approve adherence to the rules of Aristotle. Ersilia
waxes learned on the importance of plot as soul of the play, on
the disposition of *burle* and jests, on motivation, peripety, and
recognition. She opines that playwrights and *comici* (note the
union of what so many would put asunder) should imitate multiple models, notably Plautus, Terence, Piccolomini, Trissino,
Aristophanes, Calderari, and Bernadino Pino. Diomede re-
sponds that he wants to write a comedy named *Ersilia* so that
the peripety and recognition of his love may befall her. They
return to analysis of the parts of drama but Diomede's trans-
mogrification of the topic into love banter has revealed the
procedure of these *contrasti*. Leone Ebreo had sugarcoated a
philosophical bolus on the nature of love by presenting it as an
attempted seduction in a dialogue between Philo and Sophia.
In the Andreini contrasti dialogue is not a means but an end in
itself; the *piacevolezza* becomes the main point, the *gravità* of
learned discourse is an ornament.

The *contrasto* on the dignity of lovers between Attilio and a
lady with the Platonic name of Diotima, no less, reaches a conclusion no deeper than that his love for her is noble and should
be requited. The contrasto on the courtier's service is an attack
on courts as dens of flatterers in a typical late cinquecento
fashion ("the Court [*corte*] is not short [*corta*] but terribly long in
rewarding the worthy") (ibid., p. 122). In this contrasto the
distance from the *Courtier* is much greater than in the many
others full of Neoplatonic names and topoi. The tone of all of
them, too arch and precious both for modern taste and for
taste formed on the *Courtier* is, nevertheless, reminiscent of
Castiglione's provocatively witty interlocutors. I say this not to
claim reflected excellence for Andreini but to reemphasize the
theatrical tension achieved in the *Courtier*. But only the vestiges
of the humanistic art remain in the contrasti. The concern for
genres and forms, the idea of creative *contaminatio* and of
reconciling opposites have dwindled into a set of topics in each

of which the nucleus turns out to be not the tenor but a vehicle for amatory compliment.

Not always compliment, either, though always *amoroso*: the contrasto on the death of love, a sharp exchange between Eudosia and Manlio, ends with his threatening her that if the stars do not force her to love him he will do some forcing himself, and she mocks him for thinking that he is up to any such feats out of epic romance ("the time of knights-errant is past, and you are not one of these") (ibid., p. 41).

With this we are in the world of Beatrice and Benedick and come back to M. A. Scott's theory in 1901 that Shakespeare took them from Hoby's rendering of Emilia Pia and Gaspare Pallavicino. If Shakespeare used any Italian source, however, it was less likely to have been the *Courtier* than the fashionable and Channel-crossing sex-war dialogues that *comici dell'arte* had developed from a line of literary dramatists, *dialoghisti, trattatisti,* and contaminators of genre leading back to the vernacular humanistic art that was practiced better by no one than by Castiglione.

NOTES

1. Mary Augusta Scott, "*The Book of the Courtyer*: A Possible Source of Benedick and Beatrice," PMLA 16 (1901), 475–502.

2. Giorgio Padoan makes a convincing argument for Bibbiena's authorship of the "Castiglione prologue" in the introduction to his edition of *Calandaria* (Verona, 1970).

3. *La commedia del Cinquecento (aspetti e problemi)* (Vicenza, 1975), p. 32.

4. *Misure del classicismo rinascimentale* (Naples, 1967).

5. I quote *Calandaria* from the edition of Nino Borsellino, *Commedie del Cinquecento* (Milan, 1967), 2, 16–17.

6. *The Landscape of the Mind: Pastoralism and Platonic Theory in Tasso's Aminta and Shakespeare's Early Comedies* (Oxford, 1969), p. 52.

7. *Misure*, p. 27.

8. *Bembo e Castiglione: Studi sul classicismo del Cinquecento* (Rome, 1976), p. 186.

9. (Macereta: Sebastiano Martellini, 1578).

10. G. B. Giraldi Cinthio, *Discorsi intorno al comporre de i romanzi, delle comedie, e delle tragedie, e di altre maniere di poesie* (Venice, 1554), p. 225.

11. Bernardino Cenati, *La Silvia errante* (Venice: Sebastiano Combi, 1608).

208   Louise George Clubb

12. *Roselmina, favola tragisatiricomica* (Venice: Giovanni Battista Ciotti, 1595).

13. Of the plays of Pino reffered to here the first editions are as follows: *Gli ingiusti sdegni* (Rome: Valerio & Luigi Dorici, 1553); *Gli affetti* (Venice: Simberti, 1570); *I falsi sospetti* (Venice: Giovanni Battista Sessa, 1579); and *L'Evagria* (Venice: Giovanni Battista Sessa, 1584). Tasso's sonnet is in *Le Rime di Torquato Tasso*, ed. Angelo Solerti (Bologna, 1902), 4, 190. For recent work on Pino, see Walter Temelini, "The Life and Works of Bernardino Pino da Cagli," Diss., University of Toronto, 1969.

14. *Fragmenti di alcune scritture della Signora Isabella Andreini Comica Gelosa et Accademica Intenta raccolti da Francesco Andreini Comico Geloso, detto il Capitano Spaveto, e dati in luce da Flamminio Scala Comico* (Venice: Giovanni Battista Combi, 1620).

Index